HUMAN TEACHING
FOR HUMAN LEARNING

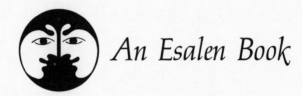 *An Esalen Book*

The Esalen Publishing Program
is edited by Stuart Miller

Human Teaching

AN INTRODUCTION TO

CONFLUENT EDUCATION

GEORGE ISAAC BROWN

for

Human Learning

NEW YORK | *The Viking Press*

AN ESALEN BOOK

First published in 1971 by The Viking Press, Inc.
625 Madison Avenue, New York, N.Y. 10022

Published simultaneously in Canada by
The Macmillan Company of Canada Limited

SBN 670-38651-0

Library of Congress catalog card number: 79-132920

Printed in U.S.A.

TO FRITZ, MY TEACHER!

We hope and think . . . that this is the beginning of a new era—
the beginning of an era when man understands the universe around
him, and the beginning of the era when man understands himself.

—NEIL ARMSTRONG
(After returning from the moon)

Preface

Although this book is subtitled "An Introduction to Confluent Education" and should be of special interest to teachers, teachers-to-be, and professional educators in general, it is also directly addressed to the concerned lay reader.

There is much confusion, suspicion, despair, and sometimes innocent expectation attending the educational scene today. Divergent groups within the community make strong demands and impositions on education; some attack out of fear, some retaliate out of frustration, and some wrangle for political or economic reasons. Some withdraw from the educational "establishment" and set up their own "free" schools. Others reject even this loose structure and turn to the extreme of a pseudo-Rousseauan back-to-nature solution to the problem of living and learning.

Although there is obvious conflict and disagreement as to method and goals and degree of formality, most people would admit that some educational process is vital (1) for survival and (2) for the enhancement of living.

There is one crucial polarity in the process of Western civilization that is of directly relevant concern: the dehumanizing versus the humanizing society. This polarity is manifested in almost all dimensions of our existence: economic, political, social, *and educational.*

We stand with those who would make education and living more human. To be sure, we hold this position because of a strong emotional and philosophical commitment to individuals. We see each individual as a unique human being with enormous potential. It is because of this potential that our position has also a sound practical base. Economically, the potential of man has barely surfaced. His political potential has just been scratched. And his potential as a social being seems to have developed only slightly beyond the primitive.

How, then, can a society transmute potentiality into actuality? The transmutation process is primarily an educational process.

This book presents one educational approach, an approach we believe to be both practical and exciting. Instead of destructively attacking the schools or denying their existence, it confronts the educational scene as it exists and demonstrates how teaching and learning can at once become both more human and more productive within that context.

We hope the reader will find the contents of this book as stimulating as we found the process of engagement that was its source.

GEORGE ISAAC BROWN

University of California, Santa Barbara
November 1969

Contents

Editor's Introduction

The problem of education is a prime concern at Esalen Institute. The first volume in the Esalen Series, Janet Lederman's *Anger and the Rocking Chair,* and a volume we will publish soon by Dr. Buryl Pane, together with this book, help form, we hope, a body of work from which teachers, administrators, and parents can take heart and instruction in helping to make education more meaningful.

Human Teaching for Human Learning derives from the Report to the Ford Foundation on the Ford-Esalen Project in Affective Education. This project, along with a number of others around the country, is the beginning of a serious attempt to renew one of the oldest traditions in education, the central tradition of Western education—education for the whole man. It is obvious that we have wandered away from this tradition. Everywhere we hear cries that education is "irrelevant." Millions of American children find that our system doesn't work for them: they fail in it, they drop out, they protest, or they are thrown out. Surely, there are many reasons for discontent with the present educational system, and surely the reasons for this discontent will have to be attacked in a great variety of ways. But one cannot help thinking that an underlying reason for this discontent is the schools' lack of attention to the total human needs of their students: specifically their emotional, physical, and spiritual needs. This book suggests that it is time to return to our central educational tradition. But not in any easy way. Not by way of a simple resurrection of educational techniques and approaches that were plausible in days before atomic bombs, computers, NASA, LSD, the Black Revolution, or the cultural transformation that has been called the "counter culture."

Instead, we must reinvent the great tradition by renewing it. One of the primary ways for such renewal is the concept of "affective education"—that is, the identification for specific educational concern of the nonintellective side of learning: the side having to do with emotions, feelings, interests, values, and character.

Human Teaching for Human Learning is a book about affective education and its relation to current educational practices. Doctor Brown and his colleagues have schooled themselves in a variety of techniques and disciplines that have started to cluster, that seem to provide the raw materials for a new affective education—one that is appropriate to our age and can be combined with cognitive concerns. These techniques and disciplines derive from the humanistic psychology of such figures as Abraham Maslow and Carl Rogers, as well as from developments in such disparate and often unlikely fields as modern dance, the contemporary theater, Eastern religions, new group therapies, physical education, and the creativity training used by certain large corporations. Indeed, the strength of this new beginning is its eclecticism, its lack of orthodoxy, and its willingness to experiment. As a consequence, Doctor Brown and his colleagues are able to draw on a rich source of material out of which to create something new and powerful.

This is not, therefore, a traditional book on education. It is not the result of enormous scientific research; it is not a manual for teachers; it is not a theoretical treatise, nor is it the outline of a new curriculum. The state of the art of reinventing affective education makes the writing of such books premature. They will come later. Because *Human Teaching for Human Learning* is not in one of the traditional genres of education books, it demands from the reader a special kind of close attention and involvement. I hope that this book will stimulate you, as it has me, to think about what is missing in the education we customarily give to children in our public schools. I hope that it will urge you to review your own education. I hope that it will stimulate you to discover how *Human Teaching for Human Learning* can be applied to your children.

STUART MILLER

HUMAN TEACHING
FOR HUMAN LEARNING

1/

Introduction and Rationale

What is "confluent education"?

At home, first graders watch a Jacques Cousteau television special on turtles. They see the frigate birds eat most of the eggs the turtles lay. The next day in class their teacher has them play the roles of turtles and frigate birds. They not only "do" this but also talk about how they feel as they do it. And they talk about similar feelings they've had in other situations. They write stories and learn to read and to spell new words. Can first graders understand tragedy? Can they experience tragedy as part of the condition of nature and life? Can they be the stronger for this? And can they learn "readin', 'ritin', and 'rithmetic" as well as they would in a conventional lesson—perhaps better?

This incident and these questions are part of what this book is about.

Confluent education is the term for the integration or flowing together of the *affective* and *cognitive* elements in individual and group learning—sometimes called humanistic or psychological education.

Affective refers to the feeling or emotional aspect of experience and learning. How a child or adult feels about wanting to learn, how he feels as he learns, and what he feels after he has learned are included in the affective domain.

Cognitive refers to the activity of the mind in knowing an object, to intellectual functioning. What an individual learns and the intellectual process of learning it would fall within the cognitive domain —unless what is learned is an attitude or value, which would be affective learning.

It should be apparent that there is no intellectual learning without some sort of feeling, and there are no feelings without the mind's being somehow involved.

As an example of how the cognitive and affective dimensions can be related, the diagram below demonstrates one way in which the approach of confluent education can be applied to the study of Columbus's discovery of America.

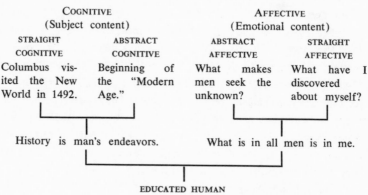

COGNITIVE		AFFECTIVE	
(Subject content)		(Emotional content)	
STRAIGHT COGNITIVE	ABSTRACT COGNITIVE	ABSTRACT AFFECTIVE	STRAIGHT AFFECTIVE
Columbus visited the New World in 1492.	Beginning of the "Modern Age."	What makes men seek the unknown?	What have I discovered about myself?

History is man's endeavors. What is in all men is in me.

EDUCATED HUMAN
What I discover about myself is what makes history.

There has been an ebb and flow of movements in American education, all ostensibly concerned with the improvement of learning. Sometimes these have focused on the child, as in the progressive-education movement under the influence of Dewey. At other times the emphasis has been on subject matter, as in the area of science and mathematics during the Sputnik era.

Throughout all this—and probably since the beginning of teaching—whether student- or subject matter-oriented or possessing some combination of both, the authentic teacher has endeavored to reach that perfect point in teaching where what the student encounters as new learning in the classroom is like Baby Bear's porridge—neither too hot nor too cold. Sometimes consciously, sometimes subconsciously, the teacher has tried to structure his teaching so that the material to be learned is not too easy—thus boring—and not too hard—thus discouraging—but just challenging enough to be exciting and at a level of difficulty that will enable the student, with a reasonable application of energy, to cope with it and succeed.

As any teacher worth his chalk will tell you, this is not easy to do, especially with a large class of students. However, it is almost impossible when a teacher's methods and curriculum are bounded by limits that ignore the student as a *feeling-thinking* human being.

After World War II, the problem of high-school dropouts and so-called "disadvantaged" students dramatically awakened the educational establishment to the obvious fact that what it had been doing for students as a whole did not work for these individuals. The initial response was to give them stiffer doses of the same stuff, and that didn't work, either. Necessarily, then, some educators began to devise different approaches. They began to consider the affective along with the cognitive dimension of learning. They were somewhat handicapped, however, because techniques for teaching in the affective domain were scarcely available. Not until recently has the bridge been made between what workers in humanistic psychology and Esalen-type activities were doing and the needs of these educators. Unfortunately still prevalent is the attitude that the disadvantaged child is more different from than like other students, and thus that what we do with the disadvantaged child and how we do it is probably not relevant to other students.

Portions of this book will demonstrate that such an attitude has little basis in reality. For many educators, the dropouts and the disadvantaged were probably the first major indications of the need for work in the affective dimension of learning.

There are other emerging areas of concern.

At the time of this writing there continues a growing schism between young people and those they consider "the establishment." This schism and other intergroup conflicts are marked by an increasing number of incidents of violence. Violence is a primitive response. A primitive response in a socialized person is often a "last" response, used when all all else has seemed to fail. When a breakdown in communication is complete, those involved are so frustrated that violence may well break out, especially when the issues are *felt* to have deep personal relevance.

This situation is another example of the need for affective learning and confluent education. Attempts at communication solely on a rational level are bound to fail when the issues involved have personal relevance for the participants. Personal relevance connotes an affective dimension; people feel and value as well as think about the position they hold. Denying or ignoring the existence of feelings in communication is like building a house without a foundation or framework. Furthermore, the primitive response of violence finds its source in feelings of impotence. An educational system can strongly influence feelings in the direction of either potency or impotence. If the system initiates or promulgates feelings of failure, low self-esteem, or self-depreciation, it can easily contribute to feelings of impotence. On the other hand, if an educational system is alert to the student as an affective organism, to how his "affectivity" relates to his cognitive experience and ultimately to his behavior as a whole person, and if the system has methods and a curriculum that deal with the evident and subtle needs of the individual student, it can do something constructive about diminishing violent response. This would seem an obviously crucial investment.

Violence, as it erupts on college and school campuses, is one of the more visible agonies of education. The sources of this violence are undoubtedly complex. But there are two factors that are often overlooked. Feeling impotent is one. For example, the ghetto black confronts the subculture of the university or the school and finds it alien, rejecting, and frustrating, offering him no immediate way to learn how to cope. This experience is overlaid on years of deprivation and so-called failure. It is no wonder that his cumulative feeling of impotence erupts in violence. The second factor is that this student is joined or supported by those who have been classified as "successful" within society and the educational establishment. These allies have been promised by the establishment, explicitly and implicitly, certain real and magical satisfactions that are "automatically" to follow academic success. Instead, these favored students find their achievement empty of personal meaning, of answers to the basic questions many young people have: Who am I? What am I doing here? And they find "plastics," as in the film *The Graduate*, an irrelevant answer. Yet the problem of student violence is only one manifestation of what seems to be a widespread social condition.

Acts of aggression, hate, and violence perpetrated by individuals, groups, and nations become more frequent and increasingly generalized. Feelings of isolation, alienation, frustration, and impotence, along with the loss of identity and purpose, at the least touch most of us; they surround many of us. A breakdown of law, an increase in disorder, a disintegration of the sense of community or tribe, and the erosion of marriage and family as a meaningful societal unit leave us personally void and socially empty.

And these conditions are so much with us that we apparently become inured to them. Moreover, we seem to numb ourselves to the sources of the conditions. We feel helpless and often hopeless as to what can be done about all this. Obviously, in terms of treatment, there are not enough psychiatrists and psychologists available even if there were a way to induce people in need to seek help.

This is compounded by a situation in which a large segment of our citizenry, out of fear, skepticism, prejudice, distrust, or ignorance, refuse to have anything to do with anything that smacks of psychology. An extreme example is the person whose lack of confidence in the professional manifests itself in the kind of rugged individualism that not only applies to his own problems but is also insisted upon as the one problem-solving approach for everybody else.

There are undoubtedly many reasons for the prodigious disintegration now so much with us. The mess is complex and, like a decomposing heap of garbage, is compounded of many ingredients. Let us look at one of the major ingredients.

The greatest potential for change and significant improvement in our individual predicaments and in our dilemma as a society lies in the school. It is the one institution in Western civilization outside the family that most profoundly affects the human condition. It is also the institution that, though resistant, is the most practical in which to innovate. Up to this point, with certain exceptions because of the dedication and skill of some teachers and administrators, schools at best have had a vacuous influence on their students. At worst, however, schools can create a hell on earth and an attitude of personal despair for some of those constrained within. Once a student is categorized and classified, it is psychologically and practically almost impossible for him to break out of his category. Once branded "slow" or a "failure," he is immutably branded.

The above condition is a dramatic and obvious one. Even more pervasive, however, for both success and failure in our educational system, is the subtle yet typical pedagogical aberration in which overconfidence in and overstress on the intellect as the exclusive way of knowing produces generations befogged in illusion and fantasy, generations critically out of touch with the only reality available to them—the reality of each moment. This will be elaborated on a bit later in this chapter.

If schools can be significantly changed—elementary through university—we can ameliorate the deleterious effects of education and contribute substantially toward improving the human condition—a contribution the schools are uniquely in a position to make.

What would be the nature of this change? A proliferation of Summerhills—sensitivity training in each classroom—therapy for all—a daily quota of ecstasy?

No.

What is proposed here is common sense, is something we've "known" about for some time, is possible within the present educational establishment, and although possibly eventually leading to considerable modification in school organization and curriculum, can be readily instituted in schools as they are now. "Readily" could be from five to ten years, for a very good beginning—a time period no longer than that of curriculum reforms like the new math.

The change would be simply to be aware that thinking is accompanied by feeling and vice versa, and to begin to take advantage of the fact.

Such a change could mean the difference between a sick society and a healthy one. A sick society at best muddles along, fumbling with patchwork stanching and binding up of its wounds, and while burying its mistakes increases the variety but not the meaning of its funeral orations and rites. A sick society at worst could totally turn on itself in a blazing necrophilic orgy of self-destruction. A healthy society learns from its mistakes and allows its members to grow toward authenticity, communication, and productivity. It makes available a continuing choice between the tranquillity of reflection and the excitement and gratification of individual and group creative endeavor no matter what the focus of the creativity.

History has recorded the place and problems of change and innovation in education as they relate to Western culture. There are a number of examples of Western man's attempts to thrust both the emerging dimensions of knowledge and the process of knowing into educational practices: In reaction to the vocational emphasis of the Sophists, Socrates stressed the pursuit of virtue; Alcuin, at the direction of Charlemagne, attempted to restore the learning of Greece and Rome; Scholasticism focused on Aristotle; the rise of the physical sciences challenged classical literature and theological speculation; Pestalozzi, Froebel, and others aroused interest in the "natural" development of human powers; in America, Dewey and Kilpatrick contributed "learning as doing"; and recently education has been enriched by the application of such technological development as television, programmed learning, and so on.

We are now at a new threshold. Simultaneously emerging in our time are a number of approaches to the extension of human consciousness and the realization of human potential. Some are dangerous, some are irresponsible, and some are exciting, holding great promise. There are a variety of exploratory practices and theories that can be grouped under the taxonomic umbrella of humanistic psychology. These have been the largest resource for work in the new area of confluent education.

To reiterate, confluent education describes a philosophy and a process of teaching and learning in which the affective domain and the cognitive domain flow together, like two streams merging into one river, and are thus integrated in individual and group learning. The term "affective," as we stated earlier, refers to the feeling or emotional aspect of experience and learning. And the more familiar "cognitive" refers to the activity of the mind in knowing an object— to intellectual functioning. Schools have focused almost exclusively on cognitive learning.

One hears much about relevance today. How, then, do we know when something is relevant? It is relevant when it is personally meaningful, when we have feelings about it, whatever "it" may be. There has been concern in the educational establishment for motivating learners, but this is usually only fancy wrapping on the package. If the contents of the package are not something the learner can feel about, real learning will not take place. We must attend not only to that which motivates but to that which *sustains* as well.

The position of most educators at all levels is that the primary function of schools is to teach the learner to be intellectually competent. The position is described by those who hold it as realistic, hardheaded, and a number of other fine-sounding things. Our belief is that this position is instead most unrealistic and illusionary. Oh, yes, it would greatly simplify matters if we could somehow isolate intellectual experience from emotional experience, but at the moment this is possible only in textbooks and experimental designs. The cold, hard, stubborn reality is that whenever one learns intellectually, there is an inseparable accompanying emotional dimension. The relationship between intellect and affect is indestructibly symbiotic. And instead of trying to deny this, it is time we made good use of the relationship. Indeed, the purest, highest form of abstract thinking is coupled with congruent feelings on the part of the thinker, even in the grossest sense of pleasure, boredom, or pain. Or, as Michael Polanyi has observed, it is the passion of the scholar that makes for truly great scholarship.

The more of reality a person has available to him, the more effective he becomes in work, in play, and in love. What has happened to most of us is that we have learned to continually substitute fantasies for reality. This is aggravated by the fact that we share many of these fantasies; that is, they are socially reinforced. This is a large and complex area. But here is a somewhat oversimplified description of how the substitution of fantasy for reality can occur.

As children, we are unable to separate the acts we do from the feelings or impulses that accompany them. When we are punished for a naughty act, we also assign the punishment to the feelings that precipitated and sustained the act. What we feel is thus as bad as what we do. As we become socialized or learn to behave in acceptable ways, we not only restrain our "bad" acts but also repress our "bad" feelings. There are a number of psychological mechanisms that enable us to do this, but whatever the means we use, we are forced to deaden ourselves. We must deny feeling. The more we deaden our bad feelings, the more we deaden all feeling, for apparently we have no way of selecting for elimination only those unacceptable feelings. The deadening is an over-all process. As the process of deadening persists, we lose touch to the extent that we are no longer aware of what we really do feel. We eventually reach a point where we have little choice about how we behave, for, deprived of feelings to tell us what we want or don't want, we react primitively, compulsively, ritualistically. It is not surprising, then, that without access to their feelings a large number of people really do not know what they want.

We do not suggest as an ideal the hedonistic, anarchistic individual who expresses his feelings no matter what, where, when, or who. This sort of person is as "out of it" as the one who has no feelings. A healthy individual has a mind and uses it—not to deny the existence of feelings but to differentiate how, when, and with whom it is appropriate to express feelings spontaneously from occasions when one must wait. When he chooses to postpone or control the *expression* of his feelings, however, he does not at the same time deny to himself that *they exist*.

The denial of the existence of genuine feelings has three unfortunate effects, which are related. These are the replacement of real feelings by pseudo-feelings—feelings we *think* we have—the fear of change, and the substitution of fantasy and illusion for reality.

An outgrowth of our struggle to keep certain feelings from emerging into consciousness is the preservation of our precious self-concept. We experience ourselves in certain ways and struggle mightily to preserve that status quo. Change is a threat, for if we open ourselves to new experience and thus allow for change to occur, we must in that opening give up control. That is precisely what we have steeled ourselves against for many years.

One way we avoid change is by creating with our minds imaginary catastrophes that might happen if we were to move into the unknown of new experience. We terrify ourselves, or at least think we are terrified. And in order to stay the way we are or the way we conceive ourseves to be we dissipate huge amounts of psychic energy in manipulating our environment—especially other persons in our personal universe—so that it will respond to us in terms of our self-concept. We believe we "need" others to support, to judge, to punish, to advise, to order, to do an infinite number of things for us that we ostensibly cannot do for ourselves. We are thus out of touch with our own strength and resources. We all do need others. But it is absurd and wasteful to believe that we need others to do things we are perfectly capable of doing ourselves—to refuse to take responsibility for ourselves and for what we do or could do. We imagine both what some people will do to us and what others must do for us. In each case this is an illusion that accompanies the fantasy of our own limitations.

The obvious waste of living in fantasy in contrast to reality is illustrated by the story of the student who finally got a date with a girl he had been hotly pursuing for two months. He had an exam the next day, so he made the date for nine o'clock, planning to study from seven until nine. He sat down to study, and instead, for two hours, thought about what he was going to do on the date. Then he went out with the girl, and spent the rest of the evening worrying about the exam for which he had not studied.

This example may seem of minor significance. But if we magnify it by how often and how much we keep ourselves out of the present by either hanging on to the past or anticipating the future, the enormity of this waste becomes readily apparent. The only reality we can experience is the reality of the moment. All else is fantasy, something we create for ourselves. We grow and mature through reality experiences. False alternatives merely reinforce our status quo, help keep us stuck.

We have touched on the need for change and growth for the individual. This need is just as important for a society. When the evolving flow of change is impeded, the result is much like what follows the continued damming of a river. Pressure accumulates, and if it is not relieved the dam will eventually burst and destroy everything in the river's path.

Heraclitus, an early Greek philosopher, described the nature of the universe as in constant flux—like the flowing of a stream, always changing. Parmenides, another philosopher, antithetically held that the universe contains absolutes. But even if we were to agree with Parmenides, we would still be confronted with the necessity of searching for these absolutes. Searching is a process, and process makes for change.

Another way to put it is as Tancredi does in Lampedusa's novel, *The Leopard*, when he says to the Prince, "If we want things to stay as they are, things will have to change."

When we total individual resistance to change, we approximate societal resistance to change. When we add to the description of the process of resisting change the prevalent use of clichés, masks, roles, and games, we find it hard not to become discouraged and overwhelmed about our future as a society. In addition, our solutions to these problems are usually utopian in form. Utopias are a hangup. Because of the imperfection of our process of socialization, where we seem either to oversocialize, without sufficient counterbalancing experiences (as in therapy), or to undersocialize, without sufficient recognition of the needs and rights of others (which thus end up frustrated and pillaged, and require expensive policing or remedial work), the chances of realizing a utopia seem minuscule at best. Furthermore, because of the uniqueness or idiosyncratic nature of each individual, an over-all, continuing, harmonious socialization process seems highly unlikely for a long time to come. And this would seem to negate the probability of the harmonious society, the utopian dream. What we can do instead of soothing ourselves with this dream, however, is to concentrate our thoughts and energies on the process of growth itself, especially within the social institutions over which ostensibly we do have some control.

What about that control? The shaping of an institution is obviously in the hands of the shapers. And if the shapers themselves are in a sense misshapen, then they will tend to create the institution in their own image. If we have learned well the lessons of denial, distortion, and repression of genuine feeling, it would seem to follow that our institutions will reflect these avoidances in their structure, goals, and operation. This is especially true of the social institution we call "school" and "university." We have developed clever and elaborate rationales for the avoidances. Furthermore, these rationales are blessed with the sanctity of tradition. And tradition quickly and subtly becomes equated with "truth." Thus, as a people, we are on a merry-go-round of avoidance reinforcement. Tickets are hawked by distinguished leaders, who are tacitly supported by a large chorus, some of whom nod their heads in placid agreement while some stand dumbly, humbly confused, perhaps not even caring.

The leaders and followers are not to be condemned, however, for—to paraphrase a certain distinguished teacher—they know no other way. And that, unfortunately, is very true.

So how can we break the chain, get off the merry-go-round, so that we can move on—if not in a straight line, at least in a healthy direction—so that change will begin to become possible?

Most of the content of the curriculum in our classrooms originally had its source in human experience. When that live experience was transmuted into what was hoped would be a more efficient ordering of the curriculum, its vitality was usually lost. The educator, when justifying the transmutation, would argue, for example, that it was not possible for each student to learn the history of mankind by re-experiencing all the events on which it was based, or, for another example, that there was not time for the student himself to complete the sequence of mathematical frustrations followed by the excitement of insight that successive mathematicians throughout time had experienced, which gave mathematics a body of knowledge.

Instead, educators, by compressing and organizing knowledge in all areas of the curriculum, have created in the classroom what Paul Tillich has called the fatal pedagogical error—"To throw answers like stones at the heads of those who have not yet asked the questions." Not only has this reinforced and compounded the pathological condition of unfeeling that we have already described, but it has also had a significant negative effect on cognitive learning itself.

Yet because much of the curriculum is founded on human experience, human dimensions can be reintroduced into classroom learning. And this is where there is hope. The aspect of what and how the learner feels can be integrated with what schools believe he should know. This integration can not only increase his desire to know but also assure that his continuing learning will be a rich, meaningful, and emotionally healthful personal experience.

For a long time we have known the importance of personal involvement in learning. Educational psychologists have, however, expressed this negatively: "If learning has no personal meaning, it will not change behavior." Seldom has the converse been stated: "If we add an emotional dimension to learning, the learner will become personally involved and, as a consequence, there will be change in the learner's behavior."

Only recently have we had knowledge of and experience with ways of incorporating the emotional dimension into learning in the classroom. The work of individuals like Maslow, Rogers, and Perls and of institutions like Esalen, the N.T.L. group, Synanon, and mental-health organizations has provided oases in the impoverished dustlands of education. And the courage and foresight of officers in bodies like the Ford Foundation have given encouragement and support to our work in this area. This book will describe some of this work.

You will see that there is much that remains to be done. There are the problems of training a large number of teachers; of further developing materials, lessons, and teaching units in the various subject areas; of implementing these approaches for use by the educational establishment as a whole. There is the problem of community education, for communities are exercising increasing control on what goes on in schools. This holds both threat and promise—threat because unless people understand what confluent education is really about they could be alienated by its innovative nature, and promise because there is so much dissatisfaction in the community with the way things are in schools today.

We need training centers, curriculum-development projects, research (both empirical and clinical), and organizations for coordination and dissemination of what we learn.

What is proposed would require an initial national expenditure of millions, leading perhaps to billions, of dollars. It is not difficult to imagine this growing eventually to a national budget larger than that for defense. This might include not only the renovation of our own educational system but also foreign aid in confluent education. The emotional-educational needs of other societies are probably as great as our own, though the need is obviously greater in some than in others. There is no society within our knowledge that is not in dramatic need of emotional education. This could be our greatest investment ever in world peace.

Semanticists and others have been pleading for years for international communication beyond conventional verbalized intellectualism, where symbols erect a thick semitranslucent screen between nations and the persons who represent and compose them.

Until we learn to respond in authentic ways to one another in our private lives, in our work, or in our political confrontations, we shall continue to ride the absurd carrousel of repeating over and over the same wasteful, destructive mistakes.

This is not inevitable.

We can learn. Man is capable of growth and maturity. But he must have a place and an opportunity. And of our social institutions the educational system, at least, must change its ways and become a major contributor toward that end. It can do that by recognizing the importance of affective or emotional learning as a primary educational function. Administrators and teachers must become cognizant of how the integration of affective learning with cognitive learning benefits both domains.

Fra Giovanni, in 1513, said: "The gloom of the world is but a shadow. Behind it, yet within reach, is joy. There is a radiance and glory in the darkness could we but see, and to see we have only to look. I beseech you to look!"

So let us take a beginning look.

2/

Background: The Ford-Esalen Project

The original Esalen Institute is located in a spectacular setting on the coast of California. Rugged hills climb steeply behind, and at the distant edge of the expanse of wide, soft front lawn sheer cliffs drop to the ever-changing purple, green, and black of the Pacific Ocean. The natural beauty that surrounds Esalen at Big Sur is most appropriate for the purposes for which Esalen was intended.

Esalen was founded by Michael Murphy and Richard Price, two young enthusiasts for the potential of human existence. With the encouragement and help of others who worked in the behavioral sciences, religion, and philosophy, they developed a growing program of workshops and seminars to explore the trends in these and related areas. Since its beginning the program has continued to provide pioneering educational experiences of a sometimes unconventional nature but always experimentally stimulating. The success of Esalen is validated to some degree by the emergence throughout the country of the many "growth centers" patterned after it.

Some idea of the breadth and variety of Esalen's program is indicated by the following list of a few of its workshop and seminar leaders: Rollo May, B. F. Skinner, Carl Rogers, Bishop John Robinson, Arnold Toynbee, the late Abraham Maslow, Aldous Huxley, Buckminster Fuller, the late Bishop James Pike, John Lilly, Colin Wilson, Frederick Perls, Paul Tillich, S. I. Hayakawa, Joseph Campbell, Ashley Montagu, Victor Frankel, Harvey Cox, Allan Watts, Albert Ellis, Abraham Caplan, and Herman Kahn.

All institutions must grow and mature if they are to survive. Esalen is maturing and growing in its service capabilities and interests. For example, it is collaborating with the State of California and the National Institute of Mental Health, under the direction of Dr. Julian Silverman, in a creative but thorough research program for working with schizophrenics. It has cosponsored with the National Council of Churches an interdisciplinary series on religion entitled "Theological Reflection on the Human Potential."

It is the hope of those of us who, like the author, have been part of Esalen's growth that a happy balance can be maintained between responsible activities and programs in the human-potential movement and the excitement and courage of working on the frontiers of knowledge without either institutional stagnation on the one hand or irresponsibility on the other. So far this balance has been admirable.

One notable example of Esalen's growth and service is the work on which much of this book is based—the Ford-Esalen project.

Because of the author's work at Esalen, originally as a leader of creativity-training workshops and later as a Gestalt therapist and awareness trainer, and in his role as a professor of education at the University of California, Santa Barbara, he was frequently involved in discussions with Mike Murphy and other members of the Esalen staff on how to move some of the so-called Esalen approaches into the educational establishment. In addition to our own recognition of the need to revitalize education, there was a growing demand for something of this kind from administrators and teachers who had attended workshops at Esalen.

For none of us was there any question but that the ideas and work developing at Esalen could make a significant potential contribution to education at all levels. At the same time, we were aware that the flamboyant and sensational should be carefully avoided. Some of the approaches at Esalen easily lend themselves to misinterpretation, satire, and overreaction from certain groups. Our apprehensions have been justified by recent attacks on sensitivity training in the schools and the patently ridiculous yet pervasive myth that equates anything in the "growth movement"—or the "nonverbal humanities," as Huxley termed it—with nude encounter groups or even sexual orgies. We will comment on this more extensively in Chapter 9, "Proceed with Caution."

A number of meetings were held; plans were drawn up and discarded. This involved a continual process of modifying and refining in an effort to determine how best to combine innovation and responsibility, originality and practicality; in short, how to integrate the exciting pioneering diversity of Esalen with the cautious, sober, conservative reality of the community, and especially of its schools. The problem was not unlike the problem of confluent education itself—the integration of the affective domain with the cognitive domain, the Dionysian with the Apollonian.

We agreed that we should begin quietly and in a relatively small way, that as we proceeded we should be our own harshest critics, and that we should continually examine and justify what we were attempting to do. Having arrived at this understanding, we felt we were ready.

The Fund for the Advancement of Education of the Ford Foundation provided the author and Esalen Institute with a small grant for "a pilot project to explore ways to adapt approaches in the affective domain to the school curriculum." The project had two overlapping phases. The first was to assemble the various approaches to affective learning both from the variety of activities in Esalen's unique workshops and from other sources. The second phase was to examine which of these approaches might be appropriate for the classroom. If there seemed reasonable promise of classroom use, the staff of the project were to experience as participants the approach being considered. Subsequently, those staff members who so desired were to try the approach in the classroom within an appropriate curriculum context and report the results.

Weekend workshops were held once a month at Esalen. Saturday morning began with a reporting and development session. (An example may be found in the Appendix.) Each staff member would describe activities in his classroom for the preceding month. Problems or questions that arose during each teacher's reporting or that were raised by other staff members were often discussed at that time by the entire staff, or a work session for those concerned was arranged for later in the weekend. Sometimes there were suggestions about reading references and sometimes there were individual meetings with the project director, the author. Frequently a teacher's reporting would stimulate new ideas from others. Many of these ideas were never followed through in the project, probably because of the very large number of them. (Examples of these unexplored ideas may be found at the end of Chapter 4.) In addition to the teachers' oral reports, a series of working papers was prepared by the project director and issued to the staff a week or two before the meetings. The working papers tended to deal with the philosophical basis and educational rationale for the work of the project. Even when no working paper had been prepared, some of the discussion inevitably dealt with this problem. At times the session would focus on other articles, papers, or books. Occasionally a member of the staff would move into an area of personal need, and this would be worked on with the group at that point. During the early meetings some time was also given to examining materials collected by Severin and Peggy Peterson, which included descriptions of affective techniques or approaches. Many papers, monographs, and books were made available to the teaching staff. Some of these are listed in the Bibliography.

Saturday-afternoon sessions were used for actually experiencing certain of the affective techniques developed at Esalen and by others. Later these also included techniques developed by the project staff. After the fourth workshop we found that we were inventing more and more of our own techniques. In fact, for our seventh and eighth workshops we assigned ourselves the task of trying to invent a technique for use in the project. We found that as the project continued, the staff could often invent techniques spontaneously during the meetings as well as in the teaching period between meetings. As a result of this experience, we believe many teachers are likewise capable of inventing techniques for their own use.

Saturday-evening meetings also included the use of affective techniques; after the fifth workshop, in February, with Dr. Frederick "Fritz" Perls, the founder of Gestalt therapy, who was in residence at Esalen Institute, we tended to include more and more Gestalt-therapy techniques, for which the Saturday-evening meetings seemed tacitly to be reserved.

In the Saturday sessions these affective techniques were experienced in an authentic manner; that is, the project staff became personally involved in experiencing whatever affective technique or approach was being used. There was no "playing a game" with the techniques.

The Sunday-morning meeting was sometimes used to finish up anything still not completed. Most of Sunday morning was spent in planning sessions, where each teacher would describe what he anticipated doing in the month ahead. Suggestions and "feedback" were presented by other members of the group. Plans were also made for the project director's visits to the classrooms of the teaching staff.

During the February meeting Dr. Perls worked with the staff on Saturday afternoon and evening. The Saturday meetings were spent in actual Gestalt-therapy sessions. On Sunday morning Dr. Perls supervised while members of the staff took over the leadership role and conducted Gestalt-therapy techniques with other members of the group. That weekend meeting thoroughly reinforced what was already a growing awareness on the part of the project staff—that the techniques and methodology of Gestalt therapy had great potential significance for our work in the project and in the classrooms.

In addition to the regular monthly workshops, a weekend and a week-long open training workshop were held at Esalen for educators at various levels.

The membership of the group changed somewhat during the project; two members of the staff had to leave after the first half of the project, and they were replaced. Other staff members were added from time to time, and during the last five months of the project there were guests at each of the workshops. The entire group shared so many of the affective experiences at so high a personal level that there was much opportunity for them, both individually and as a group, to meet their own organismic needs. When there was friction within the group, it was faced and resolved at that time. When an individual member of the group needed help, the group was available and could put into practice what had been learned to help him. As a consequence, the staff as a group seemed psychologically healthy and mature. The evidence for this was revealed, for example, in the readiness of the group to welcome and absorb strangers, and to make them feel quickly a part of the group. As another example of the health of the group—a value basic in *all* of the group's behavior during the workshops; the value essentially of allowing—members were allowed to be whatever they were at the moment. If someone wanted to be alone or seemed to want to be alone, he was allowed to be alone. If he needed companionship, the group was able to provide this. There was no forcing of individual members of the group. No one was even required to attend meetings. But there was almost no absenteeism except for illness or other unavoidable causes. In fact, there was consistently great enthusiasm for the work going on at the monthly meetings.

The results of the year's work were impressive. Chapter 7 contains reports from some of the staff on the effects of the project on their teaching. A variety of examples of confluent education in practice is presented by four members of the core staff. Gloria Castillo is a first-grade teacher in a suburban school. Her journal of day-to-day activities constitutes Chapter 6. Janet Lederman teaches a nongraded class, kindergarten through fourth grade, in a ghetto school. Her students, mostly black, are students other teachers cannot handle. She reports on her results in Chapter 7. (She is also the author of *Anger and the Rocking Chair*.) Robin Montz teaches ninth-grade social studies in a suburban junior-high school. Examples of his work are included in Chapters 4 and 7. Aaron Hillman teaches English to high-school classes of "slow learners," which are a mixture of mostly Mexican Americans, blacks, and poor whites. Chapter 5 describes in detail one day in his classroom, and many lessons and units developed by Aaron are also included in the book.

3/

Some Affective Techniques

Describing a number of affective techniques by means of a series of separate and distinct exercises tends to create the feelings generated by a cookbook or a laboratory manual. So instead we have placed forty examples of affective techniques in a working context. What we describe in this chapter is a composite workshop based on two actual workshops conducted by the Ford-Esalen staff for interested professionals throughout the country. One was a weekend workshop and the other was of five days' duration. These workshops incorporated many of the affective techniques from the Ford-Esalen inventory.

Members of the staff of the Ford-Esalen project shared the leadership of the workshops with the project director (the author) and sometimes with his wife, Judith Brown, who, as a Gestalt awareness trainer, has been a co-therapist with Dr. Perls and actively co-leads workshops with her husband. Consequently, the narrative will personalize the leadership of a particular affective technique.

There is another reason for using this format to describe the examples of affective techniques. When introducing affective learning into the curriculum, the teacher is faced with the same problem that exists in the teaching of any skill or body of knowledge—the problem of readiness. When C is dependent upon A and B for its intrinsic meaning as a piece of knowledge, or for an understanding of its function if C is a skill, before a student can understand C he has to be able to comprehend A and B.

For example, before Gloria Castillo's first-graders were ready for a trust walk, as the reader will note in her journal in Chapter 6, Gloria had gradually to prepare her students for that experience by providing a series of preliminary experiences that led up to each child's allowing himself to be blindfolded and led by a classmate. Younger children are much more reluctant to give up the use of their eyes than are older children and adults. Apparently they feel the need to see even more than those who are older.

By using a workshop format to describe these affective techniques, we can more effectively convey to the reader the problem of readiness and the consequent sequence of activities. Of course, the decision to present a particular technique is at times arbitrary and will depend on the emerging needs of the group or situation. Ideally, a teacher or leader should have an extensive repertoire of techniques and approaches and should also be able to create new techniques the moment the need arises. The instant invention of teaching approaches is by no means a novel undertaking. Time and again perceptive teachers have been confronted with the need to improvise extemporaneously when presenting materials or ideas.

INTRODUCTIONS

George Brown began the first session with an introduction of members of the staff. Next, participants were asked to tell the name they would like to be known by during the workshop and to state any fears or expectations or both they had for the workshop at that moment. George read an article by Joel Carmichael on how we use masks to avoid one another.

GENDLIN'S FOCUSING MANUAL

He then asked individuals in the group to focus on their inner selves, to move within themselves to the place "where you usually feel sad, glad, or scared." (Brief silence.) They were asked to pay attention there and to see what was happening now, and were encouraged to let their feelings come in however they might. (Half-minute pause.) "If you have not got in touch with a personal problem, choose one of real importance." (Pause.) George suggested they not think of all the various aspects of the problem but, rather, pay attention to what the whole problem felt like. (Half-minute pause.) "If one feeling emerges, stay with that feeling and follow it. If words or pictures or fantasies emerge, attend to them." (One-minute pause.) They were told to allow the feeling to change or move as it wanted and to simply pay attention to what was happening. (One-minute pause.) They were encouraged to take whatever appeared fresh or new in the feel of the problem now and to find new words or pictures or fantasies to fit into what their present feeling was as it changed, if it did. (One-minute pause.) "If in the process of doing this you become aware that there is a fresh difference in your feelings or problem, let the words, pictures, or fantasies change until they are congruent with your feelings." (One-minute pause.) The members of the group were then told to take some time to use however they wished. (Pause.) They were at last asked to "come back" to the group but to open their eyes slowly— "like the sun coming up in the morning." They were not requested to share with the group what had happened with them, even though one or two had tears in their eyes.

DYADS

George led them through a three-part exercise in communication. First, sitting back to back, they were to communicate by talking but without turning their heads. Since all of the dyads were talking at once, and since when we talk we depend on nonverbal cues in addition to words for understanding, this was a frustrating experience for members of the group. They were asked to experience this frustration.

After five minutes the partners were asked to turn their chairs around and face one another. Without talking, they were to communicate by using only their eyes. They were told to get in touch with how they felt as they did this; if they wanted to look away, that was O.K.; to be aware of whether they felt silly, embarrassed, fascinated—whatever feelings they experienced. After a few moments they were to sit back and close their eyes and "See what's with you now. Do you have some concept or idea about your new friend? Now put that aside and open your eyes and see if you can view him freshly as if you were seeing him for the first time."

The third part of the exercise involved closing eyes and communicating only by touching hands. They were then allowed to communicate in any way they wished.

The second and third parts of the exercise seemed more satisfying to the participants and helped them discover the importance of other, less conventional, ways of communication. They could feel the satisfaction of making some contact with another human being. The pedagogy of the exercise was designed to move participants from very little risk to more risk. Almost everyone talks to others, but very few in our Western culture risk touching except in routine and "socially acceptable" ways, such as shaking hands or patting someone on the back. The risk here is somewhat diminished, however, because in this exercise everyone in the room is touching and so it is "all right."

INNER AND OUTER GROUPS: STAYING IN THE "NOW"

For the final exercise of the session, groups of five dyads were formed, making groups of ten people each. George used a sensitivity-training procedure involving an inner and outer circle. One person from each dyad sat in an inner circle so that there was now a group of five all facing one another. The other person from the dyad, the "new friend," sat in an outer circle concentric with the inner circle and opposite his friend so that he could see and hear him. Only those in the inner circle could talk. The friend in the outer circle was to observe the behavior of his partner in the inner circle and later give feedback as to how he saw him in relation to the group. Members of the inner circle were instructed to limit their discussion to the Now, to how they were feeling themselves and also how they responded at a feeling level to others in their inner group, moving from moment to moment ("You make me nervous." "Now I want to be alone." "I want to know you better." etc.). After about ten minutes the discussion was halted and the partners got together for feedback. The partners then switched places, and the same procedure for the inner circle was repeated.

INNER AND OUTER GROUPS: FANTASY

The second part of the exercise involved the original inner circle's first fantasizing what it was like to feel lonely and then, still in fantasy, going to the place where they would be most lonely and experiencing what it was like there. Each shared his fantasy experience with those in the inner circle, and broke again for a second feedback session with his friend. The dyads switched places, and the members of the second inner circle were asked to fantasize what it was like to feel free, and then in fantasy to go to the place where they would be most free. This was shared with the inner circle and followed by feedback.

The session concluded with reactions by participants, some discussion and questions about what had happened, and a bit of talk about the format for the rest of the workshop.

The pedagogy of the first session is relevant. We began with going into one's self, listened to a cognitive rationale for eliminating masks and establishing real human contact, established some real contact through three forms of communication, interacted in a larger group and got immediate feedback as to the quality of that interaction, and then shared a personal fantasy with others and got feedback on that sharing process. The structure of the session went from a non-risk to a moderate-risk situation through a series of gradual steps that should have been relatively easy for the participants to accept and become involved in. People seemed to get to know one another reasonably well and quickly. It was then easier for them to participate in and learn from the remainder of the workshop experiences.

In the next session members of the workshop split, and those who were interested in elementary education met under the leadership of Janet Lederman and Gloria Castillo.

TOUCHING

Gloria began the session by asking the participants to form dyads facing each other. Each individual was to close his eyes and with his hands explore his own face very slowly and get in touch with the various textures and parts of his face. Then the partners in the dyads explored each other's faces with their hands. Gloria related this exercise to her work with first-graders in self-awareness and other-awareness.

AGGRESSION EXERCISES

Janet asked each member of the group to stay with his partner and to imagine the partner to be a student who was antagonistic toward him. Standing face to face, the partners closed their eyes and pushed against each other. They were asked to become aware of whether they were initiating action, whether they were passive or responsive, whether they were responding to a "should" or spontaneously responding. They were to become aware of whether they were using just their hands or their total body in the pushing. They next turned back to back, joined hands, and pushed against each other. Janet asked questions from time to time, such as "What is happening?" "Can you move?" "Are you stuck?" "Can you feel your legs now?" She then asked the dyads, "Can you allow yourself to be taken on someone else's back and give in to this?" Few could do so, and they responded with statements like "I'm too big." They were asked to evaluate what had happened and what happens in a classroom when the teacher gets angry.

Gloria continued with the problem of openly dealing with aggression in the classroom by asking the dyads to face each other once again and, by joining hands above their heads, to push against each other face to face. Janet led some role playing with aggression, primarily in situations between teacher and principal.

GANG AGGRESSION

Next, Janet asked the participants to form groups of six. The number is arbitrary. Three groups were formed and were told that they were to become gangs. They were to link themselves together physically in some way, move around, and be aware of what happened when they encountered other groups. A great deal of pushing and shoving ensued. They were asked to go back to their places on the floor and be aware of how their behavior differed when their individual aggression had the support of the group compared to when they were acting alone in the one-to-one situation.

IMPROVISATIONAL THEATER: "YOU'VE GOT IT, I WANT IT,"
WITH GROUPS

Gloria worked further with the gang situation, setting up a variation of an improvisational-theater game called "You've got it, I want it." In this case one of the three gangs had "it." ("It" is not usually defined or identified in this game.) The other two gangs wanted it. The first impulse of the "out" gangs was to fight for it, and a real physical bombardment followed. After a short time the gangs were sent back to their original positions. They were informed that the first gang still had it, and apparently violence hadn't worked. They were challenged to find another way to get it. They tried a disarming, wheedling kind of "loving" technique, which also was not successful. Gloria then changed the situation by stating that the first group still had it but wanted to give it to someone. The first group chose one of the other two groups, went to them, and joined them, thus creating a new structure of an "in" group of twelve people and an "out" group of six. The six were asked to be aware of how they felt at being rejected by the other two gangs. The experiment continued with the twelve that had it and the six that wanted it. On their own, the six went over to the twelve and plopped themselves in the middle of the group and refused to move.

There was extensive discussion throughout the session on the application of these techniques to the elementary-school classroom. The session began with work on self-awareness, moved to other-awareness, to the aggression that other-awareness might bring, to an open dealing with that aggression, then to alternatives to violence in getting what we want and awareness of how it feels to have or not have. These exercises were discussed in connection with a first-grader's growing awareness in a suburban classroom situation and with the ghetto child's profound anger and aggression toward another child or person.

Those participants interested in secondary education met in another room with Aaron Hillman and Robin Montz. The session began with introductions of the members of the project, what they taught and where, and any additional comments they wished to make. Aaron talked about his classes and began the session by asking each participant in turn to make some personal statement to the group ("My name is Joe, and I feel sleepy but interested." "My name is Sharon, and I feel afraid." etc.). He explained that he had used this technique at the beginning of the year to open up each of his classes to group experience.

FINDING A GROUP

Aaron asked the members of the group to get up and mill about in the center of the room and, without talking, end up in groups of exactly four people. If there were five, one had to leave; if there were three, someone had to be found to join the group. The participants then discussed the process by which the groups had been formed—what caused them to choose the group they chose, etc. Aaron related this procedure to his English classes' discussion of Crane's *Red Badge of Courage*. The protagonist of the novel enters and leaves several groups during the course of the story, encountering both acceptance and rejection. The use of this technique enabled students to get more in touch with the hero's feelings. It was used again in connection with the grouping of the boys in Golding's novel, *Lord of the Flies*, illustrating how grouping is often unconscious. Becoming aware of what causes us to choose certain groups can give us some insight into ourselves.

The group was asked to complete, in turn, the statement "It takes courage for me to . . ." (". . . look people in the eyes"; ". . . have anyone touch me"). Aaron related this to his classes' discussion of *The Red Badge of Courage* as a means of helping students understand the meaning of courage and to personalize and humanize the struggle going on in the mind of Henry Fleming, the hero of the novel.

FANTASY BODY TRIP

Robin asked the group to close their eyes, assume comfortable positions, and move into themselves. He led the group in a fantasy trip through their bodies. Each person was asked to concentrate on different parts of his body, beginning with his toes, moving gradually up to his head, experiencing any sensations he might feel emanating from that part of the body. After the group finished the fantasy trip and shared their experiences, he talked about applications of this technique in discussing the concept of "What Is Man?" and in science and physical education. In the concept-of-man sequence in social studies, an assumption was made that the most immediate example of man the students had available was themselves. Therefore, the concept question became "Who am I?" The students began with rediscovering their bodies. Other exercises in the series concentrated on other parts of the person or on the experience of being a whole.

PERSONAL LIFE MAP

Robin asked the group to close their eyes again and in their mind's eye draw an imaginary road map on the inside of their eyelids. "On the left side of the map is where you are now, not so much in terms of location but where you are in your life—your feelings, your awareness of yourself. On the right side of the map is where you want to go. Get in touch with both of those things. In the middle of your map you may have noticed some obstacles that block you from getting where you want to go. See if there is anything you can do about them *now*. If not, don't try to change them. Just be aware of what they are and how you feel about them now." The group shared some of their experiences with the road map. Robin explained how the road-map exercise fitted into the intrapersonal section of the unit "What Is Man?"

TOUCH CONVERSATION

Aaron continued the session with a "touch conversation." Grouped in dyads, the participants closed their eyes and carried on a conversation with their hands. They said hello, got acquainted, took a walk together, danced, got into a fight, made up, and said good-by. About two minutes was spent on each activity. He then explained how he had used this technique in the discussion of the lack of communication between the members of the Loman family in *Death of a Salesman*, showing his class through this experience that people can communicate in other ways than by talking, and often much more effectively.

IMPROVISATIONAL THEATER: "YOU'VE GOT
IT, I WANT IT," WITH INDIVIDUALS

The session of secondary-school participants concluded with the improvisational-theater technique "You've got it, I want it," described above. The difference here, however, was that it was staged between individuals rather than with groups or gangs. Aaron explained that he had used this technique in connection with the drama *Death of a Salesman*, also in the discussion of the lack of communication between the members of the Loman family. The technique demonstrated to students the kind of behavior that results when someone has something that someone else wants. He improvised situations for his students to work with from the drama. "You're Biff, and you have popularity. You're Willy, and you want it." Robin described how he had used this same technique in connection with his classes' discussion of the concept of human rights, the issue being a central one between the haves and the have-nots in our society.

TRUST WALK

For the next session all members of the workshop met together on the lawn in front of the dining hall. Under George Brown's direction, they were paired with the person they had worked with in the first session and were given instructions for a trust walk. One of the pair was to close his eyes, and the other was to be a guide. The guide was to provide a variety of sensory experiences in touching, feeling, smelling, tasting, body motion, and so on. He was to be as creative as he could be in selecting these experiences. Two examples were given: "It's fun to run while you're blind and being led," and "It's interesting to encounter another person while blind, especially if the other is blind also." They were told not to try to identify or categorize while they were blind. "Just experience what is happening and how you feel about it." After about twenty minutes the partners switched roles, the leader or guide becoming blind and the blind person becoming the leader. The participants were amazed at what they could tune in to in terms of experiencing the world in a fresh way and how much they could trust one another. George described some uses of this technique, including working with married couples. Gloria explained how she had used the technique in her first-grade class to build trust between the children and to open them up to discovering things in other ways than by seeing.

SHEET

Each person was then given a sheet (regular double-bed size) and was instructed to put the sheet over him completely and lie face down on the grass. George led the group through an exercise composed essentially of ten parts. In the first part of the exercise the individual was to be aware of his own universe under his sheet. He was to tune in to his body, to his environment, and to his feelings about being alone in his own little world. In the second part he was to become aware of whether he wanted to remain alone or to make contact with someone else. If he wanted to make contact, he was to rise, letting his body tell him when and in what way it wanted to get up, and, staying on his hands and knees, he was to move around until he encountered someone else, remaining under his own sheet the whole time. When contact was made, the first reaction was in most cases a playful sort of aggression followed by an exploration through touching. Music was played during the latter part of this section of the exercise, and some of the people danced to the music while under their sheets. The third part of the exercise involved disengagement from contact, returning to isolation, lying down again, and becoming aware of one's self and how it felt to be alone again. In the fourth part, led by Janet Lederman, the individual assumed a fetal position under the sheet and got in touch with what it was like to be in the womb. In the fifth section of the exercise the participants were to "give birth to themselves," to slowly wriggle their way out from under the sheet and be a baby. Sixth, they were to explore their immediate environment without moving or talking. Seventh, they were given the power to crawl, and they could meet other "babies" but could not talk to them. Eighth, they could begin to walk. Ninth, they were given only the words "I want!" Tenth, they could respond to "I want!" by saying "No!" if they wished. The participants were then divided into two groups, and the groups sat on the lawn in circles. Janet met with one group, and Robin Montz with the other. Janet and Robin began by describing in poetic language what they had seen. After they had talked for a while in poetry, others in the group began describing their experiences in poetry. After about twenty minutes of "poetic evaluation," the participants were free to leave. Since most of the group remained, the suggestion was made to develop a silly game with the sheets in which all the group could participate. A period of joyful "free play" followed, in which members of the group thought up and led various games which evidently brought the group into close contact.

MIRRORING

Robin began the next session by asking the group to form dyads with someone they did not know. He led them in an exercise called "mirroring" from *Improvisation for the Theater*, by Viola Spolin. One of the pair becomes a mirror, the other becomes the communicator. The mirror cannot talk, but it reflects everything it sees. The communicator, by observing his reflection in the mirror, can get feedback about himself. The mirror, by reflecting what he sees, can get in touch with the person he is reflecting. Roles were switched after about five minutes. After five more minutes the dyads were given the opportunity to talk about what they had experienced. Finally, the participants were instructed to become both mirror and communicator at the same time and to create with their partners a dialogue of movement. After about ten minutes of this, the group was called back into a circle for evaluation.

ROCK FANTASY

Aaron then asked the participants to close their eyes again. He gave each person a rock and asked him to explore the "object" with his fingertips, then to place it on his face, to feel its weight, to imagine that the rock was growing very large and that he was growing very small, to fantasize climbing around on it, to imagine the rock growing small again, and then to return to the room and slowly open his eyes. Those who wished shared their experiences.

CONTEMPLATION

Aaron suggested that the group members leave the room and find a place where they could be all alone, reflect on the experiences of the workshop thus far, and return to the room in about thirty minutes. Thirty minutes later the group returned, and the members were divided into groups of seven. Each person was given a piece of paper and a pencil and was asked to write down two things that he had learned about himself during the period of contemplation. Each person then shared with his small group what he had written, and the group responded to what each person had shared.

At the end of the session all the participants formed a tight group in the center of the room and swayed together for a few minutes.

The workshop participants met for the next session in the interest groups in which they had previously met.

GESTALT PROJECTION GAME

Under the leadership of Janet and Gloria, the elementary-school group began their session with questions and answers about affective learning. This moved into statements from the participants as to how they felt about the experiences they had had. Janet then asked for personal statements about how the individual felt "right now." These statements moved into encounters between individuals within the group. When certain statements were made, Janet asked the individual to turn the statement around. For example, one person said, "I would like to help you." When he turned the statement around, it became "I would like you to help me." The statement "you are" became "I am." She then asked those who could do so to place a pillow in front of them and in imagination place themselves on the pillow and talk to themselves. These techniques, taken from Gestalt therapy, were explained by Janet to the group as being ways of tuning in to what is actually happening in any given situation. She related how she had used them with disadvantaged students to help them understand what is real in situations they encounter.

TRUST CIRCLE

Under Gloria's guidance, the group next worked on the development of communication and trust. Some of the participants went around the circle talking to each individual, completing the sentence "I want to communicate with you by . . ." Later, others did the same with the sentence "I think I can/cannot trust you because . . ." After some trust had been established or identified among various members of the group, small groups of eight people formed trust circles. One of the group stood in the center of the trust circle and, letting himself go, fell and was caught and supported by those in the circle, who then passed the person around the circle. Through these techniques, the need for trust and the need for support from others was demonstrated to the group.

ANIMAL FANTASY

In the secondary-school interest section, continuing under the direction of Aaron and Robin, the split session began with Aaron passing out paper and pencils and asking the group to think of a person they couldn't stand, one they loved, and themselves, and write all three names on the paper. They were then to "turn all three into animals," visualizing animals that resembled these three people. They were asked to place an adjective in front of the name of each of the three animals. The animals were then shared with the group and arranged in lists. The group compared the animals chosen for each list and made some surprising discoveries about the character traits described. The participants were next asked to close their eyes and go in fantasy to a small clearing in a forest.

There in that clearing the animal that was self met the animal that was the hated person. The fantasy was carried on from that point and later written down. Some of the group shared with the rest what had happened in their fantasy. The group was then asked to fantasize the animal that was self meeting the animal that was the person loved. The fantasy was carried through, written down, and shared with the group. Evaluation and discussion followed the exercise, and Aaron told how he had used the technique in connection with the study of *Lord of the Flies*, in which there is much animal imagery and in which the boys visualize themselves and other members of their group as animals.

SYNECTICS: DIRECT, SYMBOLIC, AND PERSONAL ANALOGIES

Robin ended the session with an exercise from Synectics, in which the participants formed groups of five or six, sat on the floor in circles, and were given a common, ordinary object such as a salt shaker or a spoon. The exercise was constructed in three stages. In the first stage the groups were to "brainstorm" about "what else" the object could be (an ash tray could be a hat for a person who had dents in his head; a paper cup could be a bra for a turquoise-shelled zucchini beetle; etc.). In the second stage the groups were given a paper cup to concentrate on. They were asked to decide among themselves what the essence of the cup was— what its unifying principle was. In the third stage they were to concentrate on the cup until they became the cup, keeping in mind its unifying principle or essence. When most of the participants had got in touch with the feeling of being a cup, they were asked to feel themselves filling up until they were full. They were then given the opportunity, if they wished, of sharing their fullness with some-one else. Aaron discussed with the group his use of the technique of focusing on objects as part of a unit on Hinduism, giving the students a concrete example of the Hindu belief that the world of sense and the world of soul are one and the same and "That art thou." By identifying his self with concrete objects, the Hindu is able to identify with the totality of the universe.

In the next session the workshop participants were divided into two new groups to work on awareness training through Gestalt therapy. One group was led by Janet Lederman, and the other was led by George and Judy Brown.

Gestalt therapy provides a methodology for the experiencing of reality by helping the individual to complete the unfinished situations in which he is "hung up" that interfere with his experiencing the reality of the moment. Hanging on to the past and anticipating the future are both illusionary conditions that can become substitutes for contact with what is real in both substance and process. Gestalt-therapy techniques can also be used to help the individual take responsibility for himself and for what he does or avoids. Among the contributions Gestalt therapy can make to educational practices is helping the student to become aware of the resources that are available to him outside and inside himself. To the degree that the student exists in a fantasy or illusory state, to that degree will he be limited to only the ephemeral and insubstantial fragments of his fantasies, whereas if he can begin to get in touch with the real world as a real person, he will have at his command all the resources of that world to help him.

Some of the Gestalt techniques used in the two groups were:

RESENTMENT, DEMAND, APPRECIATION

1. Participants were asked to pick someone against whom they had resentments and in fantasy to put that person in front of them. They were to take time to get in touch with that person and their resentments about him. In turn, each person voiced his resentments in the Now ("I resent you. You never leave me alone!" etc.). Resentments do not have to make sense. They are feelings, so logic is irrelevant. For example, one may still resent someone who is dead. After the resentments were stated, the person stated his demands of that fantasized person (demands do not have to make sense, either) and then finished up by telling the person what he

appreciated about him. Appreciation does not necessarily include "liking." One can appreciate how well a person performs a destructive act without liking the act.

THE "NOW" TECHNIQUE OR AWARENESS CONTINUUM

2. In dyads, triads, or larger divisions the members of the group carried on conversations staying completely in the present with whatever emerged into consciousness ("Now I feel tired." "You make me angry." etc.). Participants were encouraged to move from moment to moment.

GESTALT TEACHER-PUPIL TECHNIQUE

3. The group was broken into dyads. Each person in fantasy went back to the time when he was the same age as the students he now teaches (if he was an administrator, he was to go back to the time when he was a teacher dealing with administrators). After getting in touch with himself as he was then, he was to visualize a student he now has (or teacher he now works with) who is most like what he was then. He shared both of these experiences with his partner in the dyad, staying in the Now.

SENTENCE COMPLETION

4. In groups of three or four the participants completed the following sentences, saying them in turn to each member of their group: "I avoid contact with you by . . ."; "I could make contact with you by . . ."; "I keep myself from getting involved with you by . . ."; "I want you to . . ."

IMAGINATION GAMES

In the next session the whole group met in the large meeting room to be led in exercises in fantasy and imagination. The first of these was led by Gloria Castillo. It was an imagination game called "Father" from the book *Put Your Mother on the Ceiling*, by Richard DeMille. Seated, with eyes closed, the group was instructed to imagine their fathers in various situations, some of them serious tasks, some funny situations, ending with spending some time with Father in any way they wanted to.

RITUALS

The large group was then divided into five subgroups and asked to create a new ritual. The idea was to invent either a ritual to replace one we already have or one for a situation in which no ritual at present exists. The subgroups returned, demonstrated the new ritual, and then led the whole group through the ritual. This was very enjoyable.

The next session was again divided into the two interest groups.

SENSING-AWARENESS EXERCISES

The group led by Aaron and Robin met in the large meeting room. Robin began the session by asking the participants to stand, find "their space," and close their eyes. They were instructed to tap their heads with their fingers, allowing the weight of their hands to do the work—to tap on the top of their heads, down the back of their necks, around their ears, under the chin, over the face, quickly all over the area—and then to let their hands drop to their sides and to experience the tingling sensations in their hands and head. Robin then led them through an exercise in which they grouped themselves in dyads. One member of the dyad was to bend over and let his arms hang straight down, with his back parallel to the floor. The other member of the dyad slapped quickly all over the partner's back and buttocks, then, slowing down, said good-by with his hands. The one being slapped was instructed to stand up slowly, one vertebra at a time, so that he was aware of every vertebra in his back. When he reached a standing position, he was to feel that someone had attached a string to the top of his head and was pulling him toward the ceiling. Slowly, then, he could open his eyes—"as if the sun were just coming up." Roles were switched and the sequence repeated.

Following this sequence used for toning up the system, Robin asked the participants to lie down on the floor on their backs, close their eyes, and move into themselves. They were to concentrate on their breathing, to get in touch with it. After a few moments, they were asked to get in touch with the interval between breaths without doing anything about it. They were instructed to place their hands at the lowest point on their abdomens where they could feel their breathing and then, after a short time, to try to force their breathing all the way into the groin. They resumed normal breathing and were to get in touch with the way their bodies were lying on the floor. Did they feel they were pushing on the floor, or was the floor holding them up? They were asked to be aware of any sensations emanating from any part of their bodies and to see how they felt.

Each member of the group was next to get in touch with his entire body and to begin to let his body move as *it* wanted to move. Slowly, letting his body tell him when and in what way, he was to begin to rise with his eyes closed until he was in a standing position. He was to let his body find its own rhythm and to begin to move to that rhythm. After a few moments Robin asked the participants to begin to mill about with their eyes closed, being aware of whether they wanted to remain alone or to be with someone, and "let whatever happens happen." After about five minutes they were to return to isolation and to lie down again, retreating back within themselves and getting in touch with their breathing once again and how it was to be alone again.

CAVE FANTASY

Aaron led the group on a fantasy trip into a cave. The group were still lying on the floor with their eyes closed, withdrawn into themselves. He began the fantasy with the following:

"Imagine you are floating on a river. The river is winding through a beautiful forest. You can see the trees, the beautiful golden flowers, the birds, the blue sky. Now the river reaches a mountain and flows into a cave. You float into the cave. Continue your journey and see what happens." (About five minutes elapse.) "Now very slowly leave the cave and return to this room and to this group. When you feel like it, very slowly open your eyes, as if the sun were just coming over the horizon, and sit up."

The group formed a circle and discussed their fantasy trips.

Following this, Aaron asked the participants to stand and walk around the room, looking at everything in the room—the walls, paintings, people in the room, and so on. After a few minutes he asked them to begin forming groups without saying anything. They were to end up in groups of exactly four people. If there were five, one had to leave. If there were fewer than four, someone had to join the group. After the groups were formed, they evaluated within their group of four what had caused them to choose that particular group and not another.

GESTALT CONTACT AND TRUST TECHNIQUES

Robin asked those groups of four to sit on the floor together. He led them in three Gestalt experiments. Each person within the small group communicated with each of the other three people in his group and completed the following sentences: "I can make contact with you by . . ."; "I can avoid contact with you by . . ."; and "I trust/don't trust you because . . ." Aaron then asked the participants to tell the others in the group how they thought others saw them. This completed the split session.

GESTALT TEACHER-ROLE-AWARENESS TECHNIQUE

The elementary-school interest group, led by Janet Lederman and Gloria Castillo, worked with a Gestalt experiment developed by Janet in which each person completed the sentence "In order for me to be a good teacher, you should . . . ," talking as if his students were there. Some members of the group served as devil's advocate and responded, "I don't want to do that," or "What's that going to do for me?" As the game developed, it became a role-playing situation in which two people were locked in a frustrating situation, and from time to time other members of the group became alter egos for the original two participants. Members were encouraged to allow their frustrations to emerge honestly and to begin to get in touch with their expectations of their students and also of themselves as teachers.

HOSTILITY GAME

The next session was for everyone. Aaron and Robin introduced exercises in dealing with aggression. Aaron began by demonstrating with Robin a type of karate in which all the force and action of traditional karate is used but in which no one actually touches anyone else. The group was split into dyads, and the participants were asked to spend about ten minutes in a boisterous, vociferous karate fight. This was designed for two purposes: (a) to warm the group up, to wake them up and get them ready for the activities of the morning, and (b) to allow them to begin to get in touch with any hostility or aggression they might feel.

GIBBERISH

Robin asked the group to divide into groups of three persons each. He began a series of gibberish games by demonstrating what gibberish was. The groups were instructed to converse by using only gibberish. After a few minutes Robin asked the groups to begin slowly and gradually to exclude one of the three people from the conversation without deciding ahead of time who that person would be and without using any signs or signals. The participants were instructed to be aware of whether they were "in" or whether they were being excluded and to be aware of how they felt in that position.

GROUP FANTASY

Led by Gloria, the participants formed eight-person groups and worked on group fantasy. The members of each group lay on the ground like the spokes of a wheel, with their heads in the center so they could hear each other. Anyone who wished began the fantasy, and when others were "with" the fantasy they contributed to it, with individuals spontaneously taking over. The rest of the group were to go along, as if it were their fantasy, with whoever was describing what was happening in the fantasy at the time.

GESTALT CONTACT WITHDRAWAL

The next session was led by George and Judy Brown and concentrated on Gestalt techniques. First George led the group in a contact-withdrawal technique that has as its purpose helping the individual to become more aware of his immediate state of being. Most of us have a rhythm of alternately attending to reality as it exists in the moment and withdrawing from that reality by daydreaming, fantasizing, meditating, sometimes half-listening to music, or perhaps half-watching television. It is important that we tune in to our individual rhythms without unnecessarily pushing ourselves one way or the other. When we feel the need to withdraw, and if circumstances permit, we should allow ourselves to do so. Then, when the rhythm flows the other way, we can more completely attend to the Here and Now. The technique that George directed helps the individual to learn how to tune in to his rhythm and where he is at the moment. George began by asking the participants to relax, close their eyes, and "in fantasy go away someplace, someplace where you really would like to be, alone or with someone you like." (Two-minute pause.) "Now come back to the group, open your eyes, look around, and be aware not only of what you see but of how you see—how clear or bright colors are, for example." (One-minute pause.) "Close your eyes and go away again. You might go to the same place or perhaps someplace new. Do as you wish." (One-minute pause.) "Come back again and look around. Again be aware of how you are perceiving." (One-minute pause.) "Now in your own rhythm withdraw or stay here. You may want to withdraw for the rest of the time in this exercise, or you may want to stay here. Just allow yourself to tune in to what *you* really want, from moment to moment." The group was given about five minutes for this.

GESTALT "I-HAVE-AVAILABLE" TECHNIQUE

Judy next led the group in getting in touch with their own strengths or resources. Each participant was to complete the sentence "I have available . . ." by getting in touch with whatever emerged—either personal characteristics or things or persons in his universe—that could help him cope with his world and do what he wanted.

GESTALT RESPONSIBILITY TECHNIQUE

George and Judy led another Gestalt technique, aimed at separating personal responsibility from the unrealistic responsibilities we assume on behalf of others, usually where we can do nothing or should do nothing. (A rationale for this may be found in Chapters 1, 8, and 9.) Each person was to pick someone in his life—spouse, students, principal, parent, etc.—and alternate and finish the statements "I take responsibility for . . ." and "You take responsibility for . . ."

The group then worked in Gestalt awareness training, based on principles of Gestalt therapy. Space does not permit a description here. However, excellent examples of this work may be found in *Gestalt Therapy Verbatim*, by Frederick S. Perls. Some of these approaches, as adapted for use in the classroom, are also included in Janet Lederman's book, *Anger and the Rocking Chair*.

SELF-SABOTAGE GAME

The last session of the workshop began with a technique for helping the individual to be aware of how he keeps himself stuck, keeps himself from growing or changing. George asked participants to describe how, after they had left the workshop and returned to the "other world," they would cancel out what they had learned about themselves and how they might apply the techniques they had experienced to their own professional settings ("It won't work back here; my colleagues will never tolerate it." "My wife just wouldn't understand; it would take too much effort to explain." "My students are different. Besides, their parents would get up in arms.")—whatever they might say to themselves to maintain their status quo, to sabotage their professional or personal growth.

GESTALT FINISHING-UP TECHNIQUE

The group finished with statements of resentments or appreciations or both for one another in the workshop. This is one way to complete unfinished business or situations left over from the duration of the workshop. Both leaders and participants did this. In the process many became aware of feelings for one another and the group that had remained below the surface. They expressed themselves both verbally and nonverbally. Everyone seemed to leave with very good feelings.

In the next chapter the reader will see how some of the techniques used in the workshop, along with additional techniques or approaches, can be incorporated into the curriculum.

4

Classroom Applications

The teachers in the Ford-Esalen project developed many individual lessons and whole units. We are including a generous sample of these in this chapter to illustrate how affective approaches to learning can readily be incorporated into the conventional curriculum. So far we have encountered no area of the curriculum where the introduction of experiences in affective learning cannot be merged with cognitive or intellectual learning and where the cognitive learning has not immediately become more relevant and thus richer as a consequence.

A teacher on the Ford-Esalen staff had been given the responsibility of introducing driver education to his ninth-graders. At one meeting he expressed his disgruntlement with this task. The group brainstormed the situation and came up with a number of suggestions. One was an improvisational-theater game where one student stands in front of another to whom it is important to get somewhere in a hurry. The rules are set up so that the second student cannot get around the first. The lesson is structured for the second student to experience the impatience and frustration of his situation.

The situation is acted out until real feelings emerge. The second student is helped to get in touch with these feelings and with how well or poorly he can make judgments under these circumstances. This is transferred to the driving situation. The clichés of driver caution and control then become something more than words. This teacher's unit will be found later in this chapter.

During a five-day training workshop for other teachers, one of the participants, Bertle Werny, a high-school German teacher, told us that on a recent trip to Germany she collected as many modern records in German, especially those with "sexy" implications, as she could. Her students loved them and very rapidly learned German vocabulary, most of which was quite legitimate, through the use of these records. There are at least two implications that can be drawn from her account. First, there lies here a whole new approach to foreign-language learning in the secondary schools: taking cognizance of what adolescents are like, rather than ignoring or combating these characteristics, and capitalizing on them intelligently. Second, as we knew had been true of our Ford-Esalen teaching staff, there are scattered about the land many teachers who are intuitively doing some of the things we have been doing in the project but who have no theoretical knowledge of confluent education and are without the support of others and the opportunity for professional dialogue.

What follow are units, a number of individual lesson plans, and other descriptions of possible work by teachers in the classroom. Chapters 5 and 6 will also describe work in the classroom.

We are aware that there are gaps in both grade levels in elementary education and subject matter in secondary education in these chapters. This is only because of the limited number of staff in the Ford-Esalen project, which was defined and designed as a pilot project. We are confident that if staff were available, work at all grade levels and in most subject areas could have produced similar results.

The following five units were prepared by members of the staff in secondary-school social studies and English. All five units merge affective experience with cognitive curriculum material so as to bring the cognitive material to life and make it relevant to each individual in the classroom. In reading these units and lessons, notice the variety of sources that are used by the teachers for the classroom affective experiences.

UNIT OUTLINE

(Ninth-grade social studies, all levels.   By Robin D. Montz)

WHAT IS MAN?

Place in Curriculum

This was our first unit in a course in American Government and World Geography. Our teaching team (in history and English) decided to approach the subjects we teach from a concept-oriented base. We began with the discussion of the nature of man, then moved to the nature of groups, society, nations, a discussion of the American system and its inherent concepts, and then to other systems in the world, including their geographical environments.

Sequence

1. Show pictures of people from all cultures. (Opaque projector works very well. I used Edward Steichen's picture book, *The Family of Man.*) Students are to try to perceive what is common to all the pictures shown and write one-half page about it.
2. Cognitive lecture: Theories of the nature of man.
Theories:
  Naturalistic: Man is merely a higher form of animal, and differs from other animals only slightly.
  Monotheistic: Man is created in the image of God.
  Pantheistic: Man is soul, and that soul is an eternal and inseparable part of the world soul—the essence of the universe.
Elements:
  Dualism: Body and mind.
  Tripartite: Body, mind, and soul (spirit).

Man is before he is defined.

Locke: *Tabula rasa*—environment creates who we are.

Existentialism: Our decisions create who we are.

Is man basically good or evil?

3. The self as an example of man. (Small groups of ten to fifteen.) Cognitive introduction: The unique self.

When we are small children, we are completely ourselves. We act and react on an emotional level and do what we wish to do when we want to do it. As we get older and meet other people, their reactions to us cause us to change our behavior so that they will accept us. We therefore build shells around our unique self in order to make ourselves more acceptable to the outside world.

The process of becoming an emotionally mature adult necessitates breaking through the shells we have built and finding out in some way what our true unique self is all about and dealing with what we discover. Acceptance of the shells we have built is not self-acceptance. We must break through to the real self.

Some of the things we are going to be doing in this class may help you to understand yourself better. Some of them may not. It is important to realize, however, that school is not just for the memorization of facts and the development of skills. One of the primary goals of your education should be to make you understand your true self a little better. Socrates said, "Know thyself," because we don't really understand the full meaning of anything until we can truly understand ourselves.

(Or facsimile—something to let them know why what they'll be doing is important.)

Affective exercises toward self-discovery:

a. The wardrobe of your mind.

Introduction. (Seat students in a circle.) Close your eyes for a moment. I'm going to close mine too, so no one will be looking at you. You will probably be seeing some yellow or white dots on the inside of your eyelids. Concentrate on those dots for just a moment. Now concentrate on yourself as you really are. Let your mind give to your consciousness some words that describe you. Get in touch with those words and see if they really do describe your true character. When you are satisfied that the words you are thinking of describe you, open your eyes, but remain quiet and don't look around at each other.

Exercise. (Pass out scratch paper.) Tear these pieces of paper into eight parts. They don't have to be even parts, because you're going to throw them away in a while. Now, on each of those scraps of paper, write one of the words that came into your consciousness a few moments ago—words that describe your character. If I were doing this, I might say that I'm usually pretty honest, that I tend to use people to get what I want, that I'm pushy, that I'm . . . (Etc., whatever the teacher feels at that time. GET INVOLVED YOURSELF!) Remember, one word or short phrase on each slip of paper. You are the only one who is going to see these words, so you don't have to be afraid to be honest with yourself. Now read what you have written. Arrange them in order, placing the one you are happiest about or like the most on top, and the one you like least or are least happy about on the bottom. Make a stack of them and place the stack right in front of you. Now for a while confine your eyes to the surface of your desk. Don't look at anyone or anything except the top of your desk and the pieces of paper. Take each piece of paper in order and really spend some time with that word. Stay with it for a few minutes and try on the word just as you try on clothes hanging in your closet. Our characters are like a wardrobe. We are sometimes one way, sometimes another. Today we are going through the wardrobe and examining our clothes and trying them on. Really see how they feel. Become the words you see. Accept them as *you* at one time or another, then do with the word and the piece of paper what you want to do. Put it back in your wardrobe, tear it up and throw it away, or whatever you wish. All right, you may begin. Take plenty of time with each word.

Evaluation. May be done by the students' relating their feelings to the group or by writing answers to questions dictated by the teacher.

b. Mirroring.

Divide into dyads. One member of the dyad is a person, the other is a mirror and mimics everything the person does. Can be done best in the beginning by standing and using large movements of the body, hands and arms, and head. (Later you can move to facial expression, really becoming the other person, etc., but large movement is easier the first several times.) The mirror can only reflect what it sees, so the mirror is to be aware of what he learns about the person. The person is seeing a reflection of himself, so he is to be aware of what he learns about himself.

Switch roles after about three to five minutes. This should be repeated several days later and could be an ongoing exercise that will gain in meaning as the students become more aware of each other and their own feelings.

c. Tell one special thing about someone else.

Divide into dyads. Have students carry on a normal conversation for five minutes. After two and a half minutes, if you sense the feeding of information ("I like horseback riding." "I read adventure stories." etc.), stop them and bring them back to a normal conversation. Inform the students before they start to talk that they are going to introduce the other person and tell one nice special thing about him.

At the end of five minutes stop them and go around the circle, having each person tell the special thing and introduce the other person by name. The group can then talk about how they felt during the conversation, while telling about the other, and while the other was telling about him.

d. The road map of your life: What I have available.

Introduction. (Seat students in a circle.) We're going to begin by closing our eyes again and concentrating on the spots on the

inside of our eyelids. Close out the thoughts of the outside world
and concentrate only on yourself, your breathing, and the world
inside yourself. Now concentrate on yourself as you are right
now, on the kind of person you are right now. Now concentrate
on your ideal self-image, on the kind of person you would like to
be in the future if everything you hope and wish for yourself
comes true. (NOTE: Take plenty of time between these steps for
the kids to get a good image.) Now, on the inside of your eyelids, draw a map. On the left is where you are right now. On the
right is where you want to go, the kind of person you want to be.
In the middle of your map you will probably notice some
obstacles. Be aware of what they are.

Exercise. Now concentrate on what you now have available
to you to help you get to where you want to go—people outside
yourself, things outside yourself, qualities of character inside
yourself, your body, your senses. Now slowly and quietly open
your eyes and look around at the other people in the group.
Would anyone like to tell the group what things you have available to you? (Discussion follows. If the students have really
gotten into it and if they are open enough, some very good things
can come out of this discussion.)

Another way of stating the first part of this exercise is Stu
Shapiro's* "Where am I now? Where do I want to go? What's
stopping me? Is there anything I can do about it now?" etc.

e. Sentence completion form (see pages 60–61).
f. Discussion: What is the most important thing in the world?
g. Carry on a class discussion about the nature of man entirely
   in the first person ("I am . . .").
h. What are my sub-selves?
i. Meditation and/or focusing.

Combination of Cognitive and Affective:
Write an essay entitled "Who Am I?" Then write another entitled

* Dr. Stewart B. Shapiro, Professor of Education, University of California, Santa Barbara.

"What Is Man?" Compare the two and list some things that are common to both essays.

4. Final evaluation:

Further discussion of the nature of man, deciding which interpretation the student prefers, and also evaluation of what the student has learned about man in general by studying himself in particular.

5. Possible integrative work:

Science: Biological studies of man's nature as compared to other animals.

English: Reading in short stories or novels that further illuminate the question of the nature of man.

Anthropology: Exploration of early man and primitive cultures to find what they have in common with man today.

Sociology: How does group behavior help explain the nature of man?

SENTENCE COMPLETION FORM

WHO AM I?

First name_____

1. In general, school
2. La Colina Junior High is
3. Right now this group is
4. My best friend
5. Teen-agers often
6. Ninth-grade English-History core is
7. I don't like people who
8. I am at my best when
9. Right now I feel
10. People I trust
11. The best thing that could happen to me would be
12. When I don't like something I've done, I

13. When I'm proud of myself, I
14. I'm very happy that
15. I wish my parents knew
16. Someday I hope
17. I would like to

List below five single words that you can associate with yourself now.

1.
2.
3.
4.
5.

UNIT OUTLINE

(Tenth-grade English, slow learners.   By Aaron W. Hillman)

    I. Title of the unit: The Human Jungle
   II. Teaching situation: Tenth-grade English class—homogeneous group
 III. General objectives for this unit:
      1. To gain an understanding of the novel.
      2. To gain further understanding of human beings.
      3. To see ourselves in the lives of others.
      4. To further skills in communication and critical thinking.
      5. To further skills in use of language through verbal and nonverbal means.

 IV. Text: *Lord of the Flies,* by William Golding
  V. Supplementary materials: Appropriate films, music, and poetry.
 VI. Summary of each day's activities:
      1. Daily diary: Questions from the novel relating to each person.

    a. Example: What power within you can destroy you?

    b. Example: What are you most afraid of in this group?

2. Discussions: On problems relating to the novel.

    a. Example: The joy of hunting.

    b. Example: What fears hurt our group?

3. Reading: From the novel by the students and the teacher.

4. Writing: On pertinent extracts from the novel.

    a. Example: What would happen if you were on a solitary island with a group of people and no one was in charge?

    b. Example: The boys taunt Piggy for his fatness, his glasses, and his lack of physical dexterity.

5. Classwork: Individual or personal projects of the students and pertinent affective training exercises.

6. Homework: Appropriate reading and writing papers.

    a. Example: Pride, pretense, and jealousy are other adult faults lurking beneath the innocent appearance of the boys.

    b. Example: Jack, whose choirboys have now become "hunters," would happily enforce the rules by beating up anyone who disobeyed.

7. Supplementary materials that pertain to the theme of the novel.

VII. Affective exercises to be used in conjunction with this novel:

1. First week:

    a. Short periods of eyes-closed meditation.

    b. Fantasy: Circle of students. In the middle a table with a rubber mallet. Set the problem: "You are a group on an airplane flight who have crash-landed on a remote and uncharted island in the vast Pacific. Your pilot is dead; your radio is dead. No one knows you are missing. This group, as you are now, is there. You are alone on the island. It is your problem." The teacher remains completely silent and assumes the attitude that these students are in that situation. It will take days, but eventually the students will form a government of their own in the same manner as the boys in *Lord of the Flies*.

2. Second week:
   a. Short periods of eyes-closed meditation.
   b. Unknown fears have begun to grip the boys on the island. Feeling this fear can be evoked through use of Spolin's *Improvisation for the Theater*.
      (1) Silent screaming
      (2) Immobilized by fear in a tense situation.
      (3) Exploding the fear through actual screaming.
   c. Listen to a recording in darkness of the sounds of sea and surf.

3. Third week:
   a. Short periods of eyes-closed meditation.
   b. The boys have begun adopting rituals and mock murder to ward off fears and as expressions of the unknown.
      (1) Make up rituals for use in the classroom of the students' likes and dislikes. Students perform these rituals.
      (2) Chanting and dancing and use of primitive instruments.

4. Fourth week:
   a. Short periods of eyes-closed meditation.
   b. The novel begins to bring out that evil exists in every man and is a necessary part of the human condition (the evil of unreason).
      (1) Improvisational theater. Two students in a circle of students. One student has it; the other wants it. "It" is never identified.
      (2) Have students listen to a recording of Stravin-

sky's "The Rite of Spring." Have the students enter into the music. Afterwards they record their feelings. (Part of this work includes a melodic evocation of a human sacrifice to spring.)

(3) Students prepare lists of things they like and dislike about themselves. They dispose of the dislikes as they wish and then enter into and absorb what they like about themselves.

5. Fifth week:

   a. Short periods of eyes-closed meditation.

   b. The boys in the novel have reverted to savagery, and at the last moment rescue appears in the form of traditional authority.

     (1) Students begin the series of Stu Shapiro's "Who am I?"

       (a) Who am I? (Single word.)

       (b) Write an autobiography.

       (c) Write a play about yourself.

       (d) What work do I want to leave in the world?

     (2) A class choral reading of Khalil Gibran's prose poem, "Revelation."

VIII. Summation of the unit:

  1. Is there such a thing as the "human jungle"?

  2. Does it lie in all of us?

  3. What can be done to prevent it?

  4. If you were one of the boys, what would you have done?

IX. Testing: No testing should be done. The students' writings and class participation for the unit should be evaluated with the student.

X. Miscellaneous activities: Where possible, walks to the woods, trips to civic departments, or other pertinent activities outside the walls of the school should be tried.

UNIT OUTLINE

(Tenth-grade English, slow learners. By Aaron W. Hillman)

I. Title of the unit: Courage, Non-Courage, and Being Human
II. Teaching situation: Tenth-grade English class—homogeneous group
III. General objectives for this unit:
   1. To gain an understanding of the novel.
   2. To gain further understanding of human beings.
   3. To see ourselves in the lives of others.
   4. To further skills in communication and critical thinking.
   5. To further skills in language through verbal and non-verbal means.
IV. Text: *The Red Badge of Courage,* by Stephen Crane
V. Supplementary materials: Films, music, poetry, any appropriate multimedia activity or approach.
VI. Summary of each day's activities:
   1. Daily diary: Questions from the novel relating to the reader.
      a. Example: What is your "courage"?
      b. Example: It takes courage for me to _____.
   2. Discussion: On problems relating to the novel and the reader.
      a. Example: What is the difference between youth and manhood?
      b. Example: As a man is, so will he act.
   3. Reading: From the novel and related works.
      a. Example: Choral reading from Benét's *John Brown's Body.*
      b. Example: Each student reads and reports on a work concerning the Civil War, such as McPherson's *The Negro's Civil War.*
   4. Writing: On pertinent extracts from the novel.

    a. Example: Was Henry Fleming a coward?

    b. Example: Henry's shameful deed remains hidden, his glorious one open and apparent.

  5. Classwork: Group and personal projects of the students and pertinent affective training exercises (see Section VII).

  6. Homework: Appropriate reading, writing, and experiencing exercises.

    a. Example: Interview someone who has known war.

    b. Example: Compare war poetry of the Civil War and of World War II.

    c. Example: Visit a museum and observe the older artifacts of war and how people react as they view them.

  7. Miscellaneous: Individual quests.

    a. Example: Debate: "Resolved: War is inevitable."

    b. Example: Collect a series of pictures that represent courage to you and weave them into a story.

VII. Affective exercises to be used in conjunction with the novel:

  1. First week:

    a. The novel concentrates on the hero's thoughts and actions "before the battle."

    b. Short periods in which the students "contact the environment."

      (1) Directions: Try for a few minutes to make up sentences stating what you are aware of at this moment. Begin each sentence with the word "now."

      (2) Open discussion.

    c. Differing types of courage. (Inductive.) Illustration that courage is mental as well as physical.

      (1) Double circle. Inner circle is given the single word "courage" for discussion. Outer circle is to remain silent and to evaluate the discussion

and a person in the inner circle. After a length
of time, the circles are reversed and the new
inner circle evaluates what was said, what went
on in the circle, and adds to the discussion topic.

(2) Critique.

2. Second week:

   a. The novel concentrates on the hero's thoughts and
actions in his first fight and his subsequent flight.

   b. Short periods in which the students "contact the
environment."

     (1) Directions: Try for a few minutes to make up
sentences stating what you are aware of at this
moment. Begin each sentence with the words "at
this moment."

     (2) Open discussion.

   c. Unconscious grouping habits limit our world. (Inductive.) Finding our groups without conscious selec-
tion. Finding meaning in ourselves and in the novel.

     (1) All chairs are pushed back against the wall.
Students are asked to congregate in the middle
of the room. They are asked to remain silent for
several minutes. During that time they are to
move around and to end up in groups of four.
If there are more than four in a group, then one
must leave. If there are fewer than four, someone must join that group. When the group of
four is set, they are to observe one another and
to remain silent. Then the instructor asks the
following questions. (The students are to remain
silent and only think about the questions. The
instructor makes no evaluations.) "Ask yourself
the following: (1) Who am I? (2) Who are the
people in this group? (3) What made me join
this group? (4) What feeling do I get from this

group? Now look at the other groups. Ask yourself the following: (1) How do those groups differ from mine? (2) How do those people differ from me? (3) What kept me from joining one of those groups? (4) What useful thoughts can I gain from this experience?" At the end the students resume their seats.

(2) Group critique.

3. Third week:

   a. The novel concentrates on the hero's thoughts and actions as he finds his way back to camp and rejoins his comrades.

   b. Short periods in which the students "contact the environment."

      (1) Directions: Try for a few minutes to make up sentences stating what you are aware of at this moment. Begin each sentence with the words "here and now."

      (2) Open discussion.

   c. Students are generally introduced to literature as some sort of object rather than as a form of life that has meaning to the personal being of the individual.

      (1) (Students should have paper and pencil.) Put all your present thoughts into a jar and empty it out upon the sand. Now think about the one person in the world you hate the most or like the least. Imagine that person as an animal and write down the name of the animal. Think about the one person in the world you love the most or like the most. Imagine that person as an animal and write it down. Imagine yourself as an animal and write it down. Now use an adjective and describe each animal. (Ask for volunteers and write the animal names and adjectives in

three columns on the board.) Compare the types of animals and the types of adjectives. (Where possible let the students make the comparisons.) Empty your mind again. Now imagine a huge forest. In the middle of it is a large open field. The animal that is you and the animal that is the person you hate most meet in the center of the field. Write down what happens. (Ask for volunteers and open for general discussion.) Now imagine the same forest and field. The animal that is you and the animal that is the person you love most meet in the center of the field. Write down what happens. (Ask for volunteers and open for general discussion.) Now imagine the same forest and field. The animal that is the person you love the most and the animal that is the person you hate the most meet in the center of the field. What happens? (Ask for volunteers and open for general discussion.)

    (2) Critique.

4. Fourth week

    a. The novel concentrates on the hero's thoughts and actions as he again goes into battle with his comrades (the "first charge").

    b. Short periods in which the students "contact the environment."

        (1) Directions: Write some pairs of opposites in which neither member could exist were it not for the real or implied existence of the opposite.

        (2) Open discussion.

    c. Music and war. Listening to music, seeing, and feeling.

        (1) Students are asked to relax and to have paper and pencil ready. They are to listen to a record-

ing and to jot down their thoughts and feelings as they come to them. They are not to force thoughts but simply let them come as they will. Afterwards volunteers are requested to share their thoughts with the group. (Record selected was the "Soldier's Chorus" from Gounod's *Faust.*)

(2) Critique.

d. Chants, music, and rhythm. Seeing rhythm in all things as motivation (i.e., involvement in lesson).

(1) Student brings a record of own choice and class listens to the beat. Count the beat. Point out the anapests; that is, two unaccented beats followed by a strongly accented beat. Collect students' names and write them on the blackboard. Sound out the beats and illustrate by use of symbols: ' for strong and ˘ for soft. Students tap on the desks with pencils to illustrate beat. Teacher reads Byron's poem, "The Destruction of Sennacherib," and students tap along with pencil to illustrate the beat.

(2) Critique with students "seeing rhythm in all things."

5. Fifth week:

a. The novel concentrates on the hero's thoughts and actions as he again goes into battle with his comrades (the "last charge") and his change from youth into manhood.

b. Short periods in which the students "contact the environment."

(1) Directions: Answer the following questions:

(a) What would the situation be if you hadn't got out of bed this morning?

(b) What would happen in a certain situation if you for once said "no" instead of "yes"?

      (c) What if you were four inches taller?

      (d) What if you were twenty pounds lighter?

      (e) What if you were a man instead of a woman (or vice versa)?

    (2) Open discussion.

  c. Seeing ourselves in others. In seeing others we see ourselves. The understanding of literature or language requires that you understand not only the writer and the things he creates but yourself as the reader.

    (1) Directions: Students are asked to form groups of four for discussion. After a period of time they are asked to break up into dyads and to sit facing each other. The teacher goes to each dyad and asks a student to say, "I am a mirror." After all mirrors are designated, the teacher says, "The one thing about a mirror is that it cannot talk. It can only reflect what it sees. You are you, and you have a mirror in front of you. Mirror, the person opposite you is looking into you." The teacher retires to the background. After a suitable period of time the class is called back to order.

    (2) Critique.

VIII. Summation of the unit:

  1. Summation is by individual reaction utilizing an amended version of the exercise in Laura Huxley's book *You Are Not the Target* entitled "Jump into the Other's Place."

  2. Directions: Get comfortable. Lean back. Close your eyes. Recall a specific incident of the novel *The Red Badge of Courage*. Begin to see and feel that specific situation. Feel the temperature. See those surroundings. Go through the incident once from beginning to end. And now, instead of trying to understand the incident, drop this effort entirely. And with a bounce of the

imagination jump into the other's place. Now go through
the same incident from the beginning. See the same
people and the same dialogue, but this time from inside
that other person.

3. Critique.

IX. Testing: No testing should be done. The students' writings
and class participation for the unit should be evaluated with
the student.

X. Miscellaneous activities: Where possible, walks and trips
should be taken to places where students can see people in
situations that require courage and where they can see the
differences between youth and manhood. Cultural activities
of all types would be appropriate. Observing wildlife and
observing human beings and setting up situations in which
the "territorial imperative" can be acted out would also be
singularly appropriate.

UNIT OUTLINE

(Tenth-grade English, slow learners.   By Aaron W. Hillman)

   I. Title of the unit: Listening, Hearing, and Understanding
  II. Teaching situation: Tenth-grade English class—homo-
      geneous group
 III. General objectives for this unit:
      1. To gain an understanding of the play.
      2. To gain further understanding of human beings and
         situations.
      3. To see ourselves in the lives of others.
      4. To further skills in communication and critical thinking.
      5. To further skills in the use of language through verbal
         and nonverbal means.
  IV. Text: *Death of a Salesman,* by Arthur Miller.

V. Supplementary materials: appropriate films, music, poetry, or any pertinent artifact.

VI. Summary of each day's activities:

1. Daily diary: Questions from the play relating to the person.
   a. Example: What is it you would like to do but "can't"?
   b. Example: Are you self-directed or other-directed?
2. Discussion: On problems relating to the person and the play.
   a. Example: Fathers live through sons.
   b. Example: Many people talk; few hear.
3. Reading: From the play by the students.
   a. Example: Neurological impress method.
   b. Example: Open readings with students taking parts from the play.
4. Writing: On pertinent extracts from the play.
   a. Example: The old and worn deserve respect.
   b. Example: Biff (about Willy): "He never knew who he was."
5. Classwork: Group and personal projects of the students and pertinent affective training exercises (see Section VII).
6. Homework: Appropriate reading, writing, and experiencing exercises.
   a. Example: See and report on an analogous play or film (e.g., *Life with Father*).
   b. Example: Read and report on the life of Eugene O'Neill.
   c. Example: Observe people and see if they are listening and hearing.
7. Miscellaneous: Individual quests.
   a. Example: Preparing a story with photographs and pictures.
   b. Example: Visit to a mental-health clinic.

VII. Affective exercises to be used in conjunction with the play:
  1. First week:
    a. Short improvisational-acting periods. Two students (boy and girl) play Willy and Linda. They are given the situation in Act I, Scene 1, and then improvise.
    b. One theme of the play is the lack of communication. There are four characters in the play who do not know one another even though they constitute a family.

"Touch Conversation."* Ten to fifteen minutes.
Procedure: Form dyads, close eyes while standing. With only your hands:
  (1) Carry on a conversation with the other person.
  (2) Slowly get acquainted.
  (3) One speaks, the other listens; then switch.
  (4) Do a dance together.
  (5) Have a fight.
  (6) Make up slowly. Don't hurry this.
  (7) Say good-by.

  2. Second week:
    a. Short improvisational-acting periods. Two students play Biff and Happy, the sons of Willy Loman. They are given the scene: "Biff, you are your father's favorite but have not met his expectations. You like outdoor work and drifting. Happy, you are a ladies' man, have your own car and apartment, and have an office job. You have not seen each other for some time. You are in the bedroom you shared as boys. Downstairs you hear your father talking to himself in the kitchen. Happy, you tell Biff that Willy has attempted suicide. Improvise the scene."
    b. "Experiencing the Resources of Communication," based on work of Virginia Satir (sound, sight, touch,

* Based on work of Bernard Gunther.

movements and gestures, the potential fullness of emotional expression).

Procedure: Form dyads.

(1) (Five minutes.) Pair is to sit back to back with no touching or turning their heads around. They are to use only talking to learn more of the other. (Five minutes.) Discussion and feedback of what was experienced.

(2) (Five minutes.) They are to sit face to face and express as much of themselves and learn as much about the other as they can by just looking.

(Five minutes.) Feedback and discussion.

(3) (Five minutes.) First half, looking and touching. Second half, just touching.

(Five minutes.) Feedback and discussion.

(4) (Five minutes.) They are to continue their dialogue using all of the resources—touching, facial expressions, gestures, eyes, *and* talking.

In the discussion period say what you have seen—icy stares, coy twinkles, avoidance, warmth.

3. Third week:

a. Short improvisational-acting periods. Two students play Willy and his brother, Ben. Ben is a success and Willy a failure. Ben represents self-direction and rugged individualism. Willy's philosophy is, as he states: "It's not what you do, Ben. It's who you know and the smile on your face." Improvise the scene.

b. Painting dialogue (origin unknown).

Procedure: Form dyads.

(1) (Five minutes.) Each partner is to paint the portrait of the other as he wants.

(2) (Ten minutes.) The partners explain the por-

trait to the other. Everything said is accepted. There are no questions, no aesthetic judgments, and no psychoanalyzing.

(3) (Five minutes.) The partners create a painting together.

(4) (Ten minutes.) They explain again.

c. Seeking hidden meaning (origin unknown). Procedure: Two students stand within a large circle of students. One is identified as having "it" and the other as wanting "it." "It" is never identified. The one who has it does not wish to give it up. The one who wants it wants it desperately. From these simple instructions the scene is improvised.

4. Fourth week:

a. Short improvisational-acting periods. Two students play Willy and his son Biff. Set the scene. "Biff, your theme is: 'He's got to understand that I'm not the man he thinks I am.' Willy, your theme is: 'What are you trying to do, blame it on me? If a boy lays down, is that my fault?' Improvise the scene."

b. "Evoking the Other with Listening," based on work of Gerald Goodman. Five minutes per person. Too often we think we are listening when we are actually asking questions or giving advice. For this exercise the speaker is to share with the listener some significant inner concern. The listener's task is to help the speaker express himself. Everything that is said is to be accepted. The two are working together as a team to help the speaker disclose as much as possible. Procedure: "Write two direct, clear statements about your interpersonal relations. Each should be a specific, frank, bold *statement* and not a question. Avoid statements that are comfortably abstract or nonpersonal. Chances are, reading either of these statements will be uncomfortable. The discomfort is probably a good indicator of whether or not the statement chosen is an inner concern. After the first person has read his statement, any *one* person in the group may engage him in conversation. The two-person conversation should focus on the statement—one person expanding on it and the other showing understanding (1) by repeatedly asking questions, (2) by giving advice, (3) by offering explanations for the problems, (4) by reflecting back to the individual how he appears to have felt when he expressed himself, (5) by bringing in one's own similar experiences when he expressed himself, and (6) by being quiet at times and really trying to know and feel what the person is talking about."

    c. "Listening to the Movement," transformed from work of Ann Halprin. Increasing awareness and expression of body language.

Procedure: Form a circle. Each person brings a piece of music he would like to move to, or everyone uses the music provided, or the dance is done without music. Each person in the group gets up in turn, and makes a personal statement about himself, another, the season, or whatever. (One use of this is to gain skill in expressing and reading body language.)

5. Fifth week:

    a. Short improvisational-acting periods. Three students. One plays Biff, one Happy, and the third their mother, Linda. Linda's theme is: "Pick up this stuff. I'm not your maid any more." Biff wants to please his mother but wants to be his own man. Happy acts as a pacifier. Improvise the scene.

    b. Interpersonal mirroring (encounter-group origin). Thirty-five minutes.

Procedure: Form dyads.

(1) (Two five-minute phases.) The members decide

who will be the communicator and who will be the mirror. The mirror is to reflect only nonverbally what he is experiencing of the other's message. The communicator is free to use words, movement, or whatever. They reverse after five minutes.

(Five minutes.) Feedback and group discussion.

(2) (Five minutes.) The two are to create. That is, by spontaneously interacting they are mutually to create a dialogue, a give-and-take discussion.

(Five minutes.) Feedback and group discussion.

(3) (Five minutes.) Continue Item 2 for another round.

(Five minutes.) Feedback and group discussion.

c. Telling how you feel the other person feels about you. Five minutes plus.

When: Two persons have a misunderstanding and a desire for more understanding.

How: To ask each to tell the other how he imagines the other thinks and feels about him. Some reflection and introspection is needed for this, which is likely to have a quieting influence, a self-awareness direction, and result in a heightened interest in listening to each other. After all, it's infrequent in everyday life that so much is shared.

VIII. Summation of the unit:

The unit is summarized by having each student state his beliefs and opinions of the play. This is done in an interpersonal manner, using part of a discussion technique developed by Ted Crawford in "Revolving Discussion Sequence." (The technique is also good empathy training— self–other.) An hour plus.

Procedure: One person begins as the speaker and the other

becomes the respondent. The speaker makes his point, and the respondent is to (1) show *understanding* of the words, and (2) state his maximum *agreement* with what has been said. Do not encourage artificial agreement. That is sometimes hard for people to accept, because they find it difficult to agree with much that has been said. Ask the group members to save their *disagreement* and *arguments* for the next step, (3) where the respondent now becomes the speaker and says what he wishes to say. At this point he can state his disagreement.

IX. Testing: No testing should be done. The students' writings and class participation for the unit should be evaluated with each student.

X. Miscellaneous activities: Where possible, walks and trips should be taken to places where human beings can be seen in interaction. Students could also interview people outside the class. All such activities should be directed toward finding out whether what is being said is heard and understood.

SHORT INTEGRATED CONCEPTUAL UNIT IN DRIVER EDUCATION

(Ninth-grade social studies, all levels.   By Robin D. Montz)

I. The concept of the machine.
   1. Cognitive context: The study of internal-combustion engines and other moving parts of the automobile.
   2. Affective exercises.
      a. The machine: One person starts an action accompanied by a sound. Other members of the group, as they see where something might fit in, join the machine with their own action and accompanying sound. The objective is to show the structure and function of parts making up the whole and how each part functions for

the whole. After doing the machine, have the students express how they felt being part of a machine. Some may like it; others may be frustrated if they get in touch with their individual anonymity as part of a mechanistic system.

b. Have the students draw a machine. Make up a Rube Goldberg type of "crazy" machine in which all parts have a function for "something."

II. Anger, frustration, and behavior change in driving.

1. Cognitive concept: What do the extreme emotions of anger and frustration do to your driving behavior?

2. Affective exercises:

a. Improvisational theater: "You want to go somewhere, and I won't let you."

b. Gibberish games ending with "You've got it, I want it."

3. Cognitive evaluation: How did your behavior change when you were angry? Frustrated? What would that do to your driving? How can you release these inner tensions and revert to normal behavior naturally?

III. The concept of courtesy.

1. Cognitive definition: Courtesy is stepping into the other guy's shoes, understanding, and allowing him to "do his thing."

2. Affective exercises:

a. Getting communication going.

(1) Dyad work. (See exercise by Virginia Satir, pages 74–75.)

(2) Encounter groups.

b. Getting rid of resentment: Gestalt work with the person you most resent.

c. Role reversal with resented person.

3. Cognitive evaluation:

a. Discussion of courtesy.

b. Simulation of driving situations involving the need for courteous behavior.

On the following pages are individual lessons and short series of lessons which were used as parts of other units.

The following lessons were developed by Aaron Hillman for so-called "slow learners" in tenth-grade English.

EXPERIENCING LIFE

AIM: Experiencing, illustrating, knowing, and enjoying other parts of life. Providing models and experiences to show other ways of living.

FORMAT: Five male students, sophomores in high school (fifteen to seventeen years old), so-called "slow learners," culturally and economically handicapped, had a formal dinner with the teacher at the Madonna Inn in San Luis Obispo, California.

EVENTS: Preparations by the boys were extensive. Consideration about what to wear was paramount. The idea of ties (and not having any in three cases) was a problem. On the night of the dinner one did not have a tie, three wore ties and nylon zipper jackets, and one wore a suit and tie. At the inn we were seated in the middle of the room with luxury around us. We were surrounded by other diners and had a good view of the stage. We discussed napkins (What do you do with them?) and which eating utensils to use. We had drinks (Tom Collinses without gin) and discussed the menu. Four opted for filet mignon (after learning what it was and how to pronounce it), and one had fried chicken. During the meal we talked and discussed many things, mostly their feelings about school, school personnel, and relatives. They discussed what they could do with this room at a party. One boy thought the pink satin tufted chair covers would be great for seat covers in an automobile. After dessert and listening to the band, we toured the restaurant. All the staff from bus boys on up were extremely courteous and helpful; they went out of their way to assist us and to show us the place. Before departing, we toured the rest of the complex.

CONCLUSIONS: This was an extremely informative and vibrant experience for the teacher as well as the boys. We got to know one another better, and we exchanged viewpoints on life without the necessity of their bowing to peer pressure or my bowing to social pressure. It was a frank exchange. The boys participated in and enjoyed a segment of living that they had not seen or experienced. From our conversations and their frank expressions of gratitude at the conclusion, I believe the funds were more than well spent. As a side issue, I think we gave the people at the restaurant something to remember. Some asked who we were and talked with the boys, and we received many appreciative glances from other people. As another side event, the relationships between the boys and learning, the boys and their classmates, the boys and the teacher, improved; and they settled into a subtle acceptance of one another and readiness for work in the classroom. The necessity for discipline dwindled, and more work was done by the boys during class time. In all, this was an extremely profitable venture for society, the boys, and the teacher.

ORIGIN: Funds were provided for this dinner under the Cultural Enrichment section of the Elementary and Secondary Education Act of the federal government.

DECISION BY CONSENSUS

AIM: Experiencing how group decisions are made and how groups can work together to solve a common problem. Experiencing and illustrating the novel. Understanding the characters in a novel. Becoming aware of group interaction and how to function better in a group situation.

FORMAT: NASA—Decision by Consensus

First section (to be taken by individuals). Instructions: You are a member of a space crew originally scheduled to rendezvous with a mother ship on the lighted surface of the moon. Because of mechanical difficulties, however, your ship was forced to land at a spot some two hundred miles from the rendezvous point. During the landing much of the ship and the equipment aboard were damaged, and since survival depends on reaching the mother ship, the most critical items still available must be chosen for the two-hundred-mile trip. Below are listed the fifteen items left intact and undamaged after landing. Your task is to rank them in order of their importance in allowing your crew to reach the rendezvous point. Place the number *1* by the most important item, the number *2* by the second most important, and so on through number *15,* the least important.

_____ Box of matches
_____ Food concentrate
_____ 50 feet of nylon rope
_____ Parachute silk
_____ Portable heating unit
_____ Two .45-caliber pistols
_____ One case of dehydrated milk
_____ Two 100-pound tanks of oxygen
_____ Map of the stars as seen from the moon
_____ Life raft
_____ Magnetic compass
_____ 5 gallons of water
_____ Signal flares
_____ First-aid kit containing injection needles
_____ Solar-powered FM receiver-transmitter

Second section (group consensus). This is an exercise in group decision-making. Your group is to employ the method of group consensus in reaching its decision. This means that the prediction for each of the fifteen survival items *must* be agreed upon by each group member before it becomes a part of the group decision. Consensus is difficult to reach. Therefore, not every ranking will meet with everyone's complete approval. Try, as a group, to make each ranking one with which *all* group members can at least partially agree. Here are some guides to use in reaching consensus:

1. Avoid arguing for your own individual judgments. Approach the task on the basis of logic.

2. Avoid changing your mind only in order to reach agreement and eliminate conflict. Support only solutions with which you are able to agree to some extent, at least.

3. Avoid conflict-reducing techniques such as majority vote, averaging, or trading in reaching decisions.

4. View differences of opinion as helpful rather than as a hindrance in decision-making.

On the Group Summary Sheet place the individual rankings made earlier by each group member. Take as much time as you need in reaching your group decision.

Key. Take the difference between your ranking and the ranking on the key. Add the differences. The lower the score the better. These answers are based on the best judgments that are now available to you. They are not absolute answers.

15	Box of matches	Little or no use on moon.
4	Food concentrate	Supply daily food required.
6	50 feet of nylon rope	Useful in tying injured together; helpful in climbing.
8	Parachute silk	Shelter against sun's rays.
13	Portable heating unit	Useful only if party landed on dark side of moon.
11	Two .45-caliber pistols	Self-propulsion devices could be made from them.
12	One case of dehydrated milk	Food; mixed with water for drinking.
1	Two 100-pound tanks of oxygen	Fills respiration requirement.
3	Map of the stars as seen from the moon	One of the principal means of finding directions.

9	Life raft	CO$_2$ bottles for self-propulsion across chasms, etc.
14	Magnetic compass	Probably no magnetized poles; thus useless.
2	5 gallons of water	Replenishes loss by sweating, etc.
10	Signal flares	Distress call when line of sight possible.
7	First-aid kit containing injection needles	Oral pills of injection valuable.
5	Solar-powered FM receiver-transmitter	Distress-signal transmitter—possible communication with mother ship.

Third section (critique). Following the exercise, discuss the sources of the problem-solving techniques. How often did individuals use the affective domain in working out the problem? How often did the cognitive domain dominate? What kind of balance existed? How did their knowledge of the extensional world allow them to work with the unknowns? What did they learn about their own learning styles? Did they work better in groups or alone? Did they score higher as a group, or was the individual score better? How did the scores compare with the group average? Did they enjoy the individual work more than the group work?

Fourth section (applicability). Compare with the group problems experienced by the boys in the novel *Lord of the Flies.*

EVENTS: Extremely productive. There was much concentration and thought given to the answers in the individual phase of the exercise. Some went through the items quickly, while others took considerable time and thought out each answer. There was a lot of interest in the work. During the group phase also, some groups finished quickly with little interaction, while some fought long and hard to establish the consensus. In a few cases the decisions were the result of the rest of the group's deferring to one member of that group. The boys were particularly impressed by knowing that they were working on an exercise that was part of NASA's training program. In the writing phase at the end of the exercise these were some of the evaluations:

"Nothing happened except we all came to a decision."

"Well, we kept on narrowing down the answers until we got the answer."

"We finally talked it over because we were getting out of hand; some felt like punching me in the mouth."

"We would get excited and start to explain, and everybody would stare at the one who disagreed."

There seemed to be general agreement at the end that if the boys in the novel had practiced what they had learned in the exercise, then they might have been able to solve their problems before the trouble started.

CONCLUSIONS: A perfect vehicle for working with this particular portion of the novel and an excellent way for students to experience the problems inherent in working with groups. In addition, they were able to experience and to work out the emotions that were aroused and felt during both the individual phase and the group phase.

ADDENDA: In William Golding's novel, *Lord of the Flies*, a group of boys isolated on an otherwise uninhabited island attempt to set up a provisional government to solve their problems. The attempt fails and anarchy results because of their inability to mesh their emotions, goals, and ideals. This exercise was used to show what the boys might have done.

ORIGIN: National Aeronautics and Space Administration training exercise.

PERSONAL COMMUNICATION AND LISTENING

AIM: Implementing the point of view about human relations that each person is aware and responsible and direct in his own communications and listens as fully as possible to the other person as an equal.

FORMAT: As fully and as quickly as possible the instructor asks that in all interactions that take place in the group people speak directly to each other without the use of the third person. Throughout the exercise he should discourage questions and keep a steady, gentle pressure on the direct and responsible "I–thou" relationship.

EVENTS: As occurring.

CONCLUSIONS: Staying in the Here and Now and directly communicating and listening.

ADDENDA: Relate to training in personal communication and listening, as well as to training in the art of conversation.

ORIGIN: Unpublished paper entitled "An Introduction to Gestalt Therapy," by John B. Enright, Ph.D., Langley Porter Neuropsychiatric Institute, 401 Parnassus Avenue, San Francisco, California.

LSD BRINGS OUT THE REAL YOU

AIM: Inductive. Use of drugs and knowledge of self.

FORMAT: Began as a short talk by the teacher about doors that prevent people from seeing people and doors we hide behind. Two individuals (a boy and a girl, both Mexican American) of a Group 4 (remedial) class took sides and argued their points. Discussion by the teacher was used as a summing up.

EVENTS: It began with the boy saying that only under LSD could one show his real self. He was very tense, emotional, and deep as he argued the points. He knew he was right. "Why, if one felt like it, under LSD he could go out and kiss a donkey." The girl was equally intense, deep, and moving. Her main point was that drugs or whiskey weren't necessary to life. Besides, one shouldn't show all that's behind one's cover because everyone needs some secret. Other students listened intently and talked and worked on what was being said.

CONCLUSIONS: Tremendously moving experience for the teacher as well as the students. A tenth-grade boy who could hardly read or write thought deeply and spoke eloquently. A girl, conscious of her background and her way of expression, found satisfaction in defending her significance. Students saw and heard a valid, moving argument on the drug problem. There is no question to me that inductive learning took place.

ADDENDA: Used in connection with Stephen Crane's *The Red Badge of Courage* and Henry Fleming's feelings and emotions as portrayed in the writing.

ORIGIN: Spontaneous. The class began a discussion of the hero of the novel, Henry Fleming, and the doors that had to be opened by him in order for him to take his place in the world, as well as the doors that prevented him from being his real self. When the boy stated that "LSD would open those doors," then the class interaction and the intense argument between the boy and the girl began.

THE SIGHTS OF SOUND

AIM: Inductive. Inner imagery; imagery of music. Creativity training. Finding meaning in and feeling the essence of a novel.

FORMAT: Students assumed comfortable positions and closed their eyes. The lights were turned off and the blinds drawn. Smetana's *The Moldau* was placed on the phonograph. "While at rest and alert with the mind, close your eyes and listen to this rich, evocative piece of music. Let yourself go into it and absorb it. When the music is finished, stay with your impressions. Ask yourself what images were produced." Afterwards the students were given a copy of Longfellow's poem, "The Sound of the Sea." They were asked to record (1) their impressions while they listened to *The Moldau* and (2) how Longfellow's poem expressed the sound of the music.

EVENTS: After the usual preliminaries of closing the eyes or resting the head on the desk, the students were picked up and put on by the music. They became absorbed in the sound and the sight. There were many movements of body and feet and hands in response to the audio stimulation. Subsequent to the music, the writing period produced excellent results. The following are selected samples.

"It shows how fast our emotions can change and they always do, just like the record."

"The ocean can be like humans, sometimes there's peace, and sometimes a hard tide washes all the beauty away."

"Made me think of a man standing in front of an audience playing his violence."

"I heard the sound of music in my mind and I see a sea of red blood which is pumped from my heart and will flow right into the hearts of others."

"I saw during the music at first in a big, very large room. The room looked as if it belonged in a mansion in France. Then it got very loud and it reminded me of sailors or fishermen at sea, then I thought about Moby Dick and men struggling to capture it. It was real wild and noisy. The poem, 'The Sound of the Sea,' now that I think about it, matched the music just right."

"I saw a stream of water that flowed into a river then into the sea. Then it flowed into another stream where there was a dam and the sea didn't want to stop following so the sea broke the dam with waves, waves of power almost like a hand hitting a person. Then the stream came to rest in a small valley where it stayed."

CONCLUSIONS: Music by itself in creative exercises seems to me to be of unquestionable value. Combining the music with poetry seems appropriate for understanding both the music and the poem, as well as the person himself. Combining the two further and relating them to the work we are studying enhances the knowledge of the work and possibly helps in retention of its concepts. This particular exercise is valuable also as a simple writing exercise.

ADDENDA: Used in connection with Herman Melville's novel *Moby Dick*, and the feeling of the characters in the novel about the ocean of which they were a part.

IMAGINE A CAVE

AIM: Creativity and writing exercise illustrating how a novel may be read and enjoyed. Inductive. Personal insight; inner imagery.

FORMAT: Close your eyes and relax. Imagine a countryside in a foothill setting. Large oak trees soar out of the earth as large, immobile sculptures. The sun is about to set, and long shadows are boldly clothing many of the ravines. The shadows of trees seem to be spirit partners of their parent forms. Fog patterns are rising up wraithlike from lowlands to shroud the grasses and trees in moving shapes fantastically human in form. You are walking up a ravine in the last light of day amid the swirling fog. Soon you find a cave. When you enter it, experience whatever occurs. Let yourself continue until the fantasy stops. When it does, write down or draw parts of it.

EVENTS: This was soul-satisfying to the students and myself. There was considerable reluctance on the part of the students to close their eyes, and it was extremely difficult for many to keep them closed. As long as they were quiet, I didn't press the point. The picture was presented slowly, distinctly, and softly. Some of the inner lines (i.e., the trees as sculpture) were repeated or embellished. At the conclusion we sat silently for at least three full minutes, and then I asked them to record their experiences. A few wrote very little; most wrote furiously for five to ten minutes. Some found the cave lighted; others found it dark and long. A "dinner for two" was set in one. Some examples: "I was alone in a dark and weary place." "There came shadows walking slow through a crowd." In general, every aim cited above was accomplished. In addition, and this I find the most gratifying, they enjoyed the experience and writing very much.

CONCLUSION: The students were intrigued by the exercise and enjoyed the imagining and the subsequent writing. The massive amount of work done by all was impressive. For stimulating creativity in the use of the imagination and getting students with writing problems to write a lot and to express their feelings, it is an exceptional device. The next time I use this exercise, I plan to try the idea of a trip across a desert on a cold night with subsequent entry into a warm and well-lit house; then I will compare the cave and the house as to what was experienced, what was felt, and which makes the better exercise.

ADDENDA: The class is reading and experiencing *Moby Dick*. One main character, Captain Ahab, is said to be surrounded by phantoms. After this exercise, the "cave" was likened to the world of Ahab's brain. A class discussion period followed.

WHERE AM I NOW?

AIM: Inductive and deductive. Experiencing ourselves as we are; being aware of ourselves. Preparation for creativity and understanding.

FORMAT: Mary Whitehouse exercise. Students sit where they please. "Let us try an experiment. At this moment you are sitting and listening to me in a particular physical way; let's find out what it is. Please close your eyes. You may feel slightly embarrassed or self-conscious; but once everybody has his eyes closed, the embarrassment is not located on the outside. It is not because someone else is looking, but because you are. The looking is an act of *attention*. Do not move or change your position; just be where you are. Now begin with your feet. Where *are* they? Are they touching the floor; and, if so, what part of the foot is pressing on the floor?

Are they touching each other? Are they alike or quite separate and different? Wiggle your toes inside your shoes. Can you feel them? Now travel up to your knees and do the same thing. Are they crossed over each other? Is the back of either one or both touching the chair seat? If not, at what point do the backs of the legs rest on the chair? Travel along underneath and behind yourself. How much of you is touching the chair? What are you sitting on? Go on to your back. Is it rounded or straight? Are you leaning back? Where? Are you sitting more on one side than the other? What are your arms doing? Where is each one? Finally, how does your head feel? Can you feel it, or do you just know it is there? Now try to be aware of yourself all at once, of all of these things at once so you can recognize: I am sitting *this way*. Now open your eyes." Discussion and feedback period follows.

EVENTS: My preconceptions had been that the students would resist and that much difficulty, snickering, laughter, and inability to close the eyes would result. These happened, but to a minimal degree. The room was darkened, which could have assisted in quieting embarrassment or feelings of unease. During the exercise, a majority of the students could be seen trying to sit and to move and to feel what the instructions were asking. They became absorbed in the exercise. During the discussion and feedback the comments ranged from "I didn't feel nothing" to the expressive "I discovered all of me!" When the teacher tied in this feeling to the lesson we were studying, the students seemed genuinely intrigued both by themselves and the novel.

CONCLUSIONS: All aims were satisfactorily achieved. Students became more aware of themselves and that we don't just happen to be, we *are*. They became more interested in themselves and in our lesson. It seemed to me that the exercise was also useful in overcoming embarrassment, in relaxing with the group, trusting the group, and enjoying the simple pleasures of life. I can also see this exercise as leading into a productive reading and writing exercise.

ADDENDA: Related to *Moby Dick*. In today's lesson the novel's narrator, Ishmael, says, "The problems of the universe revolve in me." This exercise and experiment was an attempt to have the students know and experience that feeling. The "problems of the universe" revolve in every one of us. However, we actively seek to avoid this fact in our daily lives.

ISOLATION

AIM: Experiencing, illustrating, knowing the feeling of isolation.

FORMAT: Students were arbitrarily set in groups of six. Sexes and races were deliberately mixed. Two students from each group were asked to step outside for a moment. The remaining four were told to accept one student when they returned and to direct their conversation and questions to that person. The other person was to be ignored entirely and was not to be talked to under any circumstances. Then two students from each group, each one alone, were sent out to walk about the campus and to return in twenty minutes. At the conclusion, each individual and group was told the circumstances and reasoning for the exercise. A critique was held. The teacher reviewed the novel and the concept of isolation.

EVENTS: The students sent out on their own were very apprehensive at the idea of leaving. In two cases the students returned in a few minutes saying that there wasn't anything out there. In another two cases they came back and requested someone to accompany them. They were, as they said, "lonely and wanted someone with them."

The two students sent out from each group were also apprehensive. The students "in the know" liked the idea and entered freely into the exercise. The students who received all the attention became very animated and delighted with the attention. In two cases, where the student was normally shy or withdrawn, he was brought out of his shell to some degree. The students who were rejected were very much concerned. They tried all sorts of ruses to speak to others and in three cases became abusive because no one would listen to them. Some rejected the whole group and wouldn't speak to them.

In the critique they stated that they felt happy, alone, sad, rejected, mad, uneasy, and in the case of those who were sent out to walk the campus alone, that their friends "didn't want to be with them." It was stated that they had experienced this isolation many times but hadn't paid much attention to it. In one case a boy stated that he wished we could do something like this often, because he got to talk to more students than he had in the classroom all year.

The teacher related to them the circumstances of isolation in the novel and spoke briefly on how groups are formed, how we often isolate people from our groups, and how we often isolate people even within the group.

CONCLUSIONS: The sense of isolation was forcefully presented. The students themselves experienced both exhilaration and isolation, and gained an understanding of how it feels and of how we consciously and unconsciously accept and reject other persons.

ADDENDA: The group was reading Herman Melville's novel *Moby Dick*. The sense of isolation felt by the hero, Ishmael, was more clearly understood.

SOURCE: Unknown.

The following lessons and lesson elements were developed by Robin Montz for use in junior-high social studies and English, all ability levels.

   I. Human-rights concept. Use of improvisational theater to get deeper understanding of the concept.
      1. Began with warmup:
        a. Divided into groups of three.
        b. "Talked" to each other in gibberish.
        c. Told them, "Now without gestures or anything, begin slowly to exclude one of the three from the conversa-

tion. The one being excluded should concentrate on how it feels."

   d. Found out by repeating this and rotating the exclusion which ones felt it most deeply.

2. Set up the scene: "You have it, he wants it." Worked in gibberish, then English, then gibberish, etc., moving in and out of these two.

3. Got to the basic situation: When there are "in"s and "out"s in a society, the "out"s get angry because they can't have what the "in"s have, and the "in"s get angry because the "out"s try to take it away from them.

4. Students really felt the anger and were able to express it well. They expressed later that they felt that they really understood for the first time how minority groups must feel.

II. *Julius Caesar*. Affective techniques:

1. Attempt to make the play more contemporary by relating it to the assassination of Kennedy.

2. Use of improvisational theater in a contemporary setting to bring out the meaning of some of the scenes. For example: "You are grieving over a friend who has just been killed. You walk out of the funeral to see all the people having a party celebrating your friend's death. They're glad he's dead! Improvise the scene. Go." (Act I, Scene 1.)

3. Use of Frederick Perls' "stage-fright techniques" to overcome reluctance of students to act out scenes. Lots of work with "top dog–underdog."

4. Ritual assassination of a dummy filled with students' gripes. Used a shaman group and chants to work group to a high emotional pitch. Dummy torn to shreds. Then worked with feelings of elation and guilt, love and hate, through use of the play's funeral oration and by evaluation.

5. Creative projects: Students took one emotion either ex-

hibited in the play or felt while reading the play and expressed that emotion through any medium—dance, music, poetry, art, etc. Many outstanding projects resulted.

All these were extremely successful both in getting across the subject content and in getting the students in touch with their feelings.

III. Simulation games. Used simulations of the electoral process (model American government, which also serves as the class governmental structure) and of a crisis involving six African nations and two major powers (a variation of the "Crisis" game, by Western Behavioral Sciences Institute).
1. Cognitive content:
   a. Experience of decision-making process.
   b. Firsthand experience of electoral process and international relations and related material.
2. Affective emphases:
   a. Feeling of responsibility for decisions.
   b. Emphasis on resentments toward major powers.
   c. Feelings of winning or losing.
   d. Feelings of being occasionally lost in complexity.
IV. Remedial work with two groups of "problem-causers."
1. Began with the "blaming" game. Discovered in both cases that they felt left out of the mainstream of school life, that they had ideas and contributions to offer but that the other students and teachers wouldn't accept them.
2. Used the Gestalt game "Resentment, Demand, Appreciation" around the group to great success. Students opened up when confronted with resentments against them and developed a real sense of communication and love through the series of appreciations.
3. At another session we worked through some basic encounter situations, both verbal and nonverbal, which resulted in a heightened awareness of other students and in

one girl the ability to break through a sense of self-depreciation and an inability to express aggression. She finally began to fight back.

4. Used some very simple and basic Gestalt methods with an empty chair and "top dog–underdog" confrontations and worked with "telling secrets."

V. Result thus far (as of April 1968).

1. General improvement in behavior, contributions, and attitudes of all but one of the students.

2. Greater acceptance of the students by other students.

3. "Smiles" and real creativity from all the students.

4. This is still a somewhat unfinished situation, as the students still feel a real need for more work. They pressure me every day for "the group," and so we meet as often as possible.

NOTE: By the end of the year all but two of the students in the two groups seemed to have reached a period of adjustment to school and an awareness of their own strength and their position and contribution to themselves, each other, the class, and the school. This was a truly successful remedial situation.

The following is a partial list of ideas and suggestions that came out of our meetings which were not used in the project and still remain to be tested in the classroom.

1. When difficulties arise in getting students to talk to each other, use nonsense talking or gibberish to try to get them involved.

2. Get people to be the parts of a sentence and actually experience the relationships between parts of speech. Devise sentences that can be used with body expressions.

3. Build a box that a student can put his head into and yell—one that muffles the sound.

4. Write gripes on a ball or something. At the end of the week kick the ball around, chanting the gripe. (Modified quite a bit and used by Robin, Aaron, and others.)

5. Use a volleyball, foam-rubber practice golf balls, or cushions as aggression-releasing devices.

6. "Brainstorm" some nonsense syllables to substitute for dirty words, swearing, etc.

7. Training program for *teachers* in using the "Now" game.

8. Have students act out the parts of speech.

9. Have students become a math problem. "What if someone added you up wrong? How would you feel?"

10. In foreign-language classes, if a student doesn't know the word for something, don't let him ask for it in English but have him show the teacher the word he needs by acting it out or doing something.

11. Institute a course combining all the languages. How does each language express the same thing?

12. (After the description of Aaron's ritual murder of the pig in *Lord of the Flies.*) Have students experience being a *victim* as well as a hunter.

13. Other universes: An exercise of moving into paintings and describing how you feel in there. Feelings can be described through body movement.

14. Have the students who are involved in some kind of encounter switch over and "move into the other guy's skin." If you were Tom, how would you feel? Be Tom; and, Tom, you be Jack.

15. Synectics: Concentration on an object. Three stages: (1) Direct analogy: What is it like? (2) Symbolic analogy: What is its essence—its symbolic meaning? (3) Personal analogy: Become the object and merge with another object.

16. Experience objects physically (rocks, jungle gym, etc.); then paint what you feel (taste, smell, etc.) instead of painting what you see.

17. Have students do some fantasy work with dying. Try to experience dying peacefully and dying violently.

18. Write secrets on a piece of paper, put them in a hat, draw, and tell the secret you draw as if it were your own, *or*

Two or three people working on two or three secrets respond individually to the same secret.

19. Divide the group into dyads. Each person is to write four or five things about the other that he wishes the other person would change. Then the other guesses what the first wrote. They then exchange lists. Do the same with appreciations.

20. Have students act out pictures in magazines or paintings, etc.

21. Develop a really neutral place to go in fantasies (as opposed to a cave, which is not neutral).

22. Build a fantasy dream house.

23. Synesthesia (mixing of sense modalities) used in writing a play: Write a play built around synesthesia.

24. Before taking tests, studying, etc., have students use the body-awakening exercises (toning up the system) and see if learning doesn't increase.

25. Encourage the use of synesthesia in writing poetry. (How does the blue sky smell?) Set up experiences for the students. (Taste the sky; smell red.) Have students describe how they felt as they moved through the experiences.

26. Define and develop statements about the intuitive process.

5|

One Day in a High School

A VIEW THROUGH THE CHALK DUST

By Aaron Hillman

I sense anticipation as I round the corner and climb to the second floor of the school. Yes, there he is. Gerald. Every morning you are there, Gerald. School will begin thirty minutes from now, but you are always down the hall looking out the window.

"Good morning, Gerald."

A smile that barely lights your young face but lifts your shoulders. "Good morning, Mr. Hillman."

This is a good room I have. Those Venetian blinds ought to be fixed. Well, maybe the Board will find the money next year, if they don't condemn the whole place. Open the doors; perhaps some of the kids will come early. Let's see. The assignments are on the board; better check them. The boards are getting dirty. John will have to wash them. LSD, love, peace symbols—the boards have sure changed the last few years. Stan is probably doing the scribbling. I wonder what makes him think he's a hippie. For an FFA boy he sure isn't cow-minded. Well, I'll erase this part of the board and see what's on there tonight. They really like to write all over the boards. A lot of creative expression and feeling goes into their scribblings. Wonder what lets them do it on the board and stops them from putting it on paper.

Might as well begin with some music today. Ah, I think we'll begin with Debussy's *The Sea*. The Beatles will come soon enough, along with Herb Alpert. Now, what have we got to work on today? We can use Longfellow's sonnet "The Sea." No, we're working on *Death of a Salesman*. What have I put on my lesson plan? . . . Here it is! I'd better keep this thing locked up or I'll lose it. Here we are. Communication is the theme. Well, English is our subject. What a beautiful play this is! Lee J. Cobb was great. They could call this "Death of Everyman" and it would be accurate. The kids are really enjoying this thing.

"Can I have a library pass, Mr. Hillman?"

"Sure, Irene. What are you working on?"

"Everything. But mostly I don't like that darn study hall. It's too boring."

Yes, everything is boring when we don't want to do anything. One can learn a lot in a library, even if one goes only to sit.

"Can I put another record on, Mr. Hillman? This thing isn't any good."

"Sure, Felix. What makes it no good?"

"It hasn't got anything."

Damn the bells! We ought to be able to get rid of those things. We've got a clock in the room; why do we need bells? Poe knew what they sound like.

"Al got busted last night."

I wonder if they ever really hear what they are saying.

"Jay came over last night and threw rocks at my window. We were talking, and my dad came and yelled at him and beat me. Why are parents so mean?"

"How long's Al been pushing grass?"

"I don't know. I didn't even know he used it."

"Mr. Hillman, you know Al's been busted?"

"No. What is he in for?"

"For pushing grass."

"I'm sorry to hear that. If you see him or hear from him, tell him that I asked about him and look forward to his returning to class."

"I'm not going to see him till he gets out. I'll let you know."

"Mr. Hillman, I'm going to be married next week."

"Why, that's just great! Who's the lucky boy?"

"Ricardo Martinez."

"I don't know him, but if you picked him I know he's O.K."

"I'll give you an invitation if you'll come."

"You couldn't keep me away. You send me the invitation. I'll be there."

"You'll get one."

How excited the girls are! They can't wait to get out of here and to start keeping house and making kids. Sophomores. Sixteen years old, fifteen years old. Wish I were as happy about their future as they are.

"Can I take the roll now, Mr. Hillman?"

"Yes, go ahead, Jessie."

Where is my pencil? Here's one. Let's see, where are we now? Right.

"Ladies and gentlemen, shall we begin?" I don't know why I say that. I know we'll begin as soon as they cool down a little.

"Mr. Hillman?"

"Ramon."

"Can they make us go to school in the summer if they want to?"

"Well, the state can. I don't know about the local Board. By state law we have to go to school at least a hundred and seventy days. I presume the local Board can prescribe more if they wish. Other than that, I don't know."

Phil hasn't changed that shirt in a week. Wonder how I could get him a new one without hurting his feelings.

"Ladies and gentlemen, let's get started with today's work. We have a lot to do, and I think some surprises for you." What makes me pace up and down like this? "We are going to work on two things today from our play. In the first case, it has to do with the hero of the play, the salesman, Willy. Willy has the idea that one of the main paths to that great goal of success is the ability to impress people." Walking around keeps them attentive and quiet anyway. "He believes that you impress people by the way you dress and talk and act. He believes that if you act a certain way people will recognize you, accept you, and you will become a success. That is the question I would like to begin with you today. Look at yourself and ask yourself the question: In what ways do I impress people? Write three lines or more on that subject and put it in your diary—unless you don't feel like writing on that subject, in which case write on anything you please." Ah, here's Grady. He looks as if he were mad or on the weed.

"What are we talking about?"

"I was just asking the class the question, Grady, in what ways they impress people."

"I know how I impress people."

"How is that, Grady?"

"Ah, I know. You impress people by being yourself."

"What do you mean by that?"

"I just let them know where they stand. They don't get away with anything with me."

"How are they impressed?"

"They know better than to mess with me."

"Do you mean you frighten them?"

"Sure I frighten them. The big phonies are scared of me."

You're scared of yourself, Grady. You're afraid to let us see you. They have frightened you so much that you've quit trying. "What would happen if you really tried to impress people by being yourself?"

"I am myself. This is me."

"What is you?"

"You know. Me. Like I am now. I go where I please, do what I please, and nobody bugs me. I can stay out late and get drunk and nobody bothers me."

The class is watching us. They are waiting for something.

"What do your parents say?"

"What can they say? I could beat them all up. When I come in at night my mother says, 'Grady, you shouldn't drink.' My dad says, 'Grady, you're going to get into trouble.' I tell them to mind their own business."

"What would happen, Grady, if they made you stop what you are doing? What would happen if they took an interest in you and really made you stop?"

"You're a phony, Mr. Hillman."

"So are you, Grady."

"The world is full of phonies."

Standoff. We've got to get to him before too long. It may be too late now.

How do you impress people? It will be interesting to see how they have answered that question. We are all trying to impress people all the time. We spend a lot of energy in that practice.

God, where does the time go? It seems as if we'd been working and talking for only a few minutes and already it's almost time for the bells.

"Will you put your work away, please. Pat, will you pick up the folders?"

This class has been good. First period is always slow. Some of the students can't seem to get up early enough to get here. I must do something about the absenteeism in this first period. But what? Threats and punishment will only make them dig in deeper and hold on to what they have.

"Hold it! Everyone keep your seats! To those of you who might be interested, a week from Saturday we are going on a trip to Ventura. Ask your parents if you can go if you are interested, and we'll get together and decide how we will select those persons to attend. The bus will only hold fifty students and I have a hundred and thirty. See you tomorrow."

Look at them go. Happy, smiling, five minutes to get from here to there, and back to whatever grind the next class calls for.

"Mr. Hillman, have you seen my history book?"

"Any books I find I put up on the shelf. When did you leave it?"

"I think it was last week, but I don't remember."

How can anyone not miss a book right away? That book hasn't been looked at since last September. Wonder if I should get a drink of water.

"Ooops. Excuse me, Mr. Hillman. Didn't mean to run into you."

"Cool it, Fritz. You might fall and hurt the floor."

The halls are full and then they are empty. It's a real race.

"Cool it, friends. Martin, will you get the folders and pass them out?"

"Mr. Hillman, what is my grade?"

"What grade do you want, Vivian?"

"I'd like an A."

"What will you do with it?"

"I've always wanted one. I think I deserve one for the work I've been doing."

"Do you know how I feel about grades?"

"Yes, but I don't think that's right. It's good to work for grades."

"I'll agree with you that grades are O.K.—that is, if the wanting and trying to know come first. If you do that, the grade will come by itself. Regardless of what it is, it still won't be anything but a letter."

"I know all that. But I'd just like to have an A on my grade card sometime."

"I'll go along with that. Why don't we discuss it with the class when evaluation time comes up again."

"Oh, they'll be too jealous to vote me an A."

"No, I don't think so. If you and I convince them of what your work has been and what you're working for, you'll get that A easily."

I wonder if anyone has ever stopped to figure how much of a teacher's time is spent figuring out grades, marking grades, computing grades, entering grades in records, putting them on report cards, discussing them with students and parents and colleagues—

and weighed all that against the pain and sorrow grades produce. I wonder how the high schools ever became the agency responsible for culling out the low achievers for colleges.

"Ladies and gentlemen, we are concerned today with a special happening in our play *Death of a Salesman*. Willy, as we know, is always trying to impress people. And he thinks the way to impress people is by putting up a big front, being a showoff. In his attempts to impress people, he often has to tell lies. Some are small; most are relatively harmless, if we want to believe that any lie is relatively harmless. But Willy's lies are believed. *He* really believes them. To him they are not lies. For Willy it is easier to lie than to tell the truth. For our discussion period today let's consider the question: What makes it 'easier' to lie than to speak the truth? Anyone have any ideas on that subject?"

Silence. Looking at one another, at the floor, out the window. What catastrophic expectations they have. Who will break the silence first?

"Mr. Hillman, I think it's better to lie than to tell the truth if you're going to get hurt by it."

"You are saying that if you tell the truth you get punished anyway?"

"Yeah. So why tell the truth? You might get away with it."

"Ron tells lies all the time. He never tells the truth."

"What do you know?"

"I know you don't tell the truth."

"So what?"

"I don't know about you two at all. I try always to tell the truth."

"Are you telling us, Bonita, that you don't always tell the truth?"

"Yes, I don't think I do. I try, but sometimes I can't help it. But when I do, I go to church and ask for forgiveness."

"What keeps you from going to the person you lied to and telling them the truth and asking for forgiveness?"

"I couldn't do that. It wouldn't help them. Then maybe they would never need to know."

Bonita, behind those thick glasses your beautiful face is searching, always searching. I see you fighting all your teachings. I see you wanting to join this group of kids your own age and live your own life. I see you hurting.

"Bonita doesn't even get to date yet."

Why did you bring that in, Ramon?

"That's none of your business."

"Well, it's true. Why don't you tell the truth?"

"O.K., so it is true. That's my business. I wish I could date, but my parents don't believe in it."

"But you have been out with boys. I've seen you out with boys."

"Sure I have. And I've got in trouble at home, too."

"Who cares about parents? What they don't know doesn't hurt them."

"They always find out. They won't let me date. Everyone else gets to date. I'm sixteen years old, and I can't date. I can't even walk home with a boy. Every time I get a boy friend he gets bored with me. Who wants to be with a girl he can only see at school?"

"If a boy really liked you, he wouldn't care."

Good old Lucy. Always the protectress. In your cage of family life and lack of "good looks" and the bag dress they hang on you, you still find others to help.

"Not for a while, maybe. But five minutes in the hall between classes doesn't amount to much."

"What makes parents do that way, Mr. Hillman?"

"What would you do as a parent, Jim?"

"I ain't a parent."

"Do you plan on getting married someday?"

"I probably will. Everyone else does."

"Well, it generally happens that when people get married they have children. O.K. So you're a parent. What would you do?"

"I know what I'd do."

"Bonita?"

"I would teach my children right. I will teach them right. And I'll trust them and I'll let them do what they want to do."

"But what if you believe they shouldn't do something they want to do?"

"Then I'll stop them."

"When we wrote on the question from the novel *Lord of the Flies*—you remember the book—that asked: 'What do you do if children don't obey their mother?', many of you wrote that you would lock them up and take any privileges away, and a great number of you said that you would beat them or otherwise physically punish them. Is that how you are going to handle your children?"

"I would talk to them. I would tell them why."

"But what happens if they still don't obey? What do you do to them?"

"Well, I would never punish them. Hitting kids never does any good. You just make them mad at you and they go out and do something bad."

"Hey, that's what you do, Bonita!"

Good point, Julius. "Julius, you remember that time you got sent to the dean this year and suspended?"

"Sure."

"What was the reason you got sent there?"

"Aw, you know."

"Yes, I do. But can you tell the class again?"

"Aw, I tore some of the paper rolls off the toilet wall and shoved them down the toilets and stopped them up."

What are they laughing at? It is nervous laughter. Are they saying something to us in the system? What is going on deep in their skulls?

"Julius, could you go back just for that day? Start at the beginning and tell us what happened to you that day."

"Everything? Right now?"

"Yes. Could you tell us?"

"Well, I got up in the morning."

More laughter.

"He's crazy, Mr. Hillman!"

"Well, after breakfast—I made it myself, no one was up—I went over to Dean's house and we rode to school on his motorbike. Then I was in school until I got thrown out."

"Did anything happen to you in school that day? Anything special before you got caught?"

"I got into a big argument in my world-history class."

"What happened?"

"Well, Mr. Richards is a nut. He hates kids. We came in and he started picking on us. He told us we weren't studying, we were all failing, and we were just dumb. I made a noise, and he jumped on me—told me I was the worst one of the whole class and I was going to get an F. I told him who cared about world history. It was just a bunch of useless junk that would never help me. I'm going to work in a garage, and I didn't need that stuff. He really got mad. He told me off and made the class get out their books, and we read and he shouted at us all period. Then he said that Cortez had conquered Mexico in two years and Spain owned it all by 1521, I said, 'So what?' He said that I was impertinent and he was tired of what I'd been doing all period and I should go see the dean. So I slammed my books down and took off."

"This was the day you were suspended."

"Yep. I got kicked out, took a three-day vacation."

"Did you go by the bathroom on your way to the dean's office?"

"Yeah, I got caught there, too."

"Did you want to get caught?"

"Heck, no. Who wants to get caught?"

"Julius, do you see any connection between what happened in the history class and what happened in the bathroom?"

"Sure. I was mad when I was in there. I didn't want to go see the dean and get kicked out of school and have my dad whip me."

"You were mad. What were you mad at?"

"At what the teacher did."

"What did you do?"

"Nothing. When he got mad, I got mad back."

"You were mad."

"Sure."

"What were you mad at?"

"I was mad at him for putting us down."

"For putting who down?"

"For putting me down."

"What made you mad?"

"What made me mad? You know—I just said it."

"There, inside you, what made you mad?"

"He called us stupid; he made us look bad."

"He called you stupid; he made you look bad."

"He did! Everyone was there; they know!"

"Julius, how could anyone get mad because someone called him stupid?"

"You ain't supposed to call anyone names."

"Aren't." Quit correcting, Lucy. You know what you are doing.

"He was calling you names?"

"Yes."

"Julius, what if he had said 'abracadabra' to you. Would that have made a difference?"

"Sure. That don't mean anything."

"But suppose he said it in the same tone of voice. He would be calling you stupid."

"That wouldn't make any difference."

"Then it's the word that bothers you."

"Yes. You shouldn't call anyone stupid."

"Julius, a word has no meaning unless you give it meaning. When he called you stupid it was you that gave that word its bad feeling. Can you see that?"

"I made it a bad word?"

"Yes."

"You mean because I think I'm stupid?"

"Yes."

"Well, I don't think I'm stupid."

"I know you're not. But we often forget that what a word means is what we want it to mean."

"Mr. Hillman, that doesn't make any sense."

Big, overgrown Fred. A puzzled look on your face. Interested in something for one of the few times in here.

"Fred, consider this. Well, all of you. Is there anyone here who doesn't know what the term 'S.O.B.' means?"

Everyone does. Yet we find learning so difficult in school.

"O.K. Now, I hear you talking in the hallways, in the cafeteria, in the gym, at football games, and other places. You are always calling each other names. The other day I heard a fellow call, 'Hey, Henry, you S.O.B.!' Now, you and I know what that meant. We know what he was calling the other guy. So did the other guy. But did he get mad? No. The other guy called back, 'I'm over here, you jackass!' Now, what was happening here?"

"That's different. They were friends."

"But those are words that you will fight over. Many of you have told me you would fight over such words."

"But it's the way they are said and who says them."

"I'll agree to that. But what does that say about words?"

"They don't mean anything unless we give them meaning."

"Good, we understand each other now. Julius, do you see?"

"I got it. I thought I was stupid when he said I was."

"I think that might be right."

"So I tore the paper off the wall because I was mad at myself?"

"That's possible, Julius, very possible."

Silence. It is *so* silent. No one is looking at anyone else. Each of us is busy with his own thoughts and a single thought. I'm tired. I'll bet they are as tired as I am.

"Mr. Hillman, can I put something on the record player?"

"Sure, anything you want."

This third-period class is my slowest class; how can they ever decide anything like that? These kids are great! Here's Howard. He sure looks troubled about something.

"Mr. Hillman, why do the white Southerners hate Negroes so?"

"Do you think they hate Negroes?"

"Sure, look what they do to Negroes down there."

"Have you ever visited there, Howard?"

"No, but I read and I hear what my friends say, and I see what goes on on television."

"The things that you see, hear, and know they are doing you are convinced are done out of hate?"

"What else is it?"

"Let me give you a problem to consider. What if you were born a white boy in Mississippi instead of a Negro boy in California? What would you be like?"

"I suppose I wouldn't like Negroes."

"Yes, but for what reasons?"

"Well, I was raised that way."

"You were raised to think the Negro was inferior. All right, now you know that. But what makes you mistreat them?"

"I don't like them. I hate them."

"But what makes you dislike them, makes you hate them?"

"That's the way I was raised."

"No, we've been over that. We agreed that you were raised to think the Negro was inferior. What we are after now is trying to figure out why you want to mistreat them, to hold them down, to keep them in their place."

"It makes me feel better."

"You get a good feeling because you can put somebody else down?"

"Sure."

"What is the basis of this good feeling? Where does it come from?"

"Everybody likes to be good at something."

"If you were born white in Mississippi, as we supposed, would you be any different than those boys are now?"

"No, I suppose not."

"I think we can say that's the biggest problem they have,

Howard. That isn't saying it's right. But it's going to take us a long time to change things. From the beginning it was all wrong. Do you know much about Negro history?"

"No, I don't know anything at all."

"Well, the Negroes were brought to this country as slaves. We all know that, I think. Sometimes we forget that some Negroes sold other Negroes to the ship captains just as the Arabs did. So the guilt, if there is any now, belongs to human nature itself rather than to groups. Anyway, they were brought here to work in the fields, a source of cheap labor. The Negroes played a big part in our history. Negroes fought in the Revolution to gain this country's independence." I wish the other kids would leave us alone. "They played a big part in the Civil War. I have a book at home called *The Negro's Role in the Civil War*. If I bring that book to you, would you read it?"

"Sure."

"O.K. I'll bring it tomorrow. Now we had better get the class started."

I sensed and saw your feelings of unease as you came into the room. Your eyes take in the desks sitting back to back, and you look at me questioningly.

"What are they like that for?"

"We will work this way today."

You do not like it. Your brows crease, eyes lift. All through the writing period you shift uneasily, look anxiously about. You mumble to your friends. I ask you to put your work away, and the babble of sound echoes in the room.

"Ron, will you sit behind Gerald?"

"Him? What for?"

"We're going to talk to each other."

"Stupid."

All of you look at me. Sixty bright eyes seeking the message.

"Keep your chair close to that of your partner but do not let your backs touch. Now, without turning your head, talk to your partner. Use only talking to learn more about each other."

You laugh. Gay talk. Shouts. Shoving with the head. You are alive.

But you, Marla, and you, Jeremy, sit forward and stare at the floor. You are not here. I see your troubled faces and the eyes that speak of fear. Some of you can't talk this way. You must speak to other people in other places. Can your partner mean so little to you?

"What did you experience?"

"That was fun."

"I felt stupid."

"Is this English?"

"Carlos has bad breath."

"I couldn't hear because my ears are turned the wrong way."

It was these things and a thousand more. It was asking you to recognize another human being as something more than an object. And it was those of you who could find no words to express your experience.

"Now, as quietly as possible, pick up your chairs and turn them so you are face to face with your partner."

Crash! Bang! Baroom! You didn't understand what I meant, did you? I am the only one who hears thirty kids talking and thirty chairs banging at once. No, not quite. I'm sure to hear from the teacher downstairs.

"Ladies and gentlemen." You are that, you know. "Sit face to face with your partner. Express as much of yourself as you can and try to learn as much about the other as you can by just looking. Do not talk."

You laugh. Some of you start making faces at each other. Dennis, I see you with your head down and your pencil tapping lightly on the desk. Simon, you are watching everyone but your partner. Juanita, I see you drinking deeply from your partner's eyes and the ease with which Della empties the pitcher for you. But Della wants something of equal value, Juanita! The noise that you make is a screen.

"Would anyone share with us what he experienced?"

"It was hard not to keep talking."

"I felt so good I couldn't keep my mouth shut."

"Ron and Gerald, you never looked at each other once. Could you share with us what you were feeling?"

"I wasn't feeling anything. I think he's ugly."

The wince that crosses Gerald's face is not noticed by you. Will you ever see beyond the range of the skin that houses us?

You are relaxed a little. You are ready again.

"Sit face to face again. Express as much of yourself as you can and learn as much about the other as you can by looking. Do not talk. However, this time add the sense of touch. Touch as you look."

Frightened laughter. Ribald laughter.

"Boy, is he queer!"

No, Ramon! It is a queer society that says two human beings cannot touch except in a formal, cold, ritualistic way.

Some of you are avoiding each other completely. There are more of you. The horror of touching is making you shift, twist, and avoid. Watch other people, Marla. You, who haven't said a word in months. We hear you screaming in the dark inside, and all our candles have not helped at all. But Jon, quiet Jon, I see you lean forward as Frank leans forward. And I see you both in all serious-ness touch and cross pencils. I see your smiles. I see the warmth of life flash between you. We share our experiences again.

"Carmen is crazy!"

"I felt funny. Sorta embarrassed, but it was fun, too."

"Why don't you find someone who will work with me?"

"It's scary. I don't like people looking at me that way."

"Liu wouldn't talk."

"I don't like touching a guy; that's queer."

A tumble of sounds and noises. You are more relaxed now. Your eyes are bright and dart this way and that.

"Ladies and gentlemen. Let's continue with our conversations and use all our resources. Touch, use facial expressions and ges-tures, speak with your eyes, and talk out loud."

Instant bedlam. Hands flash back and forth cutting the air with your rhythms. The release is good, and you speak volumes. You are finding ways of using all the resources of communication.

Marla and Jeremy, you still sit apart and do not speak or look at each other. But you are watching the others. You are talking and listening even more now than you did before.

Listen.

I am tired. It will be good to relax with the kids at lunch period. I'd better open some windows and the doors. A little piano music of Williams would be good. Carrot sticks and celery and half a sandwich. Joy. I hear some of you coming down the hallway. One of the boys has just tried to communicate with one of the girls by touching her. Her joyous and unafraid scream rockets down the hall. Clumsiness is a part of learning.

"Hey, Mr. Hillman, we had trouble coming up here. One of the hall patrols said we had to have a pass to come up here."

"I'll pass the word on again that if anyone says they are coming to this room they don't need a pass. Make sure you do come here, though, or we'll all be in trouble!"

The room is a bedlam again. God, I get so tired of the noise! What a good group they are. Cora and Sherry came in with their lunch sacks and are sitting in the corner looking at everyone again. Cora wrote the other day that she is ugly. She believes that. Sherry knows she isn't, but is too shy to speak up, to be humanly aggressive. What will they do?

Irene and Lora are dancing. Hope that shuffling doesn't bring up the wrath from downstairs. So many of them grouped around the phonograph and so few are dancing. The girls can get up courage enough to do it, but not the boys. Either they think they have to do it right or they are too intimidated. They are afraid of what their peers might say. Intimidation is a good word. We have intimidated them in our schools and our homes, and have given them nothing good to replace what we drove out of them.

Stan is at the board again. "Hippies rule." He's written a new one. "Clyde, the Funny Farmer." That's him. He chose that name after we did that television show together. That's his stage name. I can read his writing on the board. He can hardly write when he puts pen to paper.

Bonita has her usual group of boys around her. She is so beautiful that the boys are falling all over her, and she can't be anything but what she is. Beautiful, vivacious, with eyes that have secret depths of their own, and a father who is so jealous of her that he watches her every move, even through the school. She is going to break his stranglehold one of these days, and he will only think that she has betrayed him.

"Mr. Hillman, can we work on our festival program?"

"Sure, Marietta."

Marietta, Marie, Ben, and Roy, and the shy girls in their group. Together they have strength.

"Mr. Hillman, our big problem is getting the boys to do anything."

"What's our mayor, the honorable Ben, and El Presidente, Roy, doing?"

"I'm ready to be president, Mr. Hillman, but I don't know what to do."

"Have you talked to any of the groups, discussed their problems?"

"Yeah, but the boys won't do anything. Some of them said they would show up, but they won't do anything."

"Try again, Roy, and keep trying. It's slow and painful work, but they will come along."

"What's the mayor supposed to do, Mr. Hillman?"

"What does the mayor of this town do, Ben?"

"He runs the city."

"How does he run the city?"

"I don't know."

"Well, that's what you're supposed to be doing. Think about it."

"Mr. Hillman, what is this festival thing supposed to be?"

"Well, it seemed to me that it would be fun if we had a Mexican American Happening. I saw us as getting the city park and exhibiting some of the work we do as well as work that Mexican-American or Spanish people have done. We are all foreigners in this country, and every one of us has some special sort of background. I think we ought to recognize it once in a while. Since I couldn't recall when we had any sort of Mexican celebration, I thought it a good idea to have one. This doesn't mean that it can't be fun or shouldn't be fun. We ought to have as much fun as possible. But I don't want to do it all myself. I would like to have you do the work yourselves. I'll help out, but first I want you to try. That was the reason for my reply to Ben. I want him to try to find out for himself. I'll help you out and call a quick meeting if things go wrong, but I would like you to plan this and to put it on."

"Yeah, that's good; but the boys don't want to do anything."

"Work on them. But remember, accept whatever it is they will do and push them no farther than that."

"Can we get costumes?"

"We'll have some money for that, but first we'll try to make our own."

"I could get some stuff we have at home, and my dad is going to Tijuana next week. They could get some stuff."

"Sounds good. That's a good start."

"Mr. Hillman, is it all right if Marietta and I go visit the stores and pick some things?"

"Yes, go ahead. Just be sure to bring me the bill. Does anyone here know any mariachi players? It would be good to have a mariachi band simply strolling along and playing during the festival."

"I think I can get one, Mr. Hillman."

"Good, Carlene."

"Mr. Hillman, as mayor do I have a police force or anything like that?"

"Yes, I think it would be good. They could dress as you wish with badges and all and look after the exhibits. Some of those things could be stolen if we don't keep an eye on them. You are also going to need a sanitation department. Someone to help us clean up afterwards."

"Who do I get for these jobs?"

"As mayor, you have the power of appointment."

"Anybody?"

"Anybody. However, remember that it is easy to appoint but hard to get others to agree. But don't get discouraged, and keep after them."

A babble of sound. Everyone's talking at once. They are excited about the festival. I am excited myself. It will be great fun, and we will get the students and the parents interested.

Fifth period is coming up. I know I don't do as well with that group as with the others. After four periods it's rough to come back into the arena again. And they have just finished lunch.

Good God! There's Rod on a bicycle, riding in one door and out the other. Doesn't look as if he's hurting anyone. Simon is here, looking glum as usual. Fritz is bothering the twins. Interesting group. Fritz is small, wiry, and lithe, and trying to go somewhere in school. The twins are big—bigger than I am—and weigh about two hundred pounds apiece. They make a strange group, but they seem to like each other.

"Rod, could we put the bike away for the rest of the period?"

"Sure, Mr. Hillman. You want to ride it?"

"I just might give it a whirl after a while, but I don't think so now."

"Mr. Hillman, what does Rod think he's doing?"

"Ask Rod, Adele."

This class is very mature in size but less mature in an emotional sense. Half Mexican-American, one Negro, and the others low-income, low-culture white. There has to be something wrong with a system that calls these kids slow learners. They have simply been raised differently.

"In our play, *Death of a Salesman,* we are working with a family who have trouble communicating with each other. That is, they do a lot of talking but no one listens to what the others say, nor do they hear what they say themselves. It winds up in the end with the son, Biff, remarking that his father, Willy, 'never knew who he was.' For our discussion period today let's take that phrase and work on it: 'He never knew who he was.' "

A small ripple of sound, among themselves, to themselves. They very effectively block us out when something to learn comes along. We have conditioned them to this through the system and the work. And we think we have to keep doing the same old things and they will work. We are really making the child conform to the knowledge rather than setting out the knowledge for the child to eat.

"What does that mean, Mr. Hillman, that he never knew who he was?"

"What does it mean to you, Fritz?"

"Nothing to me. It don't make sense."

"Well, let's try it. The 'he' refers to Willy, the salesman. 'Never,' of course, means something that has not happened. Now to you, Fritz, who was Willy?"

"He's just some guy in this stupid play."

"Well, that may be true. But who was he?"

"He was a salesman."

"Who was he as a human being?"

"I don't get you."

"What was he as a human being?"

"Well, he was a father and he sold things for a living."

"True. However, those are things he did."

Roy is watching us intently. I wonder if he sees what we are at.

"Yeah, but he was a man, and he wanted things. He wanted money; he wanted to be something big."

"What for?"

"Why shouldn't he want it?"

"What will he gain by getting what he wants?"

"Money! Be a big wheel!"

"All right, I'll accept that. Ladies and gentlemen, you have heard Fritz and me in discussion. Now let's try something as a group. Will you form a circle, please."

From silence to bedlam in seconds. Attention is repressive to kids. Silence is repressive. Is every one of us afraid to be quiet?

"Roy, would you join me out here in the circle?"

"Out there? By myself?"

"Yes, it will be just you and I."

"What for?"

"We are going to work together for a few minutes."

"Go on, Roy. He isn't going to hit you."

"Let Fritz go. You were talking to him."

"True, but I would like to work with you, also."

"Well, O.K."

He's going to come out! He's taking the risk of moving out into the center!

"What are we going to do?"

He's as big as I am, and truculent. I'd better be careful.

"I would like to set up a scene, Roy, and have you work with me on it. O.K.?"

"I guess so."

"This may sound difficult or not understandable, but let's try it. I would like you to imagine that I have 'it.' Now, you want to get it, but I don't want to give it up. Try to get it from me."

"What is it?"

"That we don't know. But try to get it from me."

His eyes are suspicious, his mouth twisted into a funny grin.

"O.K. Why don't you give it to me?"

"I want to keep it myself."

"You don't have any need for it. Let me have it."

"That doesn't make any difference. I've got it, and I'm going to keep it."

"Yeah, but you don't need it."

"Do you need it?"

"Sure I do. You don't need it. Why don't you give it to me?"

"I don't have any reason to. It's mine, and I don't have to give it to anyone."

He's beginning to circle around me like a fighter waiting for an opening.

"You don't have any use for it. Can I buy it from you?"

"No. It's mine. I'm going to keep it. Money couldn't buy it."

"Aw, come on, I need it. I got to have it. I need it now."

"I don't see that you need it."

"Well, I can see it! What do you want to be so stubborn for?"

"I'm stubborn, just because I want to keep what's mine?"

"But you aren't using it. I can use it. Let me have it."

"I'm not concerned about you. It's mine. That's all there is to it."

"If you don't give it to me, I'm going to take it from you."

"You can't ever take it from me no matter what you do."

He's coming close and staring into my eyes.

"I could take it from you any time I want!"

"Perhaps, but I'm not going to give it to you."

"But I've got to have it. You've got to give it to me!"

"Put your hands up."

"What?"

"Put up your hands, palms out flat. Now push them against mine as hard as you can."

He is strong. I think I can hold him for a while.

"Give it to me! Give it to me!"

"Push, Roy! Push!"

"Give it to me! Give it to me!"

We are moving back and forth. I'm tired. The students are quiet.

"Roy, you can have it. I give up."

He looks dazed, exhausted, yet pleased about the whole thing.

"Is that all, Mr. Hillman?"

"That isn't all, Roy, but we are done for now."

The class is silent. Roy is sitting down and burying his head in his hands.

"Thank you, Roy and Fritz, for working."

This is as subdued as this class has ever been.

"Ladies and gentlemen, in our play the salesman, Willy, wanted success, and he wanted it badly enough to cheat, steal, lie, and sell his soul and his family to get it. Success was his god. And success to Willy meant having a lot of people liking him and having a lot of money. It is much the same with your friends you see around you. When one of the boys has to have a big car and makes it squeal and burn in the schoolyard or in front of people, he needs success. He needs, in other words, to have people see him, to be recognized, to be somebody. He cannot yet see that that kind of success doesn't bring the happiness he needs. Everyone needs success. It's how we gain it that makes the difference. Now, I would like you to record in your journals the experiences, feelings, and ideas that you had during this period. Take your time and put down exactly what you feel."

They are silent and writing well. Roy is almost attacking the paper.

Sixth-period lunch. I thought it would never come. I think I'll take my lunch and go to the cafeteria. It is my day to supervise in the cafeteria this period. After as much teaching as this, we should be relieved of the duty, but it does have its interests. Most of the students are sitting in their accustomed places. We don't assign them places, but they find their own. I think I'll sit with Jon.

"Play a game with me, Mr. Hillman?"

"Set up the board and pieces. I'm ready to go."

The place is a bedlam. Talking, talking, animated, bright, full of life. Release after the day's tedium of studies. The boys trying to figure out how to talk to the girls. One boy always seems to lead, and a group trails after him.

"Your move, Mr. Hillman."

"I'll take your king's pawn."

Our special-education students, blind and retarded, always sit together. It is lovely how they help each other.

"Can you help me with this math problem, Mr. Hillman?"

"I'm sorry, but I can't, Daphne. I'm not very good at math. Check with Arlen over there in the corner. Do you know him? He's very good at math."

"Well, O.K., but I don't like to talk to boys."

Wonder where that puts me.

"Checkmate, Mr. Hillman."

"Hmmm. Only for a minute. You forgot to check something here."

"Now you've got me."

"It looks that way, Jon. I don't think you have a move."

"I'm not sorry about that. It was a good game."

"Thank you, Jon. We'll play again soon. I think I'll wander around a bit now."

"Thank you, Mr. Hillman."

Empty lunch sacks arc toward the trash cans. Some miss. Some are picked up. Boys are hitting each other. They have no other way of showing affection or expressing what they can't speak. A good many girls are working on their lessons. Only two or three of the boys. Ella is working at the cash register.

"Good afternoon, Ella."

"Hello, Mr. Hillman."

"Enjoying your work?"

"Oh, yes. I like it. Besides, I get to eat for nothing."

Probably the only good meal she gets. Wish we could do something about clothes for these kids.

"Hello, Dan."

"Hi, Mr. Hillman. Guess you know I'm cutting class."

"No, I didn't know that. What happened?"

"I couldn't go to class again today. It gets boring after a while."

"Maybe it will pick up later."

"I don't know; it's all boring."

What are they really saying when they say it's boring? They must be telling us something, but what?

"Excuse me, sir."

Well, that's one for the day! One gets jostled a lot each day but seldom hears an apology. Well, they don't mean to push. Life is too exciting. Seventh-period bell. Best to get out of the road until the room is empty.

Think I'll look over some of the kids' papers today. I'm getting behind a little in that work. Gosh, how they mark up these folders! Simon's is covered with writing—all aimless. Roy's has a big cross on it with the words "For Sale" in the middle. Here's another cross with a Nazi swastika on it! The folders are all marked and covered with their scribblings. What are their thoughts at the moments of writing? What does it mean, these beautiful drawings with the words 'ESP,' 'LSD,' 'Love'; the drawings of scarabs, automobiles, and persons with flowing hair and weird eyes? Where are the young today?

Fred has written something on that. "The world progresses and progresses like a ship that keeps on sailing from island to island but never stopping. For example we invented the automobile and were we satisfied? No! We had to invent the atomic bomb, the missile, and other inventions!"

In answer to the question "If a person believes differently than you, can he still be your friend?" Lucian has written: "In a case such as this I believe that the person should not pick his friends just because they all believe in what he does. A person could learn more about different people, their beliefs, their problems, and learn to understand them. For these people are our neighbors, our brothers in the eye of the Lord. Oh! Yeah!! It is better to have a friend that believes differently than you than to have an enemy who has the same beliefs as you."

Good point. Good writing. Who could say it better?

Jerry's writing is poetic. "I am a mirror. I am a lovely mirror. I am a mirror that reflects loveliness. I am a mirror of body and shape. I reflect body of beauty and shape. I am a mirror. I am a lovely mirror. I am a mirror that reflects loveliness. A mirror of

which I am. One who is afraid of the dark for without light there
is no reflection."

Carmen has written: "The thing wrong with education is that
we are forced to learn the things we dislike." Where did these
dislikes come from? Why do we force students to learn such things?
If they are important, the children will learn them because they
want to. Why can't we see that learning can be fun?

Phil has written a book review of *Old Yeller*. His last sentence
is good. "The meaning I find in the book is that a dog can become
a hero and not just a man." Excellent, Phil. There is heroism in
everything.

Rosetta's work is good. She has deep and penetrating thoughts
as well as wild flights of fantasy. Yet she will marry young and lose
what gifts she may give us. She doesn't come to school often and
only stays to escape from home. "White always looks so empty,
and it looks bigger than the whole world. It makes you think of the
lonely people in the world; it makes you wonder why—you are surrounded—and why you are being drowned in this pure heaven,
when it is what you least wanted."

There are so many papers. One hundred and thirty students and
they are writing continuously. I cannot give of myself enough to
read their work fully and to correspond with them. I do what I can.
We must somehow manage to have smaller classes so that real
dialogues, learning, and respect can come to exist between students
and teachers. We must not continue to stand apart. We cannot turn
over human relations to machines.

"Hi, Mr. Hillman!"

"Hello, Dolores. Don't tell me it's eighth period already!"

"Yep. Here we are."

"Well, I'll put these papers away, and we'll see what happens
today."

The last period. Strange class, in a way. A mixture half of fresh-
men, half of sophomores. Almost two-thirds boys. The kids are
tired. I am tired. We have all been at it since eight this morning.

This class is cut quite often. I can't blame them at all. The boys finish with the writing period early. The girls will write on and on, but the boys cannot work very long.

"All finished, fellows?"

"Look, Mr. Hillman. I got six lines."

"I wrote what you asked. Ain't that enough?"

"I never know what is enough. Is it enough for you?"

"Suits me."

"O.K., then it suits me."

"Mr. Hillman, can I go home?"

"I'm sorry, Pete, but I don't have that authority."

"Oh, come on. You can let me go."

"You really want to go?"

"Sure."

"Tell you what I'll do. Suppose you go out to the campus yard and look at the trees. Imagine they are human beings. See what happens. Then come back in, say, twenty minutes and write me what you saw, felt, and heard. Will you do that?"

"O.K., but I won't write much."

"That's all right. Just so you tell me what you saw, felt, and heard."

"Can I go too, Mr. Hillman?"

"Perhaps another day. Let's make this Pete's day."

"Mr. Hillman?"

"Yes, Bella."

"Carlos keeps saying bad things to us."

"Have you talked to him about them?"

"I told him to shut up, but he won't."

"Carlos, what do you say?"

"Girls are crazy. I don't like girls."

"Do you believe that, Bella?"

"Yes, I do. He wouldn't talk like that if he didn't."

"He likes girls, Mr. Hillman."

"How do you know, Grant?"

"He talks about them all the time."

"Yes, but the girls say he doesn't say nice things."

"Mr. Hillman."

"Penny."

"He just doesn't know how to talk to girls. He likes girls, but he doesn't know how to talk to them."

"That's a good point, Penny. In our play, *Death of a Salesman*, that's one of the problems the family has. They talk to each other but they don't know how to talk. Each one is talking and saying something, but he means something else. Would you like to work on that idea for a minute?"

Instant suspicion. You can hear their fears blocking the openings.

"I would like you all to form groups of four. Arrange your chairs so that you are in groups of four facing each other."

"Do we have to?"

"This time, yes. I think you will like this exercise."

Some groups are quickly formed. But there are enough students so that we get mixed groups. Even those groups who know each other can profit from this.

"Now, for the next ten minutes I want you to talk to each other and to say nothing but positive things about each other. That is, good things. You must not make any bad remarks to each other. Look at the other people and say good things only. O.K., let's begin now."

They grin at each other. Some are looking embarrassed. They are very slow in getting started. Bella and Penny are moving very well. Two different races expressing the good they feel about each other. Voices come from all over.

"I like the way you comb your hair." One boy to another; his grin is self-conscious, but I think he means it.

"You have a good personality."

"You always seem to be happy about things. What makes you so happy?"

"Don't ask questions of each other, friends. Just say whatever comes into your mind that is good about the other person."

"You get good grades."

"Dolores, you have pretty brown eyes."

"Amanda always dresses beautifully."

"You can sure drive that wagon, Bobby. You can really lay down a patch."

Tremendously exciting, vibrant, alive, and warm with good feeling. The kids are enjoying this exercise and really telling each other what they like about each other.

"All right, friends. Let's hold up for a minute. Now move the chairs so we are all facing each other in a circle. That's good. Now, can we share our experiences?"

"It was kind of hard to say something nice."

"Yeah, it seemed easier to make some other kind of remark."

"I felt embarrassed when they were talking about me. It was uncomfortable."

"We are not used to that, are we?"

"No, we don't do it much."

"Did anyone sense or hear somebody saying something nice when he really meant something else?"

"Carlos didn't say anything."

"He didn't speak, you say?"

"Yes."

"He wasn't speaking, but he was saying something. What was it?"

"He couldn't say anything nice about someone."

"Yet some of you believe that he likes girls even when he doesn't say nice things about them."

"He just can't say nice things even when he believes them."

"Pat told me he liked my figure, but he laughed."

"Did that mean he didn't like your figure?"

"No, but he said it nasty."

"You believe he was telling you something else then?"

"He sure was!"

"I liked doing that. I felt good. Can we do it again sometime?"

"Certainly. You can even do it yourselves when you are together. Try it sometime. You will like it."

"That's for girls."

"While we are seated in this circle, let's continue the exercise a different way. All of us together, let's say positive things about each other. For example, I would like to say to Carlos that I enjoy reading his writing, that I think he is intelligent, and that his smile is one that is delightful to see."

Carlos is grinning. The other boys are grinning at him.

"You are the best teacher I've ever had, Mr. Hillman."

"Thank you, Bella. That's very warm to hear."

"Luke is too quiet, but he is very handsome."

Luke looks as though he would like to run. Amanda is grinning at him. They are all feeling the joy of conveying joy and feel the peace that comes from being liked or having good things said about them. They are relaxed now, and the words tumble from many lips. Eddie and Dave are still quiet. I imagine they didn't say a word even in the small group. They cling to each other for protection.

"You can see, friends, that it isn't really hard to see nice things in others or to tell them so. Somehow we don't seem to find it easy to talk this way. It always seems easier to say things that hurt. But how much better it would be if we could speak to each other and say what we like. That doesn't mean love. We like a lot of people. When you feel like saying something mean, ask yourself first if their isn't something nice you can say. You'll be surprised at the difference. And see if you can learn to look behind what people say to understand what they really mean. We often say things in a way that doesn't agree with the words. It is just what we were saying about the play. The people were talking to each other, but they were not hearing. Now, for the rest of the period let's just talk to each other about that. Say nice things, talk about the exercise, or anything you want, but really listen to each other and understand."

They are all moved by the class as I am moved as I sit here. I could take them all in my arms and shout.

The bell. It always comes too soon and too late. The class day is almost ended. Another day.

"Good night, Mr. Hillman."

"Good night, Bella."

The room seems so empty. The chairs are scattered in all directions. The phonograph is quiet. The books are thrown around. Paper is on the floor. It is a comfortable room.

"Well, Mr. Hillman, it looks like you had quite a day in here."

"That we did, John."

"You ought to make those kids behave better, Mr. Hillman. It sure makes it hard for me to clean up."

"I'll speak to the kids."

"I get tired sweeping up after them."

"I understand, John. Good night."

"Good night, Mr. Hillman."

The corridor is empty. The building silent. Yet the place is full of people, and the building is singing.

6

Eight Months in the First Grade

A DAY-TO-DAY JOURNAL IN
CONFLUENT EDUCATION

By Gloria Castillo, Foothill School, Goletta, California

October 23. Imagination and Language Arts

1. Lie on the floor.

2. Close your eyes.

3. Make pictures in your mind. Try not to talk so you don't disturb your neighbor's picture.

4. Think of a special friend. A very special friend. If you cannot think of a real one, make one up. Look closely at your friend. Is your friend tall or short? Fat or thin? What color is your special friend's hair? What color are your special friend's eyes? Take a very good look at your friend. Try to know exactly what your friend looks like to you.

5. Now pretend you and your friend are going to a special place. How did you get there? Did you run? walk? ride? Think of where you are now. What are you and your friend doing at your special place? Keep thinking about your friend and what you're doing. Now take your friend's hand and take your friend home with you.

6. When you get your friend safely home, leave him there and you can open your eyes. You don't have to hurry.

When they had all opened their eyes, they sat up. I asked them then to go back to their desks and try to draw a picture of their friend. They told me their stories and I wrote them, leaving space under each line so they could rewrite it underneath in correct form.

NOTE: Save stories and pictures for later comparison.

October 24. Literature and Self-Awareness (Body)
1. Read *Somebody's Slippers, Somebody's Shoes*.
2. Talk about being barefooted. Take off shoes and socks.
3. Go outside and walk on:
    a. dewy grass (cold, wet)
    b. blacktop (dry, warm, rough)
    c. concrete (dry, cool, smooth)
    d. sand (rough, warm, sticks to wet feet)
    e. climb on jungle gym
4. Come inside and feel:
    a. rubber mat
    b. vinyl floor
    c. rug
5. Put on shoes while talking about feet.
6. Write stories. Watch for drawings of feet.

While putting on his shoes, Mike yelled out, "Wow! I can really feel my feet inside my shoes now. I know right where they are."

I said, "Go draw a picture of your feet and show how they feel if you want to."

Reflections: Some boys, not necessarily the same ones as before, were very uncomfortable with this. They balked at removing their shoes and then refused to go in all the areas.

October 25. Body Awareness

Have children lie on the floor, finding their own space. Repeat chant exercise but this time keep the hands touching the head parts only.

> I am rubbing my head.
> I am feeling my hair.

I am touching my ears.
I am rubbing my neck.

After warming up on this, give them directions:

Now rub your head. Try to find out if you have bumps on your head. Now run your fingers around your ears. Feel for soft parts, hard parts, bumpy parts. Close your eyes. Put your fingertips over your eyes. Feel the eyeball move underneath by moving your eyes underneath. What does the skin on top of your eyes feel like? Soft, rough, smooth, bumpy? Now move to your eyelashes. Open and shut your eyes over your finger. Are your eyelashes long or short? Straight or curly? Soft or hard? Move to your eyebrows. Rub them one way. Now the other. What happened? Now rub them both ways again. Rub them back to where they were. Move your fingertips down your nose. Feel the hard bone underneath. Feel where the bone stops. Is your nose fat, pointed, bumpy, smooth? Do you have a scab on your nose? What does your nose feel like? Now move one finger under your nose. Breathe through your nose. Feel your breath go in and out over your finger. Is it hot or cold? Do you like the way it feels? Now move down to your lips. Trace your fingertips over your lips. How many lips do you have? Do they feel alike? How are they alike? How are they different? Now move over to the side of your lips. Open your mouth. Feel how your bones move. Go way up by your ears. Open and shut your mouth. Feel what happens. Feel your bones under your skin. Feel your teeth inside your mouth. Now move your fingertips down your throat. Swallow. What happens? Now make a noise. Listen with your ears and feel with your fingertips. Where does the noise come from? Take both your hands and fold them under your head. Close your eyes. Keep your voices quiet. Try to think about some of the things you did. What did you find was the softest part of you? The coldest part? The hardest? Warmest? What did you discover about your own face? When you are ready, go back to the mirror and take a good look at yourself if you want. Then draw a picture of your face. And write something you know about you.

NOTE: When doing this with first-graders, I broke it up into two sessions of about twenty minutes each.

October 26. Getting to Know Each Other. Moving into Other-Awareness

Have the children stand in a close circle, touching shoulders and holding hands. Actually, I had to go around and move bodies, but once placed they stayed there.

Play a game. Leader says, "This is my friend _____ and _____," naming the children he is holding on to. I asked them to look right at each other when doing this. They had some trouble with that.

Then it progressed around the circle so each child made one statement but heard his name in the sentence twice, once on each side of him.

When we were all around the circle, I asked them to sit just where they were. Remain close enough still to be able to feel their friends. Then I said, "When you really feel like it, tell us what you are feeling." I started by saying what I felt from my two friends. I had them close their eyes. Many did not stay shut, but I said nothing about it.) I was delighted that children from various parts of the circle said what they were feeling.

After this stopped, I asked them to join arms and let's see what happens. Don't try to make anything happen, just see what *does* happen. In a while part of the circle began to sway back and forth. Then another part of it began moving in and out, stretching down in front, and lying down on their backs. After a while the circle became quiet again.

I asked them to lie down, staying close to each other still. I said they could touch each other in any way they wanted.

Some seemed to want to pull away from the group. After letting them go for a while, I asked them to come up to the rug so we could talk about what we did.

At one time, when the class went from sitting to lying down, I decided to leave the group. I had a parent and a student teacher observing and thought I would look a bit silly stretched out on the floor at 10:15. But the children, from widely spaced intervals in the circle, said, "No, Mrs. Siemons, don't leave," and "You can't leave, you've got to do it too." Not in a demanding way, but as if to say, Don't miss the fun, we've just begun this! I was very happy that they wanted me to be with them and I was glad to stay.

In our discussion almost all parts of what we did were brought out. One girl said, "I liked to say, 'This is my friend, Pauline. This is my friend Carlene.'" When I asked her how she felt when they said her name, she said, "Oh-h-h, that made me real happy inside." She was just glowing.

Others mentioned lying on the floor. I was greatly surprised that many children said they liked the part where they could just go on their own the best. In watching the group, I had felt they were falling apart at that point, so I called them up to the rug after allowing them only a short time on their own.

They then wrote a story about their experience.

NOTE: Pat's story: I didn't like being in that circle.

October 27.

After having so much fun with yesterday's lesson, I decided to try it again. Again without quite knowing where the lesson would go.

We started with the circle again. Today I didn't have to move them. From there we sat down. The group wanted to rock. So we rocked. I encouraged them to rock real hard, way over to each side. Squash each other. Then I tried to get them to sit still and listen to themselves and each other. They didn't want to. Some lay down. So we all tried it. My side of the circle began to laugh, really laugh. Everyone began doing it. Me too. The other side of the circle sat up and said, "What's so funny?" Since we didn't seem to get into a one-group feeling, I suggested they move off on their own and see what happened. I asked them to continue to move on their backs, pushing themselves.

I didn't move from my place, because three children moved to me right away. One boy moved up, picked up my head, and manipulated himself around until he had my head on his stomach. Then he giggled and giggled.

After about five minutes I asked the class to try to come together into the circle again. They resisted. After about three more minutes I said to come together to a slow count of ten. After counting to ten, we all stood up. There were three separate groups. There was a close group of four or five over by the door, a large group of about sixteen in the original circle area, and a few standing apart from everyone.

I then asked them all to come up to the main group. As we began to move, two boys encountered each other in the middle of the floor. They were alone in an open space. I stopped them and suggested that they "push" each other. (I had seen this with adults just the day before.) The class became just wild watching these two. They were evenly matched in spirit, strength, and size. They thought it was great. Several other boys began to pair up on the rug, so I suggested that we all go outside and try it. They were *screaming* to get out. I got them quiet enough to get out the door and past other classrooms.

We went out on the playground between a backstop and a fence about forty feet across and *pushed*. I took on several children. Several challenged me. I challenged others that I wanted to meet. It was amazing to feel the strength of these little kids. It felt very good to feel those strong, healthy beings really take me on.

We soon found very few children pushing each other to the limits. We almost always stayed within about twenty feet of space. When we were tired and hot, we got a drink and had free play for ten minutes. When they came back, we had a very quiet, attentive reading group.

NOTE: Pat and Jay physically left the group. Pat really looked uncomfortable. However, he really threw himself into a contest with me. I let him back me up, but he knew it and said, "No, don't move." So I stood my ground until he was tired.

November 10. "Can You Imagine"

We had the videotape in today, and they knew they were going to be on camera. I asked them to sit by me, like an Indian, hands in their laps, eyes closed.

Pretend you are something furry. (I could actually see some children move into this.) Are you big or small? I had them put up their heads and tell me what they were. Close your eyes again. Keep imagining you are a furry animal. Do people like you? Why?

The class was getting wiggly, so I said, "Now try to think how you move." I had those who were big animals move on the floor. Then those who were small. I asked them how they could be their best as the animal they were now. Now favorable response. One said, "Be quieter." She was a bunny. (The class was noisy at times.)

This lesson was good, considering it was a Monday and our first day on tape. We'll try it again tomorrow. I'm finding Tuesdays and Wednesdays are good days again this year. I've always invited visitors on Tuesdays and Thursdays. Mondays and Fridays are not as good somehow.

November 22. Voyage to Inner Body.

Reporter: Peggy Peterson, student teacher. About forty minutes, twenty-six six-year-olds.

This is a report of something that happened spontaneously. My original goal was to help the children find places to hide other than under the desks, in the hall box, or in the closet.

As the hour passed, the children became very responsive about describing their bodies. I encouraged this for the purpose of guiding them to more accurate perception of their bodies. I also feel the process helps them to develop and use their imagination.

Also, Gloria and I can now use this kind of imagery in a variety of situations—when a child needs to pull away, to pull the class out of hiding places after recess, etc.

It is important in the first grade for the child to develop a more accurate image of his body.

I began by reading the poem "Hiding." I then asked the children to close their eyes and find a place in their body where they could hide. The children had a hard time closing their eyes. A hard task for first-graders. After a period of about three minutes it was obvious that most of the children were hidden. I then asked them to open their eyes and, one at a time, tell where they were. About three children had spoken when I realized that this was an opportunity to find out how they felt about their bodies. The next boy said he was in his thumb. I asked him how he got there. He told about his trip into his mouth, down his throat, through his heart, up to his shoulder, and down his arm. The other children were fascinated by the story of this trip. My standard questions for each child were, "How does it feel in your _____?" "How did you get there?" "What can you see there?" The children were extremely interested. If there had been more time I would have had them go to their seats, draw their hiding places, and write a story about it.

Many of the children talked about blood, veins, and bones—probably the only things they are really aware of inside them. For a while I talked about veins, arteries, and the heart.

I am sure that the children would not have been able to go so far if they hadn't had several days of body awareness and three days of imagination exercises. (Imagine you are furry, green, and what happens to you.) All of these elements built up their ability to imagine and be aware of their bodies to the point where they could take such an inner trip.

January 17. Good Lesson on Rhythm
    Warmups:
        Finding own space
        Moving with different parts of body, feet "stuck"
        Feet and one hand, feet and two hands
        Bottom
        Whole body stuck
    Took suggestions from class on what parts were stuck. How to

move then? When whole body was stuck, sun melted it slowly to make it unstuck. Move to music, at first in sitting position. Try dyads. Move to and away from each other, heads only.

Move from feet up.

Move entire body:

"Waltz of the Flowers"

Stamping Land

Bears

Seals

(*Music through the Day*; California State Series.)

Marvelous variety of movement shown by class:

Inchworm	Rolling	Twirling
Twisting	Stamping	Ballet movements
Running	Jumping	Tap dancing

Needs: Boys not very involved (about nine of the fourteen); silly, bashful, disruptive. Gear another lesson more to them. More structure? Be sure to get control between pieces. Needs more buildup, present in smaller steps, do warmup activities, stressing various body parts. Thirty-minute lesson too long. Needs to be done more than just once—may do just warmup on first try.

Highlights: Pauline's ability to express herself so beautifully—an unknown quality shown to me. Keith's contact with me, waiting for me and holding my hand on the way to the classroom.

Insights, learning, questions: This late I had an idea of where most of the kids were. My "problem" boys tended to do two things: (1) Stay separate and away from the group, breaking into it now and again, disrupting. (2) Pair off and meet it in their own way, Luke and Jay clasping each other and rolling over and over each other.

Perhaps this would be a good lesson early in the year, the second or third week, to get some clues as to which children have difficulty making contact. I don't know. Seems to me I remember this same kind of thing happening last year with Paul, Armand, and David.

Try to read up on dance in classrooms. I need more information on this technique.

KEITH

Keith is running around the room wildly. I wonder if his mother remembered to give him his drug. It keeps down his aggression, but I wonder. Does it also keep down all his feelings? He hasn't touched me. He hasn't let me touch him.

Music is playing softly and slowly. Many of the children are dancing around.

"Keith, what are you doing?" "I don't know." "What are you doing?" "I am running." You run away from me. Soon you are back. You are standing. I am sitting on the floor. You smile at me. You run up to me and stop short about two feet away. I invite you to join me. You come closer and then run away. This time when you come back, you slide on the floor. You still don't come very close, yet closer than last time. "Would you like to slide into me?" "Yes." "Then go back and this time slide into me." You go back. You slide. You do not touch me. "Did you slide into me?" "No." "Do you still want to?" "Yes." "Then try again." You run off. It is longer before you are back. I wait. You come running up. You slide. Your foot barely touches my knee. "What are you doing, Keith?" "I'm touching your knee." "What else are you doing?" "I'm smiling." "Would you like to touch more than just my knee?" You don't answer. You get up and run off. I wonder if you will come back. Soon you do. This time you have a great big smile. You run toward me, slide, and roll onto my lap. I hold you. We are quiet. You jump up and run to the corner and hide behind the flag. "What are you doing, Keith?" "Nothing." "Who is doing nothing?" "I am doing nothing." "May I hold your hand?" No answer. You turn to the wall. I move a step away so you are not cornered, but I stay by your side. You run out of the corner and join the rest of the class in responding to the music. I see your eyes looking at me. I see you take a deep breath. Now the class is lining up to leave. You get in line. You look back at me. You come back and hold out your hand to me. It is warm. It holds my hand firmly. You feel good to me. We walk to class. You leave me at the door. After two or three steps, you turn and smile at me, and then go on your way.

Blind walk: We're trying to get the children to the point of taking a meaningful blind walk. I'm beginning to think the experience itself won't be nearly as meaningful as all the learning that will build up to it. We may not even get that far.

January 9. Introduce Blindfolds

After much consideration I made blindfolds for the whole class. We have discovered great difficulty in keeping eyes closed.

On the first day Peggy instructed the class to put the blindfolds on and to explore first only the rug. There was a lot of chaos, bumping each other, much more fun to explore each other than the room. There was a lot of peeking. Many wore their blindfolds slightly too high so that they could see well enough to run around. We let them try to explore the whole room and then let them go outside to the grass by our room. I would say about five children seemed to be really exploring the world without sight. About half were running around (most of the boys). About five girls did not like to wear the blindfolds at all. These girls were mainly the ones who always had to be "right." In their words, "good students." They seemed very afraid of the uncertain experience without their eyes. After about twenty minutes of exploring we called them back in and talked awhile about the experience. It seemed that most of the children did not like it. Many found the blindfolds uncomfortable.

I feel that many negative responses were of a "me too" type, especially since verbal and physical response was very different in many cases. And the girls who really did not enjoy the experience are "stars" whose reactions are closely attended to by others in the class. I recommended more structure and a safer environment for the next lesson.

The following comes from that, and again Peggy is the teacher. I told the children to bring things the next day to "share and tell," things they could share while all of the class had on their blindfolds. That day we decided to start with a kind of structured experience before the sharing, which is usually first. I've forgotten exactly what I did; however, most of the kids did not like the experience. (I think I was trying to give them "mystery sounds.") Most of them peeked to see what I was doing rather than using their ears. By the time it was sharing time many of them did not want to wear their blindfolds any longer. I permitted them to take them off and not play if they didn't want to. About six started the sharing period with their blindfolds on. Some dropped out and others joined in as the period went on. After about ten minutes the disorganization was too much for me to bear, so I collected all of the blindfolds and we went on with sharing without the blindfolds.

Insights: First of all, we're having trouble timing this new, maybe fearful, experience. I feel much was lost today on two counts. First, the period should have started out with them feeling, smelling, and listening to the sharing objects, and then gone into mystery sounds if they were still with it. Second, the items shared should have been handled in a structured way, such as sitting in a circle and passing items from hand to hand rather than one child doing it. Some of the problems were those of control. Perhaps items should be teacher-chosen at first. Another insight in regard to children bringing things; be sure to include a teacher preview of the items so that they really do have a tactile quality to them.

I would like to try this: Have the children sit in the circle blindfolded. Give each child an item. Set up a sound signal. When they hear the sound, they are to pass the object to the next child. Do this only for about five minutes.

After the first two days we just let the blindfolds sit. We left them out so the kids could play with them if they wanted. All during this time I saw evidence that they had been used during indoor recesses on rainy days.

January 15.
Today Peggy used the blindfolds again in a lesson. Most of the children wanted to take them. Only about three said they didn't want to use them. These three were easily persuaded to try them. I had the kids find their own space, lie down on their backs on the lawn, and put on their blindfolds and listen to the sounds around them. Except for about five or six who had difficulty, most of the class enjoyed the experience.

Insights: Steps still needed. More experience with wearing the blindfolds and taking directions at the same time. More trust in moving without using their eyes. Perhaps instruction about how to move when you can't see. Finding and practicing a way of selecting a partner—someone you really trust. Demonstrating and practicing how to be a leader in a blind walk, how to protect and guide and show your partner what you want him to attend to.

January 19. Finding and Practicing a Way of Selecting Partners
Form a close circle as before, with a friend on each side of you. Go around with "This is my friend _____ and _____." Lie down in a close circle, feet to the inside. Get close enough to touch each other. Keep holding hands.

I originally had thought to use blindfolds with this and took them out. However, the sun was very bright, and closed eyes were more comfortable. Throughout the lesson I was noticing how many kept their eyes shut. When I said we wouldn't use the blindfolds, many children groaned.

The children were holding hands in their circle with their eyes closed. I said, "Now try to find a partner. Let go with one hand, but hold on with the other. If the person you want to hold on to keeps your hand, you are partners. If he lets go of you or won't keep your hand, he has someone on the other side who is his partner." I walked around the circle. All but three children had partners. I wanted to see if they could do this nonverbally. They could.

I then asked them all to join hands again and then get up. If I had been going into a dyad situation, I would have had them move with their partner. But I didn't go that far today. I would have the three children without partners make a triad. I did not see any evidence that they felt left out, perhaps because the whole group joined hands again.

Responding to music: Peggy played "Ebb Tide" and let the children draw pictures and write stories to the music. They responded quickly to the sounds of the sea. Their stories were mostly explanations of the pictures they had made. This is just another lesson in trying to develop more critical listening along with attentive listening.

January 20. Waking Up the Body

You are sitting on the rug after listening to sharing time for about twenty minutes. You wiggle into someone else's space and let out a yell of protest when he punches you. You look around. Others are wiggling, yelling, hitting, squirming. Random movement. Mild disorder. You stay on the rug. You do not seem very much aware of yourselves or the others around you.

I say, "I hear wide-awake mouths. Let's see if we can get wide-awake bodies." Rub your hands on the rug. That's right, only really rub. Rub until your hands burn. Now rest them on your lap. What are your hands doing? Tingling, burning, stinging. Now slump over and then fill yourself up with air. Sit up as you do it. Be like a balloon. Let all the air out and slump down again. Do it again. Fill yourself until you're about to pop. Let the air out with a whoosh! Again. Again.

This time when you fill yourself up, lift yourself from sitting to kneeling. Slump over again. Heads on the floor near your knees. Now be a puppet with someone pulling a string from the back of your head. Up, up, up, up, up, up. Oh, still higher, higher, higher. Let your arms go up to help you stretch. Now the string *snaps*. As you slump down, I realize there is no wiggling, no more moving into others' spaces. You are enjoying your own space.

Now be that puppet on a string again. Stretch as high as you can, staying on your knees. S-t-r-e-t-c-h! This time don't break the string, but come to an easy rest with your back straight and your arms down. Your eyes are watching me. Your mouths are quiet. You have a spark in your eyes that asks me, "What now?"

Stay in your own space and follow me. I move my weight from one knee to the other. As I do it, I say, "Right, left, right, left." Right away you are chanting with me. See if you can get yourself into a standing position from here without using your hands. You step up quick and crisp. (It was easy for you, hard for me.) I ask you to stamp your foot. I am surprised that you do not *really* stamp. You make noise, but you don't really get the feeling up the back of your legs. I stop you. You respond quickly and quietly. I am both surprised and pleased. I show you how you are "breaking" your stamping. I show you how to get the full jarring impact. You try again. I laugh aloud when I see your shocked looks of discovery and surprise. You have really stamped now. You like it. You may line up for recess stamping your feet—if you really stamp them.

P.S. I heard about this from the teacher next door. I plan to do this with her class as a warmup when I do some things with them.

January 20. I've Got It, You Want It

After hearing Robin talk about his experience with "I've got it, you want it," we wanted to try it.

We divided the class into two parts—boys and girls. I took the boys and divided them into two teams. They were given a long stick to want. One said, "Like Keepaway." One team wore the blindfolds like headbands so they could identify each other.

They could hardly wait for the word "Go." They seemed to

know how to play the game. I turned them loose. At first they kind of stood around. Then one boy took off with the baton and the game was on. They took off over the grass. When one got tired, he handed it to a teammate so he could catch his breath. They circled back to me. I told two on the other team to try to trap the runner between them. They did, and before I knew it all fourteen boys were in one big heap—arms, legs, elbows, knees everywhere. Yelling, fussing, whining. I was delighted with the ruckus. I cheered them on. Get in there and fight! Pass the baton out to a teammate!

One boy quit. He was heavyset and allergic. He may have stayed with it as long as he could. He quietly withdrew. Two began to wrestle on their own. They were mad at each other. Somehow the baton got out after about five minutes of this pile-up. They were off and running again. It was not as long this time before they were all in a heap again.

This time they were tired and hot and the game was much rougher. Three pairs of boys were really mad. They were pounding each other, choking from behind. I pulled them out and said, "Square up and face each other. Now push, face to face. Anything goes, but no fair jumping from behind." They started out facing each other, but they were so mad they didn't stay that way long. They got into real rough wrestling matches. I was worried. Should I stop it? What possible "educational rationale" could I give for this? What if a child really got hurt? I'm glad I was in a dilemma, because as I stood there wondering, the wrestling matches concluded. Two ended in what looked like a draw, and one boy conquered his foe, got up off him, and joined in the chase that was going on.

I called them all to me. They were sweating, panting, and quite irritable. One more boy dropped out. I asked those on one team to stand along a line. I asked the others to look at them and choose one they were mad at right now and stand in front of him. Now say what you want to each other. If you feel like it, push each other around. They all participated in this—some more vigorously than others. When they began to stand around, I told them to go get a drink and go to recess.

Problem: What to do with the anger left at the end of the session. I think a few were left feeling pretty hostile in general. I was worried about Keith's withdrawal—fear of his own aggression. How do I help him see himself as an adequate person? Try "I've got it, and I *want* to give it to *you*. Will you please take it?"

January 21. Buildings of Trust

Today we arranged it so all the children ate lunch in the room together. They chose partners and sat across from each other. I told them they were going to play a game.

Each child was to feed his partner and not himself. The class let out sounds of "No, really?" "You're kidding!" Once they realized I wasn't kidding, all but two thought it was a wonderful idea. Laura and Philip were very upset by the whole idea. I took them aside and told them to be partners, and not to say anything to the others, but each could feed himself. They calmed down and agreed to that.

I was very impressed at the joy the children expressed at this. They told their parents they had a ball, I was told later. I felt such love for them, looking at them carefully feeding each other. Their intent looks of care and concern while holding a sandwich, apple, or Frito up to their partners. I noticed that many children started out feeding each other and then moved to feeding themselves. Two things come to mind. One, they were tired of the "game" after about fifteen minutes, and, two, they're used to eating in a hurry and this did take time. I would like to try this again on a field trip to a park where we could have an unlimited lunch period and where the children could spread out more for privacy. About one-third of the class stayed with this until both partners were finished. Six didn't do it at all; of the rest, about ten did it at first. They found milk in the thermos cups the hardest to handle.

I had a chance to get to Laura before the end. She was eating a tangerine. I broke it apart and gave her a piece. She wrinkled her nose. I gave her another and told her to feel the pop of it when she bit into it. I felt she was beginning to loosen up when some children came up and stood by our open door just a few feet from her. She said, "Shut the door. I don't want them to see me." I didn't want to leave her, so I just put another piece in her mouth. She ate it and then said, "I don't want you to give me any more."

The next day several children asked me if they could do it again today.

January 23. Blindfolds

We're still trying to get the children used to wearing the blind-folds long enough to experience feeling more intently. I sat the children around in a circle wearing blindfolds. I gave each child an item from the classroom—scissors, brush, ball, pencil, chalk, eraser, etc. I asked them to feel each object. Try not to worry about what it is. Try to experience the feel of each thing. I clicked sticks when they were to pass the object to their right (a good lesson in directions). I continued to do it until each object was passed all the way around.

I was very impressed at how quiet the children were. The lesson was about twenty-five minutes, and they remained interested and in good control the whole time. I whispered any direct statements to individual children. At first a few could not resist saying out loud what they had. This stopped after about the fifth object. I stayed pretty busy picking up lost items. I was happy that the children waited until I could get them back to them rather than taking off their blindfolds to find them themselves. After that we discussed how some of the items felt rather than how they looked.

January 24. Red-Letter Day! Accidental Blind Walk

Since Monday several children have asked if they could do what Kathy and I had done. I sat, she was blindfolded, and I took her hand exploring.

Today we took the children out on the grass after asking them to choose someone they could trust. They went out in groups of two or three. Peggy instructed us to sit close to our partners. One put on the blindfold, the other directed his hand. I was working with two girls. I began moving their hands on things around us. Out of the corner of my eye I saw some movement. Looking up, I saw one girl begin to lead another on a blind walk. Others, who were sitting on the grass with "blind" partners, saw this, got up, and led their partners around. The area we were in was rather confined and not at all the area I would have chosen for this experience, and yet here it was happening. My mind raced through all the "little steps" I had thought to be prerequisites before we could do this, and yet here they were leading each other all around —to the fence, to the pillars, walls, trees, drinking fountains, even back into the room and out again. I couldn't believe it. After about ten minutes, Peggy instructed the children to change—those wearing blindfolds were to give them to their partners.

Away they went again. By now I realized that I hadn't done much for my two friends, so I joined in the blind walk. Unfortunately, recess came and we were interrupted before they could lead me.

P A T

As we come in from taking the blind walk, all of the children are clamoring for me to help them write their stories of what they have done. Pat, you come up and, holding your head down, say in a very tiny voice, "I don't want to do a story."

I remember your saying this quite often lately. I also remember your having a hard time choosing someone to trust. I ask you, "Did your partner take you for a walk?" "No." "Did you take him?" "Yes." "Do you want to go?" "No." All right then. You can now choose what you want to do. You can write a story about not taking a walk or about someone else taking a walk, or you can go on a walk now with either Mrs. Peterson or me (the advantage of two in the room).

You say in that tiny voice, "Take a walk." I ask, "With me or

Mrs. Peterson?" "You." So we go out. You put the blindfold on quickly. I believe you really want to do this. I take your hand and lead you to a tree. You touch it gingerly at first. Then you let go of my hand and really grab the tree. When you stop, I try to get you to stoop over to feel the stake near the tree. You are very stiff. Soon you realize what I want, and you move down.

We move to the fence, your hand in mine. When we get there, you let go to feel the fence with both hands. You stretch up, then go on tiptoe so you can reach the top. Once you have reached the top, you move down and reach for me again. We take about four steps. I see a piece of comb, stoop, and pick it up. I run my fingers over the teeth up near your ear. You smile. I put it in your hand. You run your fingers over the teeth while you continue to smile. You put it in your pocket. You give me your hand, and we move on to a pillar half in and half out of the sun. You feel it on all four sides. Then you wrap your arms all the way around it, resting your cheek on a warm side.

When you move again, I bend you down, push your bottom down, and get you to crawl from sunny concrete to cool concrete. You stop and feel around when you are entirely in the shade area. I am happy seeing you exploring on your own. You crawl to the grass. I lead you to a spigot by banging my ring on it. You run your quick fingers all over it. You stick your fingers into it and smile when they come out wet. You reach your wet fingers out to me. I touch them. You smile.

Now I bring you to our door. You feel it all over, find the handle, and pull it open. Once inside, you remove your blindfold. You go to your desk and write, "I like the feel of the fence." When you are done, you bring your story to me and read it. You do not use your tiny voice now.

CARLENE AND BETTY

When Mrs. Peterson asks you to sit by someone you trust, you very quickly and decidedly get up from where you are sitting and come and sit by me. I am surprised and pleased. The children don't always include me when they are picking partners. I am glad to be included.

We go outside together holding hands. I am in the middle. We sit down in a triangle. When told to put on blindfolds, you both want to do it so I leave mine off. I begin by moving your hands over the grass, your shoes, your dresses. Then my shoes, my dress. I then put your hands on each other. Now I am distracted by what others are doing while you explore each other. When I look at you again, you are both sitting with one hand on me and one on your lap. You are quiet. You are relaxed-looking.

I take your hands. We move to a tree. Betty, you let go and begin to rub your hands up and down the tree. Carlene, you just barely touch the tree and do not let go of me. We move to the fence. Again, Betty, you leave me and begin to explore the fence alone. You move down it and then back to me. Carlene, you barely touch the fence and stay by my side. Now we come to a pillar. Betty, you leave me to go all the way around the pillar. You take a few steps onto the grass and whirl around. I take Carlene's hand and rub it on the pillar. First the sunny side and then the shady side. Betty continues to explore on her own. I see her begin to crawl on the cement walkway. I take Carlene to the spigot and move her hand all over it. She laughs when her finger finds the hidden water in it. I wait for Betty to find us. She does, and we go on. Carlene, while we are walking toward our room you sigh. I feel the tightness go. What has happened? What are you thinking?

I take you to the stone wall of our room. This time both of you let go. You explore alone, then your hands touch. You keep your hands together, each one exploring now with only the outside hand. You both turn to me. I take your two hands into mine. Carlene, you sigh again. We get to the room. You both remove your blindfolds. You smile at me, then at each other. You both go to your desks to do a story.

Later this afternoon Carlene wrote: "The person I trust most is Mrs. Castillo. The person I trust least is Gail." It was a directed writing lesson up until the last word of each sentence.

January 25. Experiencing Paint

After listening to Janet talk about "experiencing paint," I decided to combine that with another idea from Aaron. The art lesson was to "experience paint."

I took large sheets of butcher paper, two clothespins, four jars of paint—blue, green, red, and yellow—and four brushes. I pinned the paper onto a chain-link fence, a baseball backstop, and told the children to line up in four relay teams. I then told them this was just like a relay. They were to take the brush and make a mark on the paper and run back. They screamed in delight. I said, "Ready . . . go!" Wow! Did the paint fly! Once through the class, and I turned the paper end for end and ran out of the way. We did this on four papers. It's possible to see first, third, and fourth, so I know which one was done second. They began rather slowly, and with organization and fear of paint spatters. But once they got spattered it didn't matter any more. The fourth painting has more overlapping of colors, smearing, and tears in the paper.

When we came in, we had quite a discussion on "What will Mother say?" since they were *really covered* with paint. (I was, too.)

Friday morning began with "What did Mother say?" I'm so happy. All but one mother was great about it. That one was pregnant so may not be in too good a humor. I sent home a note early in the year saying I would schedule any messes I could on Thursdays. Sometimes we get into it on other days but not as bad as this.

I was aware of the many different ways the children put the paint on—tender little pats, strong pats, little smears, big swipes and smears, standing back and flinging the brush at the paper. I've put the paintings up, but the children haven't said anything about them. They were through with them as soon as the game was over.

January 24 and 25. Body Rhythms

After taking the class to the cafeteria for some movement and rhythm work, Peggy began to stress the body as a rhythm instrument. She asked the children what noises they might be able to make, using parts other than their voices. They named snapping fingers, clicking tongue, clicking teeth, breathing loud, whistling, sputtering with lips, clapping hands, slapping hands (whisking motion), hitting tummy, stamping feet, rubbing hands. The whole class did each of these when it was named.

On the next day Peggy had them sit in groups. They were then given a noise to make. When she pointed to them, they were to start and keep going until she pointed to them again. The Body Band began. I was hanging up some paintings, and it sounded just like a regular orchestra—tuning up first, each section together, and then the whole thing taking shape. The first time through, the children were interested mostly in what they were doing, regardless of total effect or even the section's effect.

Peggy then asked them to listen to the total sound. Then they began again. This time I heard more of the over-all sound. When they stopped, she asked, "What happened to the tongue-clickers?" They answered, "We couldn't hear them." They tried again. Peggy then acted like a conductor, urging some to greater efforts, others to hold it down. They sounded much better and were satisfied with the sound. After this she had them change sounds and continue in the same way.

Future: Do this again to build up listening to total effect and then tape it. I think the children would enjoy hearing it replayed.

January 31.

Peggy encouraged the children to make their own rhythm instruments and bring them to school. They brought in a marvelous variety. Toy instruments—parent-made and child-made. She had them play at random. From there they went into three groups—blow, pluck, and bang—still at random. On about the third day they said it just sounded like noise. From there rhythm was introduced. Beat—fast and slow. Following the leader's beat. Choosing new leaders. Along with this, music notation was introduced by just putting it up in front of them. Perhaps we can go into that, too.

January 31–February 2 (four sessions).

Objectives:

Trying to develop readiness for committee work.

Demonstrating difficulties that arise when groups try to work together.

Changing from an "I" orientation to a "we" orientation in problem-solving.

We sent home a letter asking that each child bring a sheet or blanket big enough to cover himself. The first day we just let the children experience having the sheet in the cafeteria. Each child was to find his own space—many did so by spreading out the sheet and sitting on it. From there we had them pair up. They were then to share a space. Some did not do it, but stayed alone. Soon pairs began to move. One would sit on the sheet, the other would pull. When the period was almost over, we had them line up for races. They enjoyed that. We were able to bring out the fact that when both children worked—one pulling, the other "pumping," as they called it—they could go faster. They also saw that the one team of three could go very fast. Two were pulling one—a good review of our science unit on moving and moving faster.

During the second session we continued exploring moving as groups. They soon realized that as the groups got larger and larger, it was harder and harder to move in a determined direction. We tried some opposition teams—two children who just couldn't work together trying to move in opposite directions.

At the third session Peggy had the children fill out a questionnaire: "The two children I can work best with are _____ and _____. The two children I can work least with are _____ and _____." When they went to the cafeteria to see how true this was, they proved their statements—at first. However, if left with unworkable partners for long, they put their differences aside and joined in the games.

She had them go through "experiencing" the floor. There has been some problem in drawing this together in a meaningful way.

But I tend to want to hurry these explorations; I want results now. The fourth session was set up as a planned lesson.

February 5. Being Alone, Being Together

1. Sit in a circle, not touching.
2. Put your sheet over your head.
3. Now try to think of how you feel when no one wants you around (really get into it).
4. You know you are in a circle. As you feel like it, move from the circle as if you were in slow motion.
5. Find a place to stop. (I touched them to "stay," once there.)
6. You are all alone. No one is near. Only you, the sheet, and the floor. Be completely alone for a while. (Pause.)
7. Now lie down on the floor. Cover yourself with your sheet. Feel the floor. Only you, the sheet, and the floor. (Pause.)
8. Roll yourself up in your sheet as tightly as you can. Stay still. Feel the sheet all around you, nice and tight.
9. Now begin to roll around. If you roll into someone, you may still wish to be alone. If so, move away. If you want to be close to someone, stay near whoever you are touching.
10. Return to the circle.

When they came up, we talked about how it felt to be alone, and later they wrote stories about it. They seemed to be able to really get into it. Since we still had time, I had them lie down. I touched some, and told them that if they had been touched, to pretend they didn't want to be touched by anyone. Now the rest of you are going to try to find the ones I touched. They cannot tell you with words if they were touched or not. They have to let you know they don't want to be touched by the way they act. Now all of you begin to move around.

From this, I asked them to choose what they wanted—to be touched or not to be touched. I, too, began moving around on hands and knees. I was one that wanted to be touched. After a while I came across Laura—a beautiful girl who is very proper. She did not want to be touched. She was behind me over my right shoulder. As I got up on my knees and reached for her, she moved behind me, her eyes twinkling. She shook her head no. Before I knew what was happening, she came around in front of me and gave me a great big hug. As I was hugging her, I didn't see what happened next, but I felt children swarming all over us in one big hug. We lost our balance and went down to the floor in a heap. There were children everywhere. We laughed and giggled in delight. I sat up with children all around—one on my lap, one leaning up my back, one under each arm, my legs touching several others. One child said, "Boy, we *really* like to be touched!" I agreed.

REARRANGING THE ROOM

On the first of the month I always change the room around. This time the children wanted to do it themselves. I consented, and when we came back to the room after working in the cafeteria on the sheets, I told them they could rearrange it but that I wasn't going to help them. They thought that would be great. They began moving things about furiously. Peggy and I sat back to watch. Utter chaos. Dust flying everywhere. We opened both doors to get some air. Not one thing was left standing where it had been.

The boys began pushing desks against the wall. Girls began pushing them back. Pat wanted a desk against the wall. Philip wanted it out in the middle. They each had an end. The desk was up in the air going back and forth.

Laura and Catherine were trying to sweep the floor where the rug had been. Paul kept moving desks into their way. Finally Laura yelled at him to do it her way or else. "Or else what?" said Paul. "I'll just quit trying to get this clean," Laura said. Paul looked at her a second, shrugged his shoulders, and pushed the desk right where she was sweeping. Laura fumed, came to me, and began to tell of her plight. I didn't answer. She walked back, dropped the broom and dustpan, took another girl's hand, and left the room. She stood just outside looking in and shaking her head.

After about twenty minutes everything was in a huge pile toward the center of the room. I stopped them and asked them to look around, and asked what they suggested we do from here. The answer: "Go back to work, we're not done." Right away Jim began pushing a storage unit to the front of the room and Keith began pushing it toward the back. In their struggle they hooked one wheel up on the rug, curling it up and making the whole thing too hard to move. They left it.

By now most of the desks were pushed against the side wall, with two or three on the opposite side. Pat and Bert were struggling against each other about getting them all on one side. Bert insisted his desk was going to stay on the other side. The lunch bell rang forty-five minutes after this started. No one heard it. I didn't say anything. Soon some began seeing others go to lunch. Some quit and left right away. Others finished what they were doing and then went. David and Luke got into a wrestling match on the rug. They would fight furiously, back off, and say, "You had enough?" "No," and they would go at it again—and again, and again. Fifteen minutes later all but six had gone to lunch. Those six got together and completed arranging the room. When they were done, they all went to lunch, or what was left of lunch—fifteen minutes.

When the bell rang and they came in, Bert saw that his desk was in line with the others. He immediately grabbed it and put it on the other side of the room. Before they could begin all over again, I asked them all to come on the rug and evaluate the room the way it was now.

"I want my desk here," said Bert. We can't get to the free activities, they are pushed up against the tables. We can't get paper. The chest is against the wall. We can't see the blackboard. We're too far over. We can't get in and out of our rows; they are too close together. We can't open the door up there. We can't have noisy activities that close to the listening table.

Well, what do you like about the room as it is? We like the desks in rows. We like the rug over here. How can we keep that the way it is and still fix the other problems? Without moving anything, they began throwing out suggestions. Others would respond—that's good, that won't work, etc.

Can we manage to leave Bert's desk where it is? No. Why not? It's out in the middle. We need that space. We'll trip on it. Bert, what do you think? I want my desk here. Is it possible to leave it there? I don't know. Let's do some of the things suggested and see what happens. Small groups moved specific items. When we got the desks moved out from the walls to make movement easier, we found one row almost touched Bert's desk, which had been isolated until then. Now, Bert, what can we do with your desk? I can move it a little and turn it the other way. Then I can still be over here and we can still have rows. Do you like that solution? Yes.

After three hours the room was rearranged. I asked, "How might we do this next time so it won't take so long and cause so much noise and confusion? Or is this the only way to do it?"

Laura: "We can have just a few move things around."

Bert: "I like to do it this way."

Philip: "We can make a map of the room and arrange the things on it first."

By now it was time to go home. Thank goodness!

February 6.

Today I was working on some cupboards while the children were doing some math pages. As I was working, I began to hear some strange sounds. I looked up. A discussion was going on at the back of the room, and Betty was crying. Catherine was patting her on the shoulder. Word went around, "Betty wet her pants, Betty wet her pants." No one came to me, so I continued to be busy, watching to see what they would do on their own. Soon I heard someone say, "Leave her alone. How do you think she feels?" Others joined in. "Yeah, I bet she feels bad enough." Kathy turned around from up front and said, "That's all right, Betty. I wet my pants once. I know how awful it feels." Others said, "Yeah, I've wet my pants, too." "Me, too." "Me, too."

Bert, who was standing and had been going around helping, said, "How many have wet their pants in school?" He raised his hand. Others did, too—about one-third of them.

Luke said, "I've never wet my pants since I was a baby." Keith said, "Oh, I've seen you have wet pants." (Luke's stepmother said he was in diapers until she married his father, when Luke was four.) Then the conversation died out, and they went back to work. Betty, too. She wasn't crying any more, and she was ignoring the puddle under her. After a while I went over and asked, "Are you all right?" She said "Yes," smiled up at me, and continued working.

February 8. Trip to Tuckers Grove

We took a field trip to Tuckers Grove to begin our unit on plants. For me this is backwards. I would have done it at the end, but since reading *Toward a Contact Curriculum* (Fantini and Weinstein), I'm trying some things—backwards if necessary.

We didn't say much about why we were going. When asked what we were going to do, we answered that we were going to have a fun day together. We left early, about fifteen minutes after school had started. We walked up. Once there we let them run for about twenty minutes. Then we called them into two groups. We went on a nature walk to look at living things. After a while they were really looking. "Look at this, this moss is living." "Look, here's a spider web." "Is it alive?" "No, but the spider who made it was." We began to collect things to look at closely with the magnifying glass. We had magnifying glasses with us, but who wanted to wait his turn out here? They did pass their finds around, though.

After the walk we put our collected items on a table for all to see. They named it the "treasure table." They enjoyed being in groups of six using the magnifying glasses to see the things they brought back.

After letting them have free play again, this time on the playground equipment, I announced that I had the blindfolds if they wanted to wear them on the merry-go-round or the swings. They came running! They squealed with delight at the new feeling of motion blindfolded. I was pleased to see how many wore the blindfolds on their own.

After lunch we went on a blind walk. They enjoyed this, too. I noticed many pulling grass and handing it to their blind partner. They touched trees, grass, bushes. I was very happy to get a chance to be led by a child. I laughed at how fast, surely, and confidently she walked as she led me. It was Carlene. She seemed to enjoy sharing things with me. I was reminded of the pleasure she got when I first took her on a blind walk a few weeks ago. Now she wanted to take me. She kept me busy with things to feel and smell. As we were coming down a hill, I slipped and fell. We both laughed at me!

Again I feel an urge to get the mothers in on this. Carlene and I lay there laughing and enjoying each other as mother and daughter, as teacher and student, as two friends. Her mother might also like to experience that feeling. I would like to do this with my own girls.

Unfortunately, the bus came half an hour before I thought it would, and we were not able to continue this activity.

February 9. Science—Seeds

On Monday, Peggy and I were trying to come to some solution on problems of classroom control and having children in contact. She said something about teachers seeing their purpose but not being able to get it across. We realize that too often we try to go too fast. This morning while Peggy was teaching, I had a good chance to observe this. She had a good lesson on seeds prepared, but there was a lot of chaos. She was asking questions that had too many answers and moving on before fully developing anything. I want to state here that I sincerely feel that what Peggy was doing is not very different from what I do, too. It's just that I could observe it today.

There was constant flipping from single answers (raised hands) to group answers—everyone shouting out answers or carrying on private discussions. She was saying "I want you to be quiet" but doing nothing to keep it that way. After the lesson we felt it would have been better if we had just given the children the seeds, let them explore and discover them, and *then* asked what they found. If major concepts were skipped, we could have filled in or just let it go to another lesson. If the concept we were developing were precise enough, I'm sure they would have arrived at it on their own. The seeds were there; they could see the roots and leaves in the seed. They could see the food supply, the protective covering. Much of what was given was like the "stones of knowledge being thrown." I would like to do this lesson over, completely ignoring today's work, and see what happens. It would be hard to keep my comments to myself until they ask for them. Following this introduction, we went into the cafeteria to be the seeds we had just opened.

The period began with a free time. They still like to do a lot of random exploring with the sheets. Peggy was very pleased with the variety of activity she observed. It's not nearly as random and wild as it was a week ago. When they had been on their own awhile, she called them to a circle. After reviewing just the properties of the bean seeds, she asked them to become the seeds. They all curled up into their sheets. All but two boys, that is, and they weren't disturbing the others. She said she would touch them and then they could begin to grow. I was watching. I couldn't believe my eyes. They were just great. In *very* slow motion they began to move. Many moved around under the sheets for five minutes before they "grew" enough to come out. Many hands came poking out slowly, exploring. They really were like little plants in stop-action time lapse. They didn't move their feet.

When they were grown, Peggy had them go back down. I would have had them share what they did and go into some of the feelings. She did something I wouldn't do now. She had them go into animals being born. This turned into a lot of wild play and roughhousing. Again the problem of too much too fast.

It might have been good to go into what happens when a plant grows up. See what they think about that. Sometimes I feel like such a beginner! When to stop, when to go, when to give information, when to let them explore.

February 9. Experiencing an Orange: Science—Living Things; Shapes—Visual and Tactile Discrimination

After reading about a group of adults "experiencing an orange," I wanted to try it with my class. Since we were now on living things, I decided to try it. First of all I gave each child an orange. Then I told them to "get to know your orange." They laughed at me; there are times I'm sure they think I'm nuts. So I showed them how. Look at the color. Is it like everyone else's? Look at the shape. Is it big or little? Now look for any special spots on your orange. They were holding their oranges and watching me. I became very intent on looking at my orange. I found spots and made up stories. "My orange is rather pale. He has been sick with the flu and hasn't been out in the sun. Oh! See this spot? That's where he fell off his bike one day and got all banged up." When they were all watching and listening, I said, "Now I'm going to do my thinking in my mind. You won't hear me. So you look at your own orange and make up your own stories." They did.

Next step. Feel your orange. Feel its roundness in both hands. Feel it in one hand at a time. Next feel the weight of your orange. Let it drop into your hand. Now your other hand. Now that you know your orange, visit someone else's orange. Trade with a neighbor. Feel his orange. Look at his orange. Now get your own orange back. Soon oranges were flying all around. I got hit in the head with one. They, and I, were amazed at the difference in color, look, and feel.

After that we began to peel the orange. Feel if it wants to be peeled. Does it come off easily, or does it push against you? Maybe it doesn't care either way. Next we felt the peels. Then we peeled off the white part. Someone said it was like peeling off sunburned skin. After that we broke the orange into sections. Then we ate our first piece of orange. After that we began to share our sections—rather, we traded them. They compared them. Yours is sweeter than mine. Mine is orange, yours is yellow. Wow! Yours is really sour! Yours is soft. Mine's hard. Yours is juicy.

When we were through, I asked them, "What have you learned?" Well, not all oranges are alike. Are any two alike? No. Can you think of other things that may seem alike at first but once you really look you discover all kinds of differences? Apples and bananas. Anything else?

At this point they became restless. It had been about forty minutes, so I didn't push on. Perhaps we can tie this in with our human-relations unit later on. Perhaps not. We enjoyed the experience, and perhaps that's enough for now.

February 14. Seeds

Since we have been doing seeds for a while now, on Valentine's Day we brought in apples. These were cut in half up and down through the stem. This not only exposed the seeds of the apple but gave a heart shape, too. By cutting just a little more off the bottom part, each child had a heart block to print with. By dipping these into red paint and pressing them onto paper, the children made hearts all over. The seeds left a very special imprint, making a heart-in-a-heart in some. When we talked about what the apple was for, in relation to the bean seeds, they were pleased that they knew the purpose of the apple that we normally eat. "It's food for the seed, and we turn it into food for us. Instead of the seed growing, that food helps us grow."

The next question was "Why do we grow beans?" They quickly saw that we usually eat beans, too. Their food helps us grow. Since we had talked about needing energy to grow and move quite some time ago, they tied that in, too. Some stopped calling it the "food supply" in the bean and changed it to "energy." I feel sure we will get back to this when we study animals. The animal eats grasses and other foods, and we eat some animals.

After each child had made a valentine card and a folder to take his valentines home in, we had them use their cards during the writing lesson. We talked about how a card was different from a letter, a note, and a story. Then we wrote out some messages, and each copied the one he wanted on his card. The children also ate the apples after they were through printing with them. We washed off the paint and cut away the stained surface.

February 15. Art Lesson—Shapes

One first-grade objective is to be able to distinguish shapes. I got strips of red paper two, three, four, five, and six inches long by one inch wide. I asked a child to be the three-inch strip without showing any of the others. She was puzzled. "I can't." So I showed her the six-inch one and said, "Now be the three-inch one." She bent over. "Now be the six-inch one." She stood up straight. From there I introduced the rest of the strips. They soon saw that with five different lengths they had to pace themselves in order not to be fully let out for five inches or fully tucked up for three. One boy was standing as tall as he could for five inches. I thought he would have trouble as I held up six, but he stopped only for an instant and then stood on top of the nearest chair.

From there I had each child take two strips of each length and glue them into rings so they had ten rings. They then pasted these onto a sheet of paper, being sure not to put any two of the same size next to each other. As the work progressed, this became more and more complex, since some rings had four "neighbors." Once this was done, we moved the papers all around and looked at the abstract design.

The next step was to take a flat sheet of paper and paste it on top of the rings, making the paper big enough to cover the space between the rings and completely cover all of them, to sandwich the rings between a top and bottom sheet of paper. How much space would the top sheet need? What shape would it have to be? They enjoyed this and soon found themselves standing over the top of their work so they could see how to cut the flat paper. A great deal of association went on during all of this. "Looks like

hair rollers." "Looks like I'm a giant looking at the top of buildings." It took about two hours to do this.

February 19. Today We Have the Videotape Recorder in All Day
Peggy has been having trouble teaching first-graders. I have
been having trouble teaching her. We are both angry and frustrated
with each other and with the whole situation. I am going to use the
videotape to try to see control, purpose, and followup (control,
clarity, concepts). We begin with sharing. The camera sees everything and nothing. Most of the time I leave the camera on a closeup
of Peggy from the waist up, since she is sitting down. As time
passes, I begin to see some of the problems emerge. They are on
tape.
At recess time Peggy expresses a need to get the class settled
down. She tells me what she plans to do. It sounds good. When we
go back, the camera again records. At lunchtime when we see the
tape, Peggy is almost in tears. The morning was frustrating enough,
and then to have to watch it all over again.
Then come the questions. "What did I do wrong? What should
I have done?" We go back to the tape. She can see what she did
wrong. Just little things, taken one by one. Now I know why I feel
I'm being petty when I get after her. First-grade teaching involves
strict attention to little details. Nothing really big ever happens.
It's just one little thing after another, day after day.
We continue through the tape, stopping, talking, replaying,
talking, trying to understand. I know it was a grueling, defeating
session. I am sorry for Peggy, but at the same time thrilled at the
new insight into teaching first grade. More and more I can see not
only that all behavior is caused, but even some of the causes. As
George would say, "It's obvious."

February 21.
While doing a lesson on carrot roots, I was able to see more
clearly the contrast between Peggy and me. She still has trouble
waiting for the children to absorb one direction before giving them

another. She still wants to work with them as individuals and not as a group. She told them to wash off their carrots and then eat them. There's one sink, and there were twenty-seven dirty carrots. She completely loses the group at such times. Today she accepted my suggestion of giving them something to do while waiting. Again a little thing that has large consequences for effective classroom learning. At last I feel she has some understanding and insight into the problem.

In my mind learning and control go together. Not rigid, senseless rules and regulations, but rules that aid the flow and exchange of ideas. If everyone is shouting out (right or wrong) answers, who's learning? There must be order for learning to take place. Dewey, in *Art as Experience*.

February 23. I've Got It, I Want to Give It to You

Today we went out for free play. As usual, I sat on the grass, and several children sat with me. We just enjoyed being with each other, passing a few sunny minutes. For no accountable reason I cupped my hands and said, "I have something and I want to give it to Anita." She smiled and reached out for "it." She held it carefully for a while and then said, "I've got something and I want to give it to Pauline." The game continued. After a while Paul had it. He said, "I've got something and I want to give it to Mrs. Castillo." He reached over to me and said, "But I don't really have it. Catherine didn't give it to me." I checked my first impulse, which was to tell him there wasn't anything in the first place. I turned to Catherine and said, "Didn't you give it to Paul?" She said, "No, Rona didn't give it to me." I turned then to Rona. "Didn't you give it to Catherine?" She looked at me in wide-eyed innocence and said, "Yes, I did!" I asked her to give it to Catherine again. She cupped her hands and gave it to Catherine. I asked Catherine if she had it now. Catherine looked confused and said, "No, I guess I dropped it." I asked her if she could find it. She said, "I don't know what to look for!" She was quite upset, so I told Rona, "You give it to her again, but this time give her a great big one." I was delighted when Rona stretched out her arms and struggled to hold it now that it was great big. She staggered over to Catherine and said, "Here, take it. I can't hold it much longer." Catherine just beamed as she said, "Oh-h-h, I've got it now!" She then gave it to Paul, who gave it to me. We had to stand up now because it was so big. I gave it to Anita again. While she was looking at it, Paul walked up to it and hit it and said, "Pow!" I wish I could have had a picture of Anita's face as she said, "Oh, you've broken it!" Then she realized she could have a brand-new one. She said, "Now I've got it and I'm going to keep it." She ran off and that was the end of the game. There were about ten children playing this game, and I was so pleased to see how imaginative they could be.

February 26. Imagination

I have been working with the class on DeMille's *Put Your Mother on the Ceiling,* a book of imagination for children. The first time I took just the boys and played the first game, "Boys and Girls." I wasn't too pleased. There was a lot of talking and fooling around. The second time we did it together. Again there was a lot of fooling around. This time I asked why. Their biggest gripe was that the other kids bothered them. So we talked about "the other kids" and what we would like to do to them. The third time they really got into it. At the end it says, "Is there anything else you would like to do with your mother? Do it now." I waited quite a while before the children were through. When I asked them if they wanted to share what they did, I was amazed that so many had participated. All but two. One boy had a whole story of what he had had his mother do. The fourth time I decided to tie this in with our self-awareness, other-awareness.

After doing "Father," they again shared their stories. I was astonished at the hostility shown to fathers, but didn't say anything. One boy said he kept throwing knives at his father and missing. I reminded him that this was just his imagination. Could he bring back his father now? Yes. "Can you throw a knife and hit him in your imagination?" "Yes. Now his coat is all bloody." He touched his own chest. I became somewhat confused and frightened. I didn't know what to say. The boy didn't look upset, though, so I asked him if he could send his father away. He said, "Yes." I asked him to bring him back. "Is he still bloody?" "Not now." I bit my tongue to keep from saying "good," and said, "Send him away again." I was glad to get rid of him, I must say. (Switch to appreciation.)

I was pleased to see Philip sitting there completely at ease, with his eyes closed the whole time, even though I hadn't told them to close their eyes. Philip is the one who said "I can't" the first time I did something like this months ago. I hadn't realized how far he had come in this. After doing the game, I gave them each two dittos of a geometric man. I told them to mark one "My Father" and the other "My Imagination." We then went from head to toe drawing in details of what our fathers really looked like and then what we wanted them to look like. Since there was time and we had played "Mother" before, I told them they could do the same with their mothers if they wanted to.

I'm not sure what goals are being met by these games, but certainly I can see an increase in attention span and all kinds of language stimulation. I'm not sure I'm up to that part of it.

February 28. Flowers

Today each child had his own oxalis flower. Instead of starting from the parts leading to the whole, we went the other way. While I gave a demonstration with big chart drawings, each child took his flower apart to discover all the various parts in it. Since first-graders love new words, they quickly picked up petal, stamen, and pistil. Each part was given a name and its function explained, including the pollen and the part the bee plays in developing the seed for the flower.

From that the children went into the cafeteria to be the parts.

They were so funny when they were petals—showing off trying to attract bees. They became the stamen and the pistil. They made seeds and then let them fall. Each acted this out in his own way. At the end we played the "Waltz of the Flowers" without naming it and let them dance. This was a good lesson with hearty participation. From there we had each child draw himself as a flower. One boy drew a ship upon a sea. When questioned about this, he said, "I'm the Mayflower." Who could argue with that?

As a followup on this, I cut out a flowerpot from colored paper and had each child come up and pick a color from about seven different colors and tell me what shape of flower he would like to be. I cut his paper in that shape and asked where he wanted to be in a bouquet I was making. I then pasted the flower where he pointed and, from an extra class picture, cut out his picture and pasted it on the flower, so each flower had a face in the center of it. I pasted the picture of our school on the flowerpot along with our class identification. We then took the finished product into the office and gave it to Mr. Pearce and Mrs. Cole. The children were pleased to have something to give to them. They said, "Now everyone is in the office, not just the kids who get in trouble."

When Mr. Pearce asked them if they made it, they said, "No, Mrs. Castillo did. But she had to ask us what kind of flower we were, because she didn't know." If I do it again some year, I'll let them do their own flowers. It made a very pretty and personal poster.

March 6.

Today we made cookies for refreshments for our parents on Friday. Earlier this week we told the children we could make cookies if they would do all of the work. They agreed readily to this.

The first problem was how many we would need to make. There was quite a discussion on this. The thing they wanted to know was "How many can I have?" They finally decided three apiece was a reasonable number. They then decided their parents could each have three, too. That way, if they really wanted more, "probably my mother will give me one of hers." We then put a "3" up on the board for each child and parent. The board was covered with 3s. I asked how I could possibly count all those 3s and find out how many we really needed in all. A wide variety of answers was offered. All got groans of "It will take forever." When I asked if anyone knew of a fast way to get the answer, hoping someone knew the term "multiplication," one boy, Pat, answered, "Use the adding machine in the office." I then told them of my way, and wrote 27×3 and came up with enough cookies for them, and 25×3 for cookies for their parents, and added the two answers. I was reminded I had forgotten to add three for myself. After doing that, I asked, "Do you think we will need any more?" One child, Bert, said, "Can we eat some when we make them?" We all agreed that was a good idea. Who can smell cookies baking and not want to eat some? They decided that since we already had to make so many for Friday, we should each have just one right out of the oven. We then added that to our figure and felt we knew how many to make. Laura suggested we make a few extra, just in case. Then I read the recipe and told them it would make four to six dozen. How many in a dozen? Twelve. How many dozen would we need? By now the idea of using the office adding machine sounded pretty good. After we had decided we would need seventeen to eighteen dozen cookies, I asked what we needed to make them. They obviously had had previous experience in making cookies, because among them they came up with a complete list of utensils and ingredients. I told them I would bring the ingredients, but they had to bring the utensils. I didn't make any actual assignments. We had plenty of everything the very next morning.

The class worked in two groups in the cafeteria. They measured, sifted, beat, and blended everything. We made oatmeal cookies first. While the cookies were baking, we sat in a circle and talked about foods we liked and foods we didn't like. It was interesting that someone named eggs as a food he didn't like and someone else named them as a food he liked. From that we got into a discussion on how many foods there are, how we are taught to like foods, how unpleasant associations, such as getting sick from eating too much of a favorite food, can make us not like a food, and so on.

As soon as the first cookies were done, I took them out and gave one to each child. How they all enjoyed that! While the rest of the cookies were baking, the class wrote a story about food. It could be about the cookies, good food, bad food, anything. This kept them busy while I was checking the cookies. The children were very patient. They knew it would take a long time.

On the second day of baking we made up a story about waiting. I started with "When I wait a long time . . ." The next child added a sentence or phrase, and so on around the circle. They made it quite plain that they found waiting irritating and difficult unless there was a pretty darn good reason. Again, when the first batch was done, I gave one hot cookie to each child. These were chocolate-chip cookies, and there were differences between the hot dough, the hot walnuts, and the hot melted chips. The children were aware of this and brought it out right away. Making cookies really gets at all the senses in such a nice way!

While waiting for the other six dozen cookies to bake, we developed a dialogue between the dough being beaten and the spoon doing the beating. "Spoon, Spoon, don't beat so hard. I want to be a cookie, I'm trying." "I can't help it," said the spoon, "Arm is making me do it. Arm, why are you moving me so fast? Dough doesn't like it," and so on. I wish I had that on tape. It went on and on. From that we had little plays. Three girls wanted to act out the parts. In general they kept themselves actively busy while waiting. They felt very comfortable in the cafeteria.

When our cookies were done, I wrapped them in foil on cookie sheets. I put them in the cupboard on a shelf at the children's level. They saw me put them there, and I wondered if I was going to have to move them. Not once did a child touch those trays. I was amazed and very pleased. Even Bert, Luke, and Keith kept hands off.

In all, this was a four-day project and about ten hours of working with the children. It was well worth it.

March 8. Parents' Day

On Peggy's last day we asked the parents to come in and share our new program. Since they have asked about reading and math, we will begin with that. We'll have reading for fifteen minutes and math for fifteen minutes. This also will give time for latecomers to arrive. We began by having each child thoroughly prepared. On the day before, Peggy and I acted out the procedure, taking the parts of a child and her parent. The children loved that.

To begin the affective work, the child faced his parent across his desk, with art paper taped down between them. They each held a different colored crayon in each hand. They were instructed to color for a period of time without talking. First the child, then the parent, then together. I started them at ten seconds and worked up to their working together for a full minute. This got them into the feeling of working together without talking. It also loosened them up, because they got away from trying to do things in a "right" way. There could be no right way when moving in that way.

From there we moved into the cafeteria. I had the children wear the blindfolds and the parents close their eyes as they sat in a big circle. I gave each person an object and asked him to go beyond labeling his object. They passed their objects when I clicked sticks, as I had done once before with just the children. We continued this activity for about five minutes. From that I had them move into parent-child dyads. The parent put the blindfold on, and the child guided the parent to new experiences. Some children brought objects to their parents, while others got up and explored the cafeteria. Since it had poured the night before, I didn't expect them to go on a blind walk, but many did anyway. The mothers seemed game for anything. After about ten minutes I asked them to change places—the child wearing the blindfold and the parent leading.

When they stopped doing this, they got out the sheets and had a free-play session. I had lesson plans, but I threw them out since they were having so much fun just playing. Mrs. Hilton said, "You've got to be kidding!" and then I looked up to see her racing across the floor pulling Jim full speed ahead. When she came to the wall, she went left, Jim right. She doubled over in laughter. Keith's daddy was a sight pulling Keith, with Joe sitting Indian style on his own balled-up sheet, hitching a ride by holding on to the back of Keith's sheet. Mrs. Moreno was winding Patricia up in her sheet, round and round, with Patricia's ponytail flying and her eyes twinkling.

When they were exhausted, we went over to the room for the cookies the children had made and some much-needed punch. Just before they left, I passed out report cards to the children, since they were due to go home today, and parent and child looked at them together. I was there to answer any questions they had. It was a great day. I was so thrilled at the way the mothers and fathers joined in. They seemed so free and uninhibited I was amazed. I could have kissed them all.

When I asked the children what they thought about the morning, the first answer came instantly: "Wow!" I had to agree and felt they said it all very nicely.

March 13. Writing Lesson—Expanding Imagination

After reading *On beyond Zebra*, by Dr. Seuss, we had a writing lesson on his letters instead of our usual writing. It was very interesting, and the children were engrossed in what they were doing. They really paid attention, listened, watched, and followed directions in order to reproduce those strange letters! Bud Robinson came in with a hand-held video camera, and they paid no attention to it. They were too interested in what they were doing to care what he was doing.

When we had done six of them and got the idea, I asked them to try to make up some of their own. They went right to work. Soon their pages were covered with weird figures. They had a more difficult time naming them. I drew some of them on the board, as good a job as I could do, and the class tried to name them. The "author" of the letter then chose the name he liked best or made up one of his own after being stimulated by the class. The next thing was to draw the animal or object that went with the made-up symbol and name. Their pictures were just as creative, colorful, and original as Dr. Seuss's. From there I asked each one to make up a story about his picture. I brought in the primary typewriter so they wouldn't feel the restriction of having to print after just being freed from it.

Their stories were delightful. Long, original, and very funny. I wanted to keep them, but they didn't want to give them up. I couldn't blame them and so sent them home.

March 18. Writing Lesson—Imagination, Phonics, and Rhyming Words

Since we had so much fun with Dr. Seuss last week, I tried a similar lesson. During the reading period I wrote "A Frog on a Log" on the board. After someone read it, I asked another child to draw a picture for it on the board.

When that was done, I drew a picture of a cat on a mat and asked if anyone could guess what I wanted to write underneath it. One child knew right away, and after about three minutes seven or eight more figured it out. The answer I expected was "A cat on a mat." One child, Philip, said it could also be "A cat asleep in a heap." My drawing accounted for the different response.

From there I asked them what other animals they could think of in a rhyming situation. They had no trouble. A fish on a dish. A snail in a pail. A fly saying good-by, etc. After about twenty minutes of group discussion I asked them to write them down and draw the pictures that went with them. They really enjoyed doing this. This time when they were through, with most of the children doing from three to six of them, I read them the book *Did You Ever See?* This used a form different from the one we had used, and they noticed it by the second page.

Did you ever see a goat [turn the page] float?
Did you ever see a fish . . . wish?

They did this orally after a while, using animals not in the book. They soon realized it was harder to do with most animals. Some children wanted to try this form, but most were tired by now. Those who were interested made take-home books and did them on their own. Four very good ones came back.

March 21. *Put Your Mother on the Ceiling*—"Father" (Rerun)

After seeing such violent reactions against fathers when we played "Father" the last time, I asked the class to play the game again. And again we got a long list of bloody tales from the boys. This time I went into the "I resent, I demand, I appreciate" game with them. We did it as a group, and yet I felt each one was able to participate. We started around in a circle. I went first. "The thing I hate the most about my father is . . ." I tried to accept everything said and did not interrupt anyone. I gave those who were timid about the whole thing an out by saying, "If you really cannot think of anything to say or do not feel like saying it out loud, you can say, 'The thing I hate most about my father cannot be said now.' " Only one child, Pauline, used this.

When the game came back to me, I said, "Now I'm going to change the game. I'm going to tell my father how he should be. 'Daddy, you should not act like a spoiled little boy. You should not yell at me like you do either.' " I nodded to the child next to me. They took it all the way around the circle. When it came back to me, I said, "Now we'll play the last part of the game. I'm going to tell him the things I like about him. 'Daddy, I like you always being near when I need you. I like knowing you are at work while I'm at school. I like the way you laugh!' "

They really liked this game. I felt much better about it than I did the first time we talked about Father. I'm for the anger's being released, in a safe way, but I felt upset the first time. This time we said more things about Father that were "bad" than we did the first time, but following it with the "I resent, I demand, I appreciate" game seemed to bring things into sharper focus and put them into a perspective. The children didn't register the horror and disbelief at what classmates were saying. I felt things were said with more sincerity and less shock appeal as we progressed with it, too. They still have a tendency to play "Can you top this?" when talking about "bad" things. I didn't notice as much of that in the game part as I did in the imagination part. The next time something happens concerning a fear of what Mother will do or say, as in the paint relay, I hope we can do this with Mother.

March 26. Dealing with Anxiety

We began the day knowing our parents were coming in at 10:00. We also knew *Life* magazine was sending a reporter and a photographer to see what I was going to do with the parents. I couldn't sleep the night before for butterflies. Pat and Janice arrived, and I was even more jittery. The kids came in a bit wild, too. I couldn't seem to reach them. I had them come to the rug and make a circle, but still no quiet. On the spur of the moment, thinking on my feet, I sat in the circle with them and said, "I am going to play a new game. I will do it first, and anyone who wants can take a turn at it when I'm through."

All of you get into your stomach. Feel around in there and find out what's going on. Now, in my stomach I feel butterflies, knots, worry, tension, anxiety, and a lot of things I cannot name. They are all things I don't want. I'm taking all of those things. I'm wrapping them into one huge ball. I'm putting the ball here in my hands. Now I'm taking all of this "stuff" and I'm throwing it out here in the middle of the rug. This was great! Wow! Did I have a sense of release! I've never had such a lightening feeling as that. Somehow it worked.

While I was sitting there amazed, Bert started talking. He had worms, grass, dirt, snakes, and lots more. He, too, put it all in the middle. Laura was really concerned. She hadn't prepared her mother for finger painting and was afraid she would object. She put that worry in the middle, too. Some children still seemed funny but had not talked. So I asked them, "All of you who still have something inside that you would like to get rid of, do it now. You don't have to share out loud. Get in touch with it. Put it in your hands and stick it out in the middle." Pauline smiled a great smile of relief, stuck something out there, and beamed at me. Many others followed. From that we went outside. Pat followed. He had suggested I put him in a circle. Not knowing what would follow, I asked the children to circle him when we got out by the hill. We went out there to unwind and give Pat an idea of the layout.

They made a huge spread-out circle around Pat. He had all of his camera equipment on. I said, "We have Pat in a circle; now what would you like to do with him?" Soon someone said, "Squish him." Before anyone could plan anything, they all began to walk in on him. They continued to close in until they actually knocked him over. He was great. He just laughed and went down easily. They then sat down all over him. He did not protest or reject. Soon they got up and began running down the hill. We went down the hill a few times, around the bottom to look at the items brought in for later, and then up and around the sixth-grade classes and back to the room. By then parents were beginning to arrive.

March 26. *Life* magazine—Pat and Janice

Since the parents were so enthusiastic the first time I had them in, I don't know why I was surprised when they all offered to come back again. Luke's mother wasn't coming in, so George Brown offered to be a father for an hour. We began with an extension of the crayon activity of last time. While waiting for latecomers and to loosen up the group, I started by having them wake up their hands—rubbing harder and harder, clapping, slapping, shaking, feeling what was happening. Then I had them pour some starch they had on their desks onto the taped-down paper. As before, parent was facing child. They were then to move as before—together without talking. I went around the room for pacing clues. Seeing many mothers using only one hand, I asked that they simply become aware of both of their hands and then of all four hands. They did not have to paint with both—only become more aware of themselves. When they were all moving freely and hands were full of starch, I asked them to touch each other's hands only, holding them up between them. From that I asked each to dip into one of the colors (dry tempera) that were on the desk and to continue to move nonverbally. They could make a picture of something, but a design might be easier to accomplish if they were going to continue without words. I continued to circulate, but they did not seem to need any more suggestions. When I noticed paper beginning to curl from rubbing and starch beginning to dry, I asked that they get to some state of completeness when they could. Some will finish quickly; others will need more time. When they finished, they had a horrible clean-up task. I asked that they leave their desks as they were for later cleaning and just wash their hands. Children went out to the bathrooms. I had provided washcloths, but they were very inadequate.

They were cleaning up at varying times, and as they finished I had the child take a blindfold and go out to the hill area with his parent. Today, unlike last time, it was beautiful—sunny and warm. Early this morning Jon helped me get things ready. We brought some buckets from home and some driftwood. We put water in the buckets and put them all in the hill area. Bruce brought in two big rocks. One was flat and smooth, the other very sharp and rough. He also stuck great boughs of lemon trees into the fence. They had leaves, blossoms, and fruit on them. When we were all ready, the children took their parents on a blind walk. After about ten minutes they switched roles. They continued to use the blindfolds, mostly out of habit perhaps. They really enjoyed doing it this time. They ran, crawled, touched, smelled, and laughed! It was very joyful and so thrilling to watch.

From that I had them come into the cafeteria. I did not allow them to play with the sheets this time. As they came in, they got a sheet and sat down together. When they were all quiet, I asked the children to go through the seed sequence. Each started in his own "shell." When they "felt watered and strong," they began to grow. Upon reaching maturity, they created more seeds and began to die. As they died, they were to change from the plant to the new seed, getting under their sheets again. This went very well.

From that I asked the parents to get under the sheets and assume a prenatal position. As they felt like it, they were to come out of the sheets. They began to talk as they came out. I asked them if they wanted to talk to do it as a baby. Then they began to crawl. From there I asked them to get to their knees and really look at their child. I asked them to try not talking as they did this. As they continued in this way, I asked that they try to become acutely aware of their child as a person, as an individual. Become aware of how they felt when looking at their child. I then asked them to rise slowly to their full height, keeping eye contact with their child if possible. From that position they were to try to raise their child to their eye level. There were many groans as they tried this. I suggested to some that they put their child on the benches on the side. Either way, they soon found this uncomfortable. I told them to now get in the most comfortable position they had experienced with their child. They went back to their knees and stayed that way. From there they sat down together. The warmth and affection openly displayed were overwhelming to see. They stayed like this for about seven minutes. Since the hour was more than over, I asked the children to say good-by when they wanted and go out on the playground. Bob had agreed to watch the class while I met with Pat, Janice, and Bruce for a questioning period.

Before leaving, many of the parents engaged in a free-play session, as they had really worked in the last session. Again I was delighted with the joy and freedom they expressed while being with their children. What wonderful people to work with! Mrs. Kyle even went out with Jerry and remained with him until lunch. Bob said several parents went out to the playground with their children after leaving the cafeteria. It was a long time before they were ready to leave—up to forty-five minutes. I hadn't seen this, since I had been in conference. Another "Wow" day gone by.

March 28. Dizzy

Bob Dorn, of the *Goleta Gazette-Citizen*, and Jean Fowler, of the district office, wanted to come in, since they had heard that *Life* was interested. I didn't have the energy or desire to go through a big production again, but I did want to get some ideas across.

To begin the lesson, I had the children wrap themselves in the sheets and roll down the hill like a cocoon. They really felt dizzy that way. When they got down, I asked them to choose a partner and go on a smelling walk. Blindfolds were available if they preferred a blind walk. There were some of both.

After that I asked those who wanted to to join me in a game. We played "I've got it, I want to give it to you" as we once had played it on the lawn during free play. A large group played it with me. When I got them going, I left the game. There were about four activities going at once: blind walks, smelling walks, free play, and the game. When we were through, I stayed out and talked to Bob during lunchtime. He was interested enough to stay and come back to the room. He watched as the children turned this experience into a creative-writing lesson. I was very pleased with the stories produced by the children. They are getting to be quite hammy, performing at their peak when cameras and visitors are around. I guess we're all like that.

I feel Bob handled the newspaper article very nicely. I appreciated it and let him know it. I hope to get copies of pictures taken to include in this journal.

April 1. Goofy Day

Mid Squier had been given the assignment of being goofy at our last meeting. My class and I had been under a lot of pressure last week, so I sent home a note asking that the children be allowed to come to school outlandishly dressed on April Fool's Day. *We* were going to be goofy. Chris Braynard and I decided to get together and really turn our program topsy-turvy. We got goofy names for the kids and us, dressed funny, and switched classes. I took her class and she took mine for the first hour. We even switched schedules—math first, sharing last. We also made a code, using numbers for letters. When decoded, it said, "Go stand in the wastebasket now. Tap your head ten times. Go write your April Fool name on the board. Draw a circle around it." The children had a grand time with that. They couldn't read it very well, but once someone had done it, he helped someone else. In math, right answers were wrong.

This was the first rainy day I really enjoyed. I wore my housecoat (over regular clothes), a baseball cap backwards, mismatched stockings and shoes, etc. The children went way out. Their costumes were really great. Clowns, hoboes, mismatched, backwards, over- and undersized, cowboys, etc. Every single child had on something different, something goofy. We really had a time calling each other names like Ezekiel, Maud, Clementine, and Orville. Too bad it comes only once a year.

April 4. Drawing Bunnies

The children have been fussing about making bunnies. "I can't do it. You do it for me." To get them out of this, I had them draw bunnies in the air first. From that I asked them to draw a circle in one line to the count of ten. They had to put down their crayons on "one" and not pick them up again until "ten." They could not stop and start but had to keep going. The shapes got more and more difficult. When they got the feeling of this, I told them to outline a bunny. I did a couple quickly in two different positions to show how it could be done, and erased them right away. Each child had a large pile of scratch paper. I had them do five bunnies. They then chose the most interesting one and colored it in. They were encouraged to make it as "goofy" as possible—flowers, stripes, zigzags, etc. After that they could either pin them up or throw them away. All but two children wanted theirs up. No more fussing about "I can't."

This is a good lesson to help them get over the feeling that some particular thing has to be a certain way when drawn. This, like the drawing with the parents, does not allow for *a* right way for a painting to turn out. It is wild, free, even frustrating. But it breaks down the coloring-book stereotype in such a fun way. It can be used any time children are saying "I can't."

April 16. Science—Sea Turtles

We are beginning a unit on dinosaurs. After reading through the material in the science book, I felt there wasn't enough in it to keep the children interested very long. And from past experience I know first-graders, especially the boys, are really fascinated by dinosaurs.

In reading the *TV Guide*, I discovered that another Jacques Cousteau program was going to be on, dealing with the life cycle of the sea turtle. I announced this to the class and asked them to try to watch it. Today we began the science period with a discussion of what they had seen. Most of the children had seen it, and through our discussion those who hadn't were filled in. After about twenty minutes of talk I asked them to dictate a story to me, with a beginning, a middle, and an end. They could do it together, and I would write one story on the board. Again pertinent information was repeated.

From there we went into the cafeteria with our sheets. This was the first time for that in about three weeks. I started them in a circle for direction and control. We were being videotaped, and I was feeling a little tense. They were instructed to become the four-hundred-pound sea turtle, using their sheets as a carapace. Be the turtle underwater. Children were down on the floor using arms and legs as flippers. Now move up on the sand—heavy, lumbering movements. Build your nest and lay your eggs. Even the boys were actively participating. Once you've laid your eggs, become one of them. Children were moving under their sheets. At this point, from across the room I heard Jerry, who is usually disrupting others, yell out, "Eggs don't move!" I turned to see him push someone under a sheet out of his space. Once they were all in the egg, I told them to come out and move to the sea. We hadn't talked about this in the room, but every child moved to the south wall, the sea side of the room. By what agreement did they do this? Follow the leader? I will use this later in the development of "instinct" as a meaningful word in their vocabulary.

After they got to the sea, I asked them to review the role of the frigate birds in relation to the turtles. They were then told to be frigate birds. Sheets became wings, children became birds. Now, boys, become turtle eggs in one nest. Girls, be frigate birds. Eggs, hatch. Move to the sea. Frigate birds catch baby turtles. Only three make it to the sea. Switch roles. No turtles survive.

From that I pulled them back to the original circle and asked questions. Why do turtles lay so many eggs—four million—in a year? What would happen if they laid only twenty-seven? Good responses came forth. The idea of "extinct" became clear. The next day we went to the library and looked up sea turtles, and from that we moved into our study of dinosaurs. Turtles were alive in those days.

April 18. Cuisenaire Rods

I think a great deal of affective learning can be achieved by using these rods. Just following the directions in the manual will lead the children into *feeling* numerical concepts. After all we have done, the children have moved into this area with more freedom and ease than my classes have in the past. I've known from the beginning of the year that this was a great class, so it's hard to know exactly what is cause and what is effect.

Once before in an art lesson I had the children be different lengths of paper. After using the rods three times, I had them be each of the rods. They responded quickly. Since the biggest problem I have with rods is getting them all picked up at the end of the period, I had them act out being the rod that doesn't get put back. Since it is usually the white rod, they became that rod. That was fun. As the problem comes up, I hope to go back to having them be the lost rod. Perhaps it will help.

Perhaps next year I will have the courage to start out with the rods. They quite literally give the child something to hang on to in the area of math. And yet the children seem to love to have that math workbook. Maybe because it's the one thing in the room that has their own name on it. That's something I've never thought of before.

April 19. Literature—Science

Keith told us *The Wonderful Egg* was going to be on television and that we should watch it because it was about a dinosaur. Today we talked about it. The first response was that the triceratops was make-believe. Keith was quite angry about it. He said, "In the book it was real, but on TV it was only a pretend animal." Melanie said, "It couldn't be true even in the book." I asked, "Why not?" Karen said, "There are no dinosaurs now. Man didn't live when dinosaurs lived." Keith, do you believe that? No. It was real in the book. Well, say a boy did get a dinosaur egg and it did hatch. What would happen then? It would be just like it was in the story. Why did some people want to outlaw the dinosaur? They were afraid of it. They couldn't get enough food for it. It cost too much money to keep it. Would you like to have a dinosaur? Well, yes and no. Why not? What is the "no" part of your answer? It caused a lot of fuss. People were running all over the place. The boy had to leave his home to be with the dinosaur. What is the "yes" part of your answer? It would be nice to have one to study. Then we could learn more about it. What would you like to know? Oh, just what it would be like to have a dinosaur around. Do you think you would like to have one around? Not too many. Why not? They're so big and they eat too much.

From all of this I asked them to imagine what it would be like if they had a dinosaur, and to write a story about it. I reminded them to try to get a beginning, a middle, and an end to their stories. Some of them were very good.

Anita wrote:

I have a pet dinosaur.
It is a triceratops.
It is a gentle pet.
I have to climb up a ladder so I can pet him.
I like him for a pet.

I tried to get the book, but neither the school nor county library had it.

April 22. Creative Play

After being at Esalen and trying Robin's idea of forming groups and building things, I decided to try it with the children. They formed groups of threes and fours.

1. Using only your hands, make a house. They had some trouble with this, so I helped one group while the others watched. I had had the same feeling when I did it. After seeing what I meant, they had no trouble at all.

2. Make a school. One girl used her fingers as people moving in and out of the group's structure.

3. Make a car. You can use more than your hands if you want. One group of four had two wheels—boys swinging their arms around like windmills—a body, and a driver riding the body and holding an imaginary steering wheel.

4. A living thing. One group of three became a butterfly. The one in the middle was the body, the ones on each side the wings, jumping up and down.

After doing this we talked about it. How did it feel? How well did all of you work together as one unit? (More development of committee work.) What happened when someone didn't work?

It was a good beginning. They should do it some more. Perhaps it would be a good five-minute thing to do before moving into a group project.

April 30. Literature

I've been reading *Mary Poppins* and *Mary Poppins Comes Back* to the class. In many ways I think it is quite advanced for first-graders, but since Walt Disney is getting to them with his version, I feel a need to offer the "real" Mary Poppins. I cannot stand the way he sugar-coats everything, and, of course, they eat it up. In Walt Disney's version Mary is a dear, sweet, lively mother substitute. In P. L. Travers' book she is stern, vain, and uncompromising. Throughout the book I have helped them to see the likenesses and differences, mostly the latter, between the two. It's often hard to believe the book is the original source. Since I am so anti-Disney, I have played the music to the movie, because I do appreciate that.

After reading the chapter "Topsy-Turvy," we went outside and stood on our heads for a while and turned "Catherine wheels." We had quite a discussion on what it would be like to turn the world upside down. At times I believe these children are quite capable of doing just that.

I've also compared the real *Pinocchio* and Walt Disney's. Here, too, he simplifies everything and makes everything black or white. I've read all the Pooh stories and many of the poems by A. A. Milne—in fact, that was the first series of stories I read to them. Again, I resent what has been done to Pooh and Christopher Robin. Catherine had the records that follow the book verbatim and are beautifully done, so I played those. This year Disney has come out with *The Jungle Book*. It is far too difficult in the original form. I don't feel I can revise it any better than the Walt Disney Studios can, so I've told the class it is a book they will enjoy when they are in fourth grade. But I have shown them how different the books we have read are from his films, so they will have some idea of the variance.

May 2 and 3. Art—Creative Writing

Today we did mono prints. Each child chose the color he wanted to do his painting in. He squeezed a big pancake of paint from the jar onto a Formica square, smeared it around, created a design on it, and put a piece of paper over it. Then he peeled off the paper and saw his mono print. I really enjoyed watching their faces when they saw what they had made.

Surprise, pleasure, disappointment: After the prints were dry the next day, each child took his painting and studied it. I reminded them of the time we had the paper called "Jimmy's Idea," when they turned it all ways and made up stories about it. I asked them to do that now, using their mono print as the stimulus. I was very pleased to see how many could find a different story when the print was turned a different way. Some could even find four stories in their pictures.

Paul, who was disappointed as soon as he took his picture off the board, said he couldn't find anything at all in his. Just red and white spaces. I held it up and asked if anyone could help him find something. Many children saw something. They offered ideas. Paul listened. Soon he too saw what they saw.

From that I had them write a story, again reminding them to try to get a beginning, a middle, and an ending. Bruce happened to come in while we were working. I didn't hear him, and no one made a comment. The first thing I knew he was standing beside me. He said, "I couldn't find you when I came in." The children wrote long, good stories. I am pleased with the progress most of them are making. I'm still concerned about the problems some of them are having getting all of their ideas down. Some, like Keith, Luke, David, and Melanie, still have a hard time writing anything. At these times I wish I had some help to take dictation, or even a primary or standard typewriter to type some of their stories for them. I've tried sixth-grade helpers, but this type of thing doesn't often occur at regulated times.

May 6. Lion Hunt

I read "The Lion Hunt" as it is on the sheet. After doing it once on the rug, I had them line up and go around the room follow-the-leader style, acting out the story. The next step was to call them to the circle and ask each one, on his own, to go on a hunt again, but this time all in their imagination. First of all, what kind of hunt are you going on? What will you take? How are you moving? (Walking, running, crawling, etc.) What things do you see along the way? What is happening to your feet? Are they dry, wet, muddy? Do you see anything difficult to cross, climb, or get around? Continue. What do you see now? Go a little faster. Go a little slower. Quiet now, you're almost there. Where are you? Look around. Go on. Finish the hunt on your own. When they were through, I had them talk about it. Most of the children talked about going into a cave and what they saw and did there. After that they wrote their stories and drew a picture.

Some time after doing this, when I asked a child to find his pencil, he said, "I'll go on a pencil hunt. My desk is like a cave." I asked, "Is there anything scary in there?" He said, "No, not really." But he found his pencil with a smile on his face, when it had been his habit to grumble and groan about such things.

May 20. Science—Imagination

After doing the lion hunt with such enthusiastic response, I took the children on an underwater trip. I used the same form as the lion hunt but changed everything to suit a trip under the sea. The children enjoyed this a great deal. After the first time through they suggested taking other things. After playing with *Put Your Mother on the Ceiling*, they felt they didn't need any scuba equipment, as I had suggested, and they made other changes. I asked them to help me write out the trip, and they changed still more things.

I feel the children are happy to go on these trips, but the lion hunt and the one under the sea are not particularly good. Since DeMille doesn't have these in his book, I want to create some extras this summer. It will take time and planning. I don't feel I have the time to think it through just now. The class had fun talking about the trip and then trying to change it. They didn't feel satisfied that it was just the way they wanted it to be, but they gave it a good try. We did not write about this lesson, since the group conversation lasted a long time and they were restless.

May 20. Student Teachers' Meeting

Today I met with Bud Robinson and six student teachers who are trying some of these techniques. I had talked to one on the phone, and another had read part of the journal. I feel very disappointed in their response. Everyone said they were trying things and having very little success. They talk as though they were trying very hard, and yet they are accomplishing little. I feel they are uncertain as to just where they are with this material and just where their classes are. They have seen what this class is doing, and it looks great to them. They hear us talk, and they think it sounds easy. Perhaps they are only seeing the top of the iceberg. They don't see the work, worry, planning, overplanning, trying to visualize this program from how to begin to how to offer some closure that go into one hour of teaching. They think it's the pink pill. We must avoid that in further work.

May 21.

Just to see, Bud and I developed a lesson plan for next Monday, when the district-office people are coming in. We had done this before, so we had quite a bit of material to build on. Even so, it took the two of us one hour and fifteen minutes just to make a rough draft. We went over every minute so we would both know what to do and why we were going to do it. If he talked ahead of me, I asked him to explain. When I suggested something, he would follow or add his own twist. I continued to work for another hour and fifteen minutes after he left. A total of three hours and forty-five minutes for one hour of teaching. I realize that not every lesson requires this amount of time, but the fact is that some do need it. Perhaps for a student teacher all of them do. Nightmares of working with Peggy return.

May 27. Lesson-Planning Session in Action

Today the district-office people were in. To begin with, they were late and I was scrambling to fit everything in. After about ten minutes I realized this was awful, so I settled into the routine as I had planned it. It was already cut to a minimum as far as I could tell. Once I decided to give them a full hour from start to finish, things moved right along.

The work in the room with the crayons was an excellent warmup. From there we went into the cafeteria. At the end of that there was good contact between adults and children. This led to a successful blind walk.

I was delighted to see how completely these people participated. Mr. Hal Ulery and Mr. Bob Welling (assistant superintendents for the Goleta Union School District) really surprised me. They are such big men and so removed from the classroom and yet they really came through with the children. I have much more respect for them now after seeing how much they really care about children.

When we came back to the room, I had the children write about what happened. Their stories were so long I brought in the typewriter and did them for them. When we were done, I put their stories with the pictures they drew into a book and sent it over to the district office for their enjoyment.

June 3.

The student teachers' meeting was much more stimulating this time. Three of the student teachers are really getting involved. I guess they just need lots and lots of encouragement and *pushing*. I hate being pushy, but if that is what it takes I'll be that way. The thrill of confluent learning is worth some initial pushing and grinding. Once they get a taste of it, they will be hooked themselves.

June 3 to 13.

As the end of the year is here, I don't plan to do any new things. Frankly, I am tired and need a rest. However, there are many things I will do over again.

"I have it, I want to give it to you."

"I have it, you want it."

More of *Put Your Mother on the Ceiling* and other imagination games.

Staying in the Now—"What are you doing now?"

Body awareness and sensory awareness, especially in changing activities and beginning new ones.

We have had a lot of visitors in our room in the last two months. Now I want to sit back and just enjoy being here, and take a long last look at these children who have come to mean so much to me.

7|

How Teachers Appraise Confluent Education, Including "The 'Big H' Happening"

In this chapter four teachers and one teacher's wife describe what working in confluent education has meant to them professionally, and sometimes personally. For the reader who would like "hard" data on the results of confluent education, we have only one such set. This was obtained unintentionally, but became noticeable because of some striking classroom test results. We hope extensive empirical research eventually will be pursued.

Our work in the Ford-Esalen project was essentially exploratory and clinically oriented. As a consequence, this chapter consists primarily of a mosaic of clinical response. We hope that the reader will be tolerant of the not infrequent fervor of this response, as at times it may seem to border on the religious testimonial. However, it would seem in keeping with a project which focuses on feeling that participants should tend to air their own feelings in reporting on that project. If statements are made with fervor, be assured that they are also made with honesty and candor. Also, we include some related responses from parents concerning the confluent education of their children.

First, the "hard" data. Robin Montz, ninth-grade social-studies teacher, was startled by the results of the fall-semester test on the American Constitution. He checked out comparative SCAT and STEP test scores for classes over the two previous years to see if his present class had scored as "more intelligent." This was not so. The test on the Constitution was almost identical with the previous year's test. The following chart contains the results. To receive an A, a student had to miss fewer than six questions out of a total of eighty.

	Class, 1966–1967	Class, 1967–1968*
As	39	210
Bs	83	72
Cs	225	71
Ds	8	8
Fs	10	2
Total	365	363
SCAT verbal median	78.5	78.5
STEP reading median	79	74.5

* Confluently taught.

Although this was not a "tight" research study, the implications of these results should be especially reassuring to those more conservative elements in our society who have been concerned that anti-American "brainwashing" might result when some of the methods of humanistic psychology are applied in the public schools.

There follow five descriptions of how individuals saw the effects of working in confluent education on students:

First, an evaluation by Robin Montz, who reported the data given above. He teaches in a junior high school serving mostly middle-class suburban families.

THIS YEAR: AN EVALUATION

Several years ago I suddenly became aware that I was going "dry" in my relationships with my students. I had always been interested in making education relevant to the students I was working with and had done everything I could think of to improve the quality of the educational experience they were receiving. I began struggling to institute changes in curriculum, changes in scheduling, changes in team-teaching structure, and the like, without appreciable change in relationship between teacher and pupil. My students were doing well—they seemed creative and able to learn what I had to teach—but I knew that something was missing in the quality of our relationship and in the curricular program itself. I just couldn't put my finger on what it was.

In August 1967, when my principal called me in and told me about the conversation he had had with Dr. Brown, something clicked in the back of my mind, and I became excited immediately by the prospect that this project might help to supply some solution to my dilemma.

I attended the first weekend workshop at Esalen much like a small child who, after being starved for some time, finally attends a great banquet. I was terribly naïve and inexperienced in the whole area of affective experience, but I found that this kind of experience made a great deal of sense to me both personally and professionally.

School started, and I began to weave into our curriculum some of the affective exercises I had experienced or read about. And I saw some "miraculous" things begin to take place. I saw students form meaningful relationships in the classroom. I saw students who had been bored and in trouble much of the time begin to desire to learn and begin to take a genuine interest in life and learning. I saw myself and my own role as teacher begin to change and to take on new meanings. And I saw genuine relationships begin to develop between myself and my students, not so much as teacher and pupil but as people, human beings meeting each other and learning from each other.

Through succeeding Esalen meetings I developed greater facility and sophistication in the use of affective techniques, and I gained much from the reporting of other teachers in the project. At the same time my students benefited from the facility, diversity, and sophistication I was able to bring back to the classroom.

The use of affective-learning techniques integrated with the cognitive material in our ninth-grade history and English courses has aided our students in *at least* the following ways:

1. *Better learning of cognitive material.* This has been demonstrated in almost every major examination the students took this year, as compared with scores on practically identical examinations over the past three years. This class scores lower than the last two years' classes on the standard achievement tests (SCAT and STEP) by about 5 percentile points on the average. However, on the major examination on the United States Constitution, for example, over one-half of the ninth-grade class missed fewer than six out of eighty questions, compared to less than one-eighth of the class scoring in the same range the preceding two years.

2. *Heightened motivation and response to learning situations.* This can be demonstrated by their performance in learning the cognitive material (Paragraph 1), and also by the excitement and intensity of the discussions and other activities that were held during the year.

3. *Greater appreciation of self, nature, others, feelings, etc.* During the year, opportunity was given for a variety of papers, projects, creative work, expression, etc. The depth of feeling that the students had developed became increasingly more evident throughout the year. Relationships developed between students, and a beautiful spirit of community was apparent by the year's end.

4. *Greater pupil responsibility.* Through the use of some Gestalt games centering on individual responsibility, students began to assume responsibility for their own actions. About midway through the school year a group of students who in the past had been "problem-causers" were able to break through their frustrations and resentments and began to contribute to the activities and organization of the ninth-grade class and the school. A group of

top students, members of the Junior Statesmen of America, worked so diligently and contributed so much to a regional convention of the organization that they were named "Chapter of the Day," and in this competition they were competing with chapters from high schools in the South Coast area, including high-school juniors and seniors.

5. *Lessened desire for drug use by some students and for "mind-blowing" by others.* A significant number of students in the class had been experimenting with drugs or other methods of escaping from their problems. Many used drugs in the attempt to find a more meaningful reality to which they could relate. The use of affective techniques in connection with conventional curriculum showed them another, and a better, way to achieve this same result. Many of them discontinued the use of drugs. Other students, who were ready to drop out of society, were brought back into the mainstream of life because they were able to find knowledge and experience that was relevant to them.

In general, the use of affective techniques has resulted in behavioral change on the part of students that has made them better students, better able to relate to other human beings, and has shown other teachers that motivation, interest, awareness, learning, and so on, can be increased if students are "tuned in."

The growth in the relationship between myself and my students and the fact that the students appreciated the kind of program we had provided for them was demonstrated by the following event:

A week after school was out, one of my colleagues invited my wife and me to go out with him to celebrate the end of school. After we were on our way, he turned into one of the nicer neighborhoods to, as he said, "pick up my sister who is at her boss's house." As we pulled into a large estate, about fifty students jumped out from behind the bushes and yelled, "Surprise, Mr. Montz!" There followed one of the most beautiful, warm, and memorable experiences of my life. The students had arranged for the use of the recreation room (complete with indoor swimming pool) of one of their number, hired a band composed of students, fixed food, baked me a cake, got me some token and very meaningful presents, and arranged one of the most delightful surprise parties I have ever seen. After talking, eating, dancing, listening to the music, and spending a lovely evening with the kids, as the three of us left, I was surrounded by fifty kids, arms, kisses, hugs, handshakes, and parting words that I will remember all of my life.

Since that time, during summer vacation, I have been visited in my home by at least half of the kids who were at the party, some of them several times. In spite of the passing of the school year, we still have a warm friendship for each other.

This year is the first in which I have felt like a real educator and not just a purveyor of information and a "people-pusher." I feel that as a result of the Ford-Esalen project I have grown as a person and as a teacher. If that were all the project had done, it would have been worth while.

However, the change in the students has also been fantastic. They have grown and matured faster this year than in any other I have experienced. They are more aware, more creative, and better students as a result of this project. It has been a truly wonderful year. As I put it earlier in the year, in somewhat poetic form:

The rewards?

> A smile where once a frown grew.
> A "slow" group grasping difficult concepts because they experienced them.
> Outcasts becoming involved.
> "Behavior problems" trying to contribute.
> Young people concerned about their world, and my world too.
> Teen-agers seeking responsible solutions to their problems, and the problems of mankind.
> Unafraid,

Committed,
   Searching,
      Open,
         Communicative people, finding the joy of life.
Kids who once were bored now bursting with new dis-
   coveries.
Almost an entire grade level far surpassing those who pre-
   ceded them.
Not only in grades,
But also in maturity,
        responsibility,
         creativity,
          appreciation,
           concern.
I am changing.
Others are too: other teachers,
                but most of all,
                    our students.

Perhaps it is not too surprising to find students from a middle-class to upper-middle-class background, like Robin's, giving him a surprise party. But read the following account of what happened to Aaron Hillman, as described by his wife. Aaron teaches English to the slow, the disadvantaged, the C, D, and F students, a mixed group of blacks, Mexican Americans, poor whites, and surly semi-dropouts—kids who usually hate the school and everything that goes with it, including the teachers.

THE "BIG H" HAPPENING *By Rosemary Hillman*

School had closed for the summer at three o'clock. Now, four hours later, we were driving up to the clubhouse on a public playground in Santa Maria.

"If this is supposed to be a surprise party for you, how come we know about it?"

Aaron grinned. "You know how subtle tenth-graders are. They

told me it's a surprise birthday party for Ben and that Ben would be hurt if we didn't come."

"The only surprise," I retorted, "would be if it turned out really to be Ben's birthday party."

We walked up to the front door and found it locked. There were a lot of cars in the parking area, but no one was in sight. We were just about to try a side door when a girl appeared. She opened the door and greeted us in a stiff, controlled manner and led the way through a large entry toward a partitioned wall. It was very quiet. Suddenly the entire wall folded back and about one hundred and fifty grinning faces screamed, *"Surprise!"* Balloons cascaded down on our heads, kids jumped and screamed and hugged and shook hands with my husband. He disappeared into the mass. Music blared, the entire place had exploded, and I shrank back into a corner to take care of a sudden lump in my throat.

These were my husband's kids . . . students who were classified as "slow" learners in our present school system. I looked around the large room. Two long tables were arranged in an L shape and covered with lace tablecloths. The tables held several elaborate floral arrangements surrounded by large platters of meats, relishes, salads, breads of all descriptions, leading to a series of pastries, desserts, and a huge punch bowl. Behind the tables stood girls of all sizes busily serving the unending crowd. At one end of the table seven or eight beautifully wrapped gifts were neatly stacked. Across the room three boys stood by the record player, looking over the record supply. The room was ringed with chairs occupied by bright-eyed, excited kids. The kitchen was full of activity. Must have been about eight girls out there. The middle of the room was a wild, jumping scene of dancing to the pounding beat they call music. Once in a while I could see Aaron's perspiring head as he danced with the crowd. It was wild and beautiful, and my heart beat with the crazy music.

"Would you like some punch, Mrs. Hillman?" I could hardly hear the soft voice in the sea of noise. I nodded to Carlene and watched her struggle back through the crowd with the drink. Soft-eyed, soft-voiced Carlene. We'd shared secret phone calls for several months as she struggled with arrangements for this surprise party. The door opened, and about fifteen leather-jacketed boys threaded their way through the crowd. They nodded to Carlene. She turned to me and smiled. "You know, every kid you see here chipped in for the rent on this place. Do you think Mr. Hillman was really surprised?"

"Oh, Carlene! How could he not be? I'm surprised, too. How did you manage all of this, and on the last day of school?"

"Well, we've been planning this for weeks, and we just arranged committees and each one did his part. The hardest part was getting Mr. Hillman out of the room so we could do our planning. A lot of our parents baked the cakes and stuff, but we did all the rest by ourselves. We wanted it to be really good for Mr. Hillman."

I pushed over to an empty chair to finish my punch. "Hi!" shouted the girl next to me. "You're Mrs. Hillman, and I want to know one thing." Her eyes flashed directly into mine. "Why is Mr. Hillman leaving us?"

"After tonight," I shouted back, "I'm sure he's wondering the same thing!"

"You mean he might not leave? We don't want him to leave. He's the best teacher we've ever had."

I squirmed under the gaze of this girl and several others who crowded around nodding their agreement. "What makes him such a good teacher?" I asked, hoping to avoid the inquisition. How do you explain to kids that there's a bigger world with other opportunities in another city without hurting their feelings?

Another girl pushed forward and said, "For me, it's not just the teacher-student bit. It's not all those field trips he took us on, but it's what he did for me as a person." Her eyes grew bigger behind her thick glasses, and her hands gestured wildly in front of her. "I'm a better person because of him! I mean, I can tell him anything and he listens and he understands. I'm a better person," she repeated softly. Her chorus of friends nodded in the background.

The decibels had soared to an all-time high. Kids kept crushing around Aaron. Someone had pushed a plate of food into his hand, and somehow he seemed to alternate the food with dancing and greeting the sea of faces around him. Wild shouts of laughter, the music, and the increasing push of youthful humanity. The door flushed in an endless stream of late arrivals. When the psychedelic lights started up, they seemed to catapult the entire scene into a realm of feelings. Nothing was visually clear. The sounds were pushed into oblivion. The room pulsed with a total feeling of excitement . . . joy . . . love. It was electric and it held me transfixed. It went on and on. Suddenly someone stopped the music, and the overhead lights came on. Kids pushed more food toward Aaron, and for the first time I saw him lean against the wall. I realized I was dizzy, so I walked toward the door and stood watching while I gasped for air. One of the leather-jacketed boys ambled over and stood beside me with his arms crossed in front of him. He nudged me and, without any introduction, nodded his head toward Aaron. "There goes one heck of a teacher." Not waiting for an answer, he kept nodding his head. "Yes, sir, that's a teacher and a half! Ya know, I wouldn't be in continuation school if there were more teachers like him. I mean, ya know, that guy really understands us kids. Ya know, he knows when to let up and let us goof off and yet he knows how to get us to work. I mean we'd really work for him, but he always seemed to know how we were feeling. Yes, sir!" He nudged me again with his shoulder. "You take good care of him, ya hear!"

Jessie, a girl I'd met on several field trips, motioned me over to a corner. "I just have to know something, Mrs. Hillman." Her face was anxious. The noise was competing, so we pushed toward the door. "I just wanted your opinion on something." She paused, trying to match words to her feelings. Finally she said, "Are you aware that some of the kids in Mr. Hillman's classes call him 'Big H'?"

I nodded and smiled.

She looked shocked. "Well," she stammered, "how . . . how do you feel about that? I mean, I think it's disrespectful, and I've talked to the kids about this, but they won't listen. Don't you think that's terrible, calling him 'Big H'?"

"Jessie, what are the kids feeling when they call him that?"

She stared at me. "How do those kids feel about Mr. Hillman?"

"Well, they all think he's the greatest, and he is, and I just want them to treat him with respect."

"When you call him Mr. Hillman and others call him 'Big H,' what are each of you really telling him?"

The music stopped, and someone yelled, "Speech!" Aaron was standing on a chair with the gifts thrust into his hands. The shrieks of laughter and applause as each gift was opened and as Aaron spoke to the crowd were tremendous, and I was suddenly aware that no camera was recording these excited and smiling faces. As he picked up the last gift, a girl told me that this was the big "expensive" gift. She also said they'd had many meetings before they decided that this was one gift Mr. Hillman would really love. I pushed closer to see. Out of all the paper came a large silver tray. It flashed under the lights, and there was a momentary silence as Aaron read the inscription:

To "Big H"
from
Sophomore Class
1970

My eyes swept across the smiling crowd, and there stood Jessie. We grinned at each other, and she looked back at Aaron with what I think was a sigh of relief.

The punch was gone, the food was gone, the speeches were finished, parents poured in to shake hands and say their farewells, but the dancing continued. Here was a happening that we had thought would last only an hour but now, four hours later, the place was still swinging. I dragged out to the kitchen and asked four girls if I could help.

"Oh, no, thank you. This entire party was all arranged by com-mittees, and we are on the kitchen clean-up committee."

I returned to the jumping group and noticed that Aaron had gathered up his gifts and was making his way through the dancers, shaking everyone's hand and making a final round of good-bys.

A mother stood by me watching. She smiled and said, "You know, Mrs. Hillman, these kids just love your husband, and I know why. What he's done for Rachel this year is wonderful! She's just thrilled because he thinks she's a good writer. She always hated English until this year. She woke up this morning and said this was a special day, and it had to be perfect because it's Mr. Hillman's day. She told me she wanted to kiss him good-by, but she'd be too embarrassed. I told her if she felt that way to just go up to him at the party and put her arms around him and give him a good-by kiss." The mother laughed. "I know she'll be too shy."

We watched Aaron shaking hands, and as he got closer to the door several girls rushed up and threw their arms around him, and suddenly he was swamped with kids hugging and kissing him. I saw Rachel on one side of the group and hoped he'd notice. As he struggled along slowly with the embraces and handshakes, he routed the group toward Rachel, swept her into the group, and managed a big hug. It was easy for her to reach up to his cheek. No camera to record that smile! The dancing continued, but at the entry Aaron turned around, waved at the entire crowd, and said softly, "Well, good-by, everybody!"

We turned to go, and as we crossed the large entry hall it was as though a magnet had swept out into the room. The music thumped on as every soul followed us out to the door, down the steps, and along the sidewalk. Following us softly, silently . . . over a hundred kids shuffling along beside us, behind us, boys thrusting out awkward handshakes, quiet fingers on Aaron's shoulder. They were all with us. We reached the car, and now there wasn't a word heard. One boy opened the car door and nodded to Aaron. We climbed in, and there, facing us, silently watching, were one hundred kids. Aaron started the car, and hands began to reach up in slow, heavy motions of good-by. Voices quietly saying, "Good luck, come back and visit. I'll write to you." Aaron backed out and waved. I couldn't look back because it was all a blur.

We drove in silence for ten miles. "No tape recorder, no cameras," I moaned. Aaron, lost in his own thoughts, finally said, "You know, a teacher is filled with doubts every day about whether he's doing the right things in the right way. But after tonight I guess . . . I guess I can say . . . that something important did happen this year. But how . . . how in the world . . . could anyone describe what really happened tonight? It's impossible!" I stared at the black road ahead and mumbled, "You're right. It's impossible."

And now Aaron's attempt to describe what he felt happened the year of the project.

IT'S BEEN A VERY GOOD YEAR *By Aaron Hillman*

What has occurred this year is something that I doubt can ever be gauged by means other than intuition and observation. When a student, silent and withdrawn, begins to speak and contact other human beings, that is an accomplishment. When a student who is always "acting out" begins to understand what he is doing and to take responsibility for his actions, that is an accomplishment. When a student begins to read and write more than ever, that is an accomplishment. There can be no real measurement of his movement, his achievement. The accomplishment is uniquely his, and only he knows how deep it goes. We can observe and be aware that change has taken place, but only to a small degree. We are aware that this change may not come or take hold for years to come. But somehow, across that gulf that separates human being from human being, we know that profound things have happened. That is how I know that a unique and substantial change occurred in the students as a result of our work in merging cognitive and affective education.

In the measurement of what has been accomplished there is little concrete data. I did not attempt any numerical or statistical analysis. My "measurement" was simply an awareness of the outward signs of internal change and of the changes occurring in the students' writing and speaking and reading.

The intuitive and observational knowledge of change rests in the area of the human development of each student. I could, for example, cite numbers of students who either spoke to me or have written to me since the end of school about changes in their lives. However, it is my personal knowledge of the student and our symbiotic relationship because of his education that have shown the change. Each student changed in terms of human development, which I believe is the goal of all education.

I began the year with the assumption that slow learners were merely children blocked by their circumstances, and that cognitive and affective education could be merged in such a way as to provide for the human development of the student. I ended the year with the assumption not only intact but strengthened.

In terms of accomplishment, by the end of the year the students seemed to have partially answered the questions of who they were as well as what they were. They had gained some measure of insight that gave them a place in the world and some strength to hold that place.

The primary objective and accomplishment in the cognitive field was the improvement in the students' reading and writing abilities. The students began to approach reading as something more than a chore forced upon them. The subject matter began to intrigue them, possibly because they were not compelled to read it, and this in itself led them to explore other readings. They also became aware of the infinite variety of reading experience; that is, that reading was more than sitting down and reading aloud from a book. It could be sung, danced, felt, and experienced as a person.

Their writing also became a means of self-expression. The writing was a moving out of their inwardness, and each new paper they completed was a step toward facing life. The content of the themes showed significant improvement, but there was a correlative improvement in the writing itself, its style and grammar.

Perhaps more significant than this was the desire, the need, of the students to approach reading and writing. In varying degrees it became something they looked forward to. In the beginning some of the students stated in their papers that they "hated reading" or they "hated writing." Toward the end of the year their attitudes ranged from grudging willingness to read and write more to such enthusiasm that some students were pouring out more work than I could keep up with.

This brings us to the students' accomplishment in the affective domain. I see the primary change here as being a release from inhibitions to learning. The affective work was instrumental in removing barriers that blocked their learning. They became aware of what it was in them that impeded learning—that is, what made them "hate reading" or "hate writing."

A secondary, but very vital, accomplishment of the students was to learn how and to want to express themselves. Feeling free to express oneself and one's feelings leads to self-confidence. Confidence in oneself leads to a greater appreciation of life and, in the case of students, a desire to want to know and to learn more. It also leads to the ability to take the knocks of life in stride and to move on. In general, slow learners are stuck in their place because they have been "put down" frequently and do not want to risk further hurt by attempting new things. It is easier for them to be negative. As a result of this year's work, the students were able to express their fears and desires quite openly and to work with one another. Not the least outcome was their ability to state and demonstrate that they liked each other.

To my great surprise and delight, I discovered that working with the students in this program led to accomplishments of my own— my own life and my teaching ability were enhanced by the program. I was learning right along with the students. I became more aware of my students, my surroundings, and myself. Increased awareness leads to more knowledge of the cognitive and affective worlds, and that leads directly back to the individual.

The cognitive accomplishments led me to delve deeper into the work in question and to understand more of what I was reading. The subject matter—the cognitive material—became much more meaningful to me. I think I may also have developed some intolerance; I will never again be able to accept the traditional teaching of literature.

The affective accomplishments for me were primarily a new awareness of self and of students. We—the students and I— became an entity searching and loving together. The students were able to accept me in my role as leader, but they nevertheless felt free to pursue their interests, to challenge me, and to relate to me. I have often read papers putting forth the argument that teachers, parents, or other authority figures should not attempt to become one of the students, boys, and so forth. As one result of this year, I am happy to report that I was seen as a person by the students and loved every minute of it. The students accepted me. I did not lose status by it nor did anarchy result. We were aware of each other, our needs, and our societal roles.

Nowhere have I meant to imply that there were no hardships or mistakes during the year or that this program is a panacea. There were hardships, mistakes, and frustrations. But these seem to be minor and what one would normally expect. There were, however, no major adversities or adverse reactions from any source. Granted, some kept a wary eye on us, some shook their heads in disapproval; but their objections were minor and did not result in any direct action. I think perhaps they realized that something profound was happening, and it made them uneasy.

The measurement and proof of the value of this year and this research program lie in the personal growth of the students and the teacher. Personal growth includes the fact that these students improved academically. I received many letters from my students this summer. Many of them told me what the last year had meant to them as people. I would like to end this paper with an excerpt from a letter I received from a sixteen-year-old Mexican American student. I enjoyed the feeling she gave me in the letter, but primarily I rejoiced in what had happened to her and that she could express it in her way.

> Mr. Hillman, I want you to know that I didn't forget you one minute! Every time I heard the song "To Sir with Love" I even remembered you more. I want you to know that I really miss you and that you were my best teacher I ever had. I wish the pages would turn back and start my freshman and sophomore year over again. I wish I could have a festival again, go on all the trips we had, but most of all have you teach me English and history again. In those two years I think I learned a lot of things, especially how to communicate with people. But I guess I can't turn them back.

She can't turn back. She will go on.

Gloria Castillo taught first grade in a suburban elementary school. In Chapter 6 she describes how, toward the end of the year, she invited the parents to come to school for a morning and participate in some of the experiences their first-graders were having. All but one or two mothers came. The following are letters from parents in response to her request for reactions.

> It was the first time I have ever been anything but a spectator in a classroom, and I think the interaction of mother and child in your program that Friday morning was very rewarding—and fun! It's too bad that fathers couldn't experience the same activities with their child in the classroom.
>
> I am so happy with M.'s attitude about first grade. He seems relaxed and so interested in learning which I am certain have come about because of your methods. I wish my older children could have had the same learning opportunity in first grade.
>
> Sincerely,
> MRS. T.

The morning spent with D. in his classroom was very enjoyable. You are an exceptional teacher and your realistic approach is exciting. I was made "aware" of the pride and pure joy the children so obviously feel in having a parent "in attendance." It was interesting to me also to watch other parents' reactions to their children in a "do it together" atmosphere. I imagine these feelings were not what was expected of me—but in truth—this is my comment. I would be most interested in learning what comments you might have to make on the morning's activities.

Sincerely,
MRS. G.

I particularly enjoyed the few minutes spent drawing hand to hand with K. This contact made me appreciate her as an individual and gave me a feeling of closeness. The object passing, blindfolded, was interesting and makes one more aware of their senses and develops a good use of the imagination I'm sure. I wish the parents could have seen each child under their own sheet as I did, but I know this would be a bit difficult, perhaps, with all the parents present. I appreciated the opportunity you gave us to see our children as individuals. We are so busy these days we need reminding.

Sincerely,
MRS. S.

I was particularly interested in the group work on the floor with the blindfolds and the way in which the children enjoyed the feeling of the items passed around. I thought the walk D. took me on was very good for making one aware of things taken for granted.

MRS. P.

Thank you for the invitation to participate in some of the classroom activities with our children. L. and I particularly enjoyed the physical activity involved in the work with the sheet because we have so few moments together like that.

During the reading and math periods L. had trouble concentrating and I found myself in the position of wanting to "nag" her to keep her mind on her work. (We do better together at this at home.) The art we enjoyed very much and I felt this could have been expanded a bit.

I'm not sure what the children "take away" from a blind walk or handling things while using a blindfold. I felt interested as well as puzzled as I left as to the direction of all this and how much time it takes away from the academic endeavor, or if it adds to it in any way, such as in the area of creative writing.

At any rate, L. and I both enjoyed our time there. It let us know what you were doing with them, how and if they were responding, and let parents participate, which is in itself a unique experience.

Sincerely,
M.R.

I found this experience very enjoyable. I was particularly surprised at the ease which the children had when wearing the blindfolds. They seem quite keen in their observations of what they felt when blindfolded. We have tried since that day to become more aware of the properties of everyday objects.

Mrs. F.

I shall try real hard to be with K. again on Tuesday morning. I felt that K. really enjoyed my being there. The morning was fascinating and very rewarding. You are to be commended on your understanding of the needs of this age group. I wish that I could give you additional suggestive help in routine—but all I can say is that I was fascinated by the morning. Thank you.

C.L.

I liked the art study better than the experiment with the blankets. I will do more such drawings as we did together (child and mother) that Friday morning. Besides C. likes to do it too.

M.H.S.

In regard to my reaction to my visit to your class last Friday, I believe the thing I enjoyed most was merely observing. Helping our children with reading and math and art are not entirely new experiences but doing it in an atmosphere where our children are so in command is. I was very impressed by the whole class's attitude. They seemed extremely secure in their world away from home and it is a wonderful feeling for any parent to feel their child has been introduced to the world of learning with such enthusiasm.

If there is ever anything I can do to help my child or help you to help my child I will be more than willing to participate; but I left Friday feeling that the whole class was a very well-adjusted group.

This is perhaps not answering your questions but it will serve to thank you for what you have done for my child.

J.H.

I enjoyed very much the first-grade activities I shared with my daughter. The art project was interesting and I experienced a feeling of complete helplessness when blindfolded and led around the room—my safety in the hands entirely of B. She did a good job of selecting objects for me to touch, feel, and discover.

With a large family, it is difficult to spend enough time individually with your children—story time, game time, camping, etc. and all shared by all. I think what I enjoyed most of all was spending a morning with just B., sharing her world.

M.L.B.

Really, what I enjoyed the most wasn't the activities we did as much as the chance to *share* in these activities with my son. It was enjoyable, in fact thoroughly delightful, to see him surrounded by his peers, and completely happy to let "mommy" share it with him for a few hours.

In some ways I was watching a different little boy than the

boy we see at home. His reactions to the other children and Mrs. Castillo were interesting to watch as I have never seen him so free of thinking inwardly about himself in such a situation. He seemed quite concerned of other children and of my welfare which I have never seen him use in large groups before. He can often be this way at home but never in a group as far as I have observed.

I felt very close to him that day and came home glowing with good reports—so much so that his Daddy *asked* if he could go next time. J. is delighted that Daddy wants to come and keeps saying he can hardly wait.

I've been spending one hour with the boys almost every night—30 minutes with each boy. My husband helps with one boy while I help the other. For J., we listen to him read and Daddy plays math games with him.

I've noticed a more pliable, happier, secure little boy—we all seem much closer and willing to understand each others' idiosyncrasies. I hope it will continue. It has been delightful.

W.M.

You know that I greatly admire your work with reading and other subjects in the classroom. To be perfectly frank I feel that I cannot comment on the new space or sensual perception program. I don't understand enough about the goals you are trying to achieve and how they relate to the school program. I also do not understand how important the program is for the majority of children. I hope in the future to find out more about the program's goals and successes. However, I will never cease to admire and publicize your courage in trying new things and your interest and dedication to children.

Personally, I am so pleased with K.'s skill in reading but more so in her enthusiasm and love for books which I feel was largely inspired by your teaching.

Sincerely,
J.L.

I thoroughly enjoyed Friday's program with the children. My only complaint is that the morning went by so quickly.

My most enjoyable part of the program was the blindfold game, mainly because I had complete trust that B. would not let me harm myself, at the same time he did not have this complete trust in me.

The morning made me realize that since the arrival of the baby, I have not had as much physical contact with B. as we had before, and being we are rather a close family he very probably has missed this contact with me.

This could be the behavior problem that we find on his report card. Since Friday, I am striving to build this contact up again.

Time will tell.

J.D.

And now Gloria herself reflects on the year.

EVALUATION OF THE FORD-ESALEN PROJECT
By Gloria Castillo

My first-grade class sits in front of me as I sit here at the back of the room trying to formulate an evaluation of the project. I watch them as they work, unaware of my being here.

Jay and Jerry are sitting together working on a writing assignment. Jay was not able to trust anybody or give much warmth or affection all year. Yet there they sit, arm in arm, heads together, working together, and I realize that something has happened to him.

Keith turns around and sees me writing. He comes over. "What are you writing?" "A story about first-graders." "Am I in it?" "Yes. You are smiling. Does that make you happy?" "Yes." And he leans over me, touching my shoulder. I am pleased that Keith is touching me. He is no longer on tranquilizers and yet he is calm, relaxed, and happy to be here. Sure, he still has some rough times. He still becomes angry and frustrated. And yet somehow these times are farther and farther apart. When they do occur, he is more able to cope with them and with himself. He can fight, cry, scream, and then move on. No longer does he hide under a chair or behind a desk, cowering away from me and everyone else in his world. He has made contact with peers and adults at school for the first time. I am reminded of the joyful phone call just two nights ago, when his mother called to report similar contact being made at home with siblings and parents.

Anita, who at the beginning of the year wanted to be told the answers so she could tell them back, walked up and said, "Listen, Mrs. Castillo." I stopped writing as she read from a third-grade reader written more than forty years ago.

" 'Ma started a fire, put on some greens and noodles to cook, and made coffee.' That doesn't make sense. If she 'started' a fire and put the noodles on 'to cook,' shouldn't that word be 'make' instead of 'made'?"

I am pleased that she is able to question both me and written words. Perhaps there's a different way to say this. No longer is it necessary for her to have just one right way.

I see Philip helping Jerry with reading flash cards. Philip has been retained in first grade. That in itself is nothing new. But to see his growth and development along with his enthusiasm and pleasure at first-grade activities is. I have not applied any new materials this year. Only a new focus that changes so many old things and adds a new excitement. Philip has said "School's fun this year" more than once. I agree with him and am happy because he feels that way.

Paul, who says the best time of his day is 2:30, when he goes home, is still in the room now, twenty minutes after all the children are gone. He is playing with our two pet rats. He sees they have a messy cage and says, "I am going to clean the cage." He gets the job done all on his own. I can remember the day when he would not do anything for anyone. He was too busy trying to find his own sense of worth to be able to worry about the comfort or care of others. He does not stop me from my writing or worry about who "should" clean the cage.

And so it goes throughout the classroom. Happy, healthy first-graders, growing in academic skills; learning to get along with each other; offering help and support to each other; accepting others for what they are and not what the teacher wants them to be or what they "should" be; allowing the other child to be better or worse than they themselves are. Together we have grown.

Throughout the work in the project I have been able to begin to help these children see their world, feel it, smell it, touch it, separate it from the world of fantasy, imagination, and expectations. What is real, what is make-believe? What is fact, what is fiction? How do we confuse the two? When is it best to use one or the other? What gets in our way of really knowing, feeling, trusting others? I have no set answers, no "sure-to-work-for-everyone" ideas. I have touched upon many things that need further exploration in the years to come. Was it just this class and this year that was so alive, so rewarding? Or have I really discovered something about myself, my teaching, and my effectiveness with children that will carry over in years to come?

I do have the memory of the most eventful teaching year of my career. I do have the feeling I am sending happy, open, capable children on their educational way with all I could have done. I am satisfied at this, the last week of the year. I have been a successful teacher in a successful classroom. I could not want more from any year's work.

Janet Lederman, who is also the author of *Anger and the Rocking Chair*, during the Ford-Esalen project taught a special non-graded class, kindergarten through fourth grade, of children from a predominantly black neighborhood whom other teachers could not handle. All were behavior problems. She describes what happened.

CONFLUENT LEARNING — PERSONAL VIEWPOINT
By Janet Lederman

Often I am asked how I evaluate the "techniques" I use with children. How do I know what to do? How do I know if I am succeeding in my efforts to "teach" effectively? My first impulse is to answer, "I have no elaborate system of evaluation." I wonder if this is so. I am an affective being; that is, I have and use such emotions as love, anger, grief, and joy. I have a great deal of cognitive information stored and ready for use—information accumulated from study and experience. Therefore, when I am teaching I am affectively (emotionally) and cognitively (thoughtfully) encountering the child who is also responding both affectively and cognitively. The balance and the percentage of each component is a constantly changing sum within me and within the child. We are formed by both affective and cognitive domains as a sculpture is formed by both positive and negative space. There is no way in reality of separating the two without changing the "beast." Therefore, I use both in a continuing evaluation system.

I would like to take you with me, in reflection, as I expose my "system": my attitudes, my expectations, my intuitive responses, and my computations—my affective and cognitive domains.

I do not plan for children I have not met. How can I? I have no idea of "where they are" in either domain. I have enough teaching experience to be able to pass out paper; I have enough teaching experience to be able to create a lesson on the spot or lead a discussion or a game until the true needs of the children make themselves apparent. It is then that real educational environment begins to develop. With some children the time of waiting is almost nonexistent; with others the time of waiting is long. I will wait. The children come into a barren room. The room begins to fill as they begin to *live* within the environment we create together.

Now I ask the reader to enter inside of me and listen in to my senses, my intuition, and also my computations. I shall not address you now, for I am directing my attention to the children.

Roderick, you walk into the classroom. It is your first day. You hit every child in your path as you cross the room. There are several toys on the floor, and you step on each one of them. You do not sit in the circle with the other children. You sit just outside the circle. You are in touch with being "angry," and that you are able to communicate. You seem busy protecting yourself. I imagine you could use some help. I want to find ways of showing you I want to protect you. Words won't do. Then I imagine you will *allow* me to protect you (trust) and then perhaps some of your energy will be released for other things—like learning to write. Now you need to be a big shot or bully. This way you imagine you are safe. I won't get too close to you. I will give you space. I watch you until I discover something that you like to do. Something you do well. It takes awhile and I wait. You like to work with wood. I ask you to saw many pieces for me. You do. I don't let anyone take the job away from you. I only ask you to do things in which you will succeed. Your experience with frustration is ample. One day after recess some bigger boy chases you into the room. I have no idea whether you provoked the situation. This is the time to protect you. I do. We don't talk about it. The action stands for itself. I am beginning to feel love for you. I enjoy your aggression. When you start to take over the class, I do not respond with pleasure. I do not tolerate your violence. I don't imagine you want that kind of power. You are testing to see if I am strong enough to take care of you. Yes, I am. We even wrestle to prove it to you. You are very much in your senses. Words have little meaning for you. I use very few words. My messages to you are through action. We will build words after our relationship has developed a meaning. How will I know? You begin to arrive at school on time. If you need to go play for a while, you put your lunch bag by the door for me to see you are here. You begin to call me by my name. You have your temper tantrum in the room instead of stealing something and running away. Your body begins to relax, and you

smile now from time to time. You begin to work on numbers when
I sit with you. You begin to learn to print when I sit with you. I am
not going to push you to work away from me yet—not until you are
ready. The first time I will ask you to work on something I know
you can do and that *you know* you can do. How will I know you
are ready? You will not mind if I am giving attention to some other
child when you sit next to me. I might get up and move away for
a few minutes, and you will keep working. I am watching you. I
am listening with my eyes and ears, all the time thinking what the
next step is to be. I watch for the first time you make a mistake and
are able to go on instead of tearing up your paper. I assume you
feel safe in the room when I see that you don't have to be a bully
for the entire time. I begin to send you on small errands, and I give
you points for returning right away. I mark down the time you
leave and return so that you have some structure. I know you are
beginning to trust *you* and me when you don't need that structure.
And I imagine you trust me when you are in stress and ask for it
back from time to time—before disaster strikes. I do not ask you
to do things that are impossible for you. You have enough contact
with frustration and you don't need more! You begin to trust that
I will not ask the impossible of you; therefore, you begin to take
a few risks—such as writing a story. I make sure you succeed.
Soon you are willing to try arithmetic, and you find you love adding
numbers. You do pages of adding. Then comes a crisis. You have
been doing what you thought impossible and this scares you. How
do I know? You become a bully once again. You try all your old
techniques—almost to make sure that they are still there. I won't
let you use them in the classroom any more. This time I tell you,
"Roderick, I won't accept this kind of behavior any more. You
needed it when you came. You knew no other way to behave. Now
you do. I have seen you. I won't let you stay in class today." I send
you home. You want to stay. You cry. I send you home and hope
you get the message. The next day you return. You got the message.
You left the bully outside the door. We don't talk about what hap-

pened. We go on. I felt you wanted someone to control that bully. You begin to use other things available to you in the room—puzzles, games, the chalk board. You sit with us in the circle. You like to sit next to me while I read stories. You like to select the book, and you begin to make your wants known—not by fighting but by asking. You can even wait and take turns. You put your arms around me, and you allow me to hold and comfort you and play with you. You begin to say, "This is my teacher, my room, my school."

Stanley, you spent two years with me. I am remembering when you first arrived. You are sullen. You do no schoolwork. You steal things from the room. I say nothing yet. I give you time to be wherever you are. I will meet you there first. You cry a great deal. You have no friends. I am wondering if you remember this day? You are frowning and angry. You walk over to the chalk board and you write in large letters, "FUCK." You look at me. You see I am looking at you. I accept your message. You stand there for a time, then you slowly erase the word. You do not steal anything today. Thereafter you use that technique to show me your anger. Sometimes the letters are huge, sometimes they are very tiny. You start to print, and then you want to write stories. You love to paint and build boats. At the end of the second year you are ready to move on to a regular room. A room you have tested and found to be comfortable for you. You come back for visits. Your visits become shorter and shorter. Soon you visit only when there is a substitute teacher or when you are under stress. Then comes the time when I push you from the nest. I tell you, "Stanley, you are too big to visit during the school day. Come see me after school and tell me what you are doing." You are ready, and somehow that gives you more confidence in yourself. Then comes the *day*, that wonderful day your teacher and I stopped you from reading. Your eyes were red-rimmed. Were you "reached," as they say? I think so. Do I have a systematic test to prove it? No!

Willis, on your first day you came in fighting. You ran away when you couldn't take charge of the classroom. You got frustrated the instant you made one mistake. You tore up your paper and found someone to hit. You tried to hit me, we wrestled, and you cried. When you calmed down, I gave you a hammer and nails and you fixed the tool cart. You could have thrown the hammer at me, but you didn't. For several months you only worked with wood. Oh, you built so many airplanes! You wouldn't touch a pencil. You loved to clean and organize the room. I arranged for you to work in the kindergarten, and you loved taking care of the small children. You were in the second grade, yet you still seemed to need the kindergarten experience, but with status. You never bullied the little children. You were gentle and patient. Gradually you began to work with a pencil. You wanted to practice your printing. You wanted to be perfect. You could not stand failure. With a community volunteer by your side you were able to get through your intense frustration. You have been in a regular room for a year. You still fight and you still get frustrated, but you can also wait and give yourself a chance before you tear up your work. You can now wait while the teacher gives directions. You are not removed from the classroom. You are there and you can learn.

Nora, oh, Nora! You have not talked for two years, ever since you started school. You talk at home and when there is no teacher around, but you will not talk in the classroom. That takes a great deal of strength on your part. You walk around, you go through all the motions of school, but you never talk. You pretend to write stories. You scribble. Soon you begin to learn to write your name and then other letters. You want to write a story. How can I give you the words you need when you won't ask for them? I see the frustration. But not talking is still more important. Today is your special day, a day I will always remember. Raymond comes over and socks you. Mrs. Chalmers, a volunteer, is working with you at the time. You look at Raymond. You have never hit anyone in the classroom before. This time you do. You sock him, and Mrs. Chalmers gives you a lollipop. You look shocked! You whisper your first words in school. I feel as though you just grew a head taller and put on ten pounds. Soon you begin to whisper the words you want for your story. You write stories every day. You begin to learn arithmetic. You begin to read. Your whisper is getting louder and louder. You are smiling more and more. You have been in a regular room for a year. Mrs. Chalmers keeps working with you twice a week. You don't need me at all.

Christine, you came into the room with a reputation for biting, and you fulfilled that expectation on the second day. Now, two years later, I point to my arm and we both start laughing. We were together for a year and a half. You used to be in a fight every day. Now you are in a regular room, and you have a delightful sense of humor. I enjoy our time together—we visit and talk. You have an occasional fight. You have a very live temper. You are very alive. You write interesting stories, you do lovely art work, you enjoy coming to school. You have been in two regular rooms, and you are making it.

George Henry, they threw you out of kindergarten. You beat up the kids. George Henry, the big bully of the kindergarten set. You wouldn't change activities every ten minutes like the other children. No, not you! You enter the room. You spend days just walking around. You explore. You talk with no one. I soon discover you have your very own rhythm and you are not about to sell it short. You sit and play with a hammer and nails for an hour, quietly and all-absorbed. You cannot print and you don't want to learn. You love to work puzzles, and you work with them for hours. You come in each morning and go over to a chair and eat half your lunch. If I stop you, you are impossible the rest of the day. For two years you eat half your lunch the first thing each morning. You learn to saw. You begin to build trucks and boats. You like to paint, and you continue working puzzles. You love music. You play with the toy piano, and you are very methodical. I learn that you enjoy staying with an activity you are interested in, and you do not like to change as often as most children your age. You stay with me until the end of the first grade. Now you love to print and practice words on the chalk board. You begin to write stories. You love to add, and you laugh with delight as you keep asking for more and more work. You enjoy going back to the kindergarten and working for your former teacher, and she enjoys having you there. You are helpful. Soon you become bored, but first you fully enjoy the pleasure of being the returning hero who made good.

As I reflect, I am also aware of the failures. Raymond, the school failed you. There is no one at home who wants you. Your needs are too great for the school. You have grown too big—you are eleven years old—and the school is too small. You cannot maintain yourself in a regular room, and the school has no facilities to care for you. The adjustment between home, streets, and school is too much. Several organizations are "trying" to find a twenty-four-hour youth facility that *can* provide the care you need. I do remember the times you came to the room for contact. You didn't like being away from school. We talked, and I let you stay for a while. Soon the younger children became frightened with you there. You began to demand more time than I had available. I asked you to leave. I know you have to return to the streets. I cannot be with you all the time. You are still a very hungry boy.

I could go on with each child as he came and went. But I feel that these examples are enough. Each relationship is unique in its intensity and depth; each relationship is unique in the "system."

8|

Three Relevant Issues

As we mentioned before, undergirding the actual work of the Ford-Esalen project was a continuing dialogue among the staff as to a philosophical rationale to justify what we were trying to do. A number of issues or themes emerged from time to time, but three issues seemed central to our reflections. These were freedom and responsibility, innovation versus revolution, and Americanism and patriotism.

Although it is not possible in the space of this short chapter to describe in detail the progress of our thinking about these themes, here are some of the conclusions and positions we reached.

FREEDOM AND RESPONSIBILITY

When we confronted the basic questions, "Why introduce affective experiences into the classroom?" and "Why is it important to integrate the affective and cognitive domains and, accordingly, modify the curriculum?" we became aware that something besides our own prejudices was involved, especially if we were to answer these questions reasonably when they were put to us by people not in the project.

One dimension of these questions is that of the relationship between freedom and responsibility in a democratic society. A goal we were striving for in our work was to help students become both *more free* and *more responsible*. We believed this could be done by increasing the student's sense of his own power to take responsibility for his behavior. Further, by providing experiences that made available ways to become free, followed by the actual experience of increasing freedom, we could help the student attain the personal satisfaction that is unique to feeling free. It was crucial that the two qualities, freedom and responsibility, be thought of as existing in an indivisible relationship. Just as we tried to achieve a balance between affective and cognitive learning, we also sought for ourselves and our students a balance between freedom and responsibility.

In the kind of society which for the individual overstresses responsibility—and this is what our schools seem to do—it is likely that totalitarian conditions will rapidly emerge. It is true that one is responsible to someone or something or some group unless one is responsible only to oneself, which can lead to anarchy. However, when responsibility is stressed at the expense of freedom to make changes, the repression of freedom also suppresses any possibilities for change. As a consequence, the status-quo situation or establishment becomes entrenched, and the prevailing rules and regulations continue to be enforced, resulting in a totalitarian or authoritarian society.

On the other hand, when individual or collective freedom is stressed without an accompanying appropriate emphasis on responsibility—when one is responsible only to oneself—chaos and anarchy can swiftly follow. Some current examples are riots and, to a degree, certain aspects of the hippie movement.

For a democratic society to flourish and increase in health and realistic productivity, as a society and also in terms of the welfare of the individual, its members must learn how to combine freedom with responsibility and responsibility with freedom. Each is crucial; and their combination is essential for the continued health of our society. This integration has been poorly taught in the schools, if it has been taught at all. Much of the work a student does in learning about democracy, its importance, and how it functions consists commonly of a series of verbalizations with little personal relevance. It seems a game which teachers and students play; a ritual non-happening whose non-discursive meaning has been lost in the dimness of the past.

Interestingly, in our language we do not say "I think responsible" but, instead, "I feel responsible." And yet when we teach responsibility in school, we teach it as thinking, not as feeling. Furthermore, we usually begin by stressing responsibility to others. Before one can be responsible to or for others, one must know what feeling responsible is like, what it means. The meaning that makes most sense to an individual, whether child or adult, is personal meaning. It follows, then, that one must begin with learning to feel responsible and to take responsibility for oneself. From here one can move meaningfully into the experience of taking responsibility for others, and can recognize when this is important and when it should be avoided. There are times when taking responsibility for someone else deprives him of the opportunity to stand on his own two feet, thereby interfering with his own learning of the first step.

Among the techniques we used, Gestalt-therapy experiments were especially productive in teaching the relationship between freedom and responsibility.

INNOVATION VERSUS REVOLUTION

Following the theme that freedom and responsibility are essential and inseparable values to be learned by members of a democratic society in order for that society to continue to flourish, the next question is, "What if the educational system in a democracy is not teaching these and other important concepts? Do we throw the whole thing out, as some demand, or do we attempt innovation within the present system?"

We are sympathetic with such critics as Paul Goodman, who cry out that the present curriculum is anachronistic or even, in some instances, archaic. However, believing that significant change can occur within the educational establishment, we hold that it does not make sense to throw everything out and begin again. Change should be brought about through commitment and involvement rather than by edict or revolution. The democratic process is not merely a chauvinistic cliché. Nor is it *just* a political theory. As a political and social process, democracy provides a system that is psychologically sound in its potential for allowing healthy and gradual change.

Change occurs when frustration is (1) encountered, (2) confronted, (3) experienced, and (4) worked through. When life is experienced as smooth and easy, there is no need for change. There is no dissatisfaction with what is. However, when frustration does exist, reality-based resolutions of the frustration occur, again when emotion and intellect work together.

Too much overbalance toward emotional reaction, or the affective, can lead to violent revolution. Though, historically, violent revolution may have been unavoidable in some cases, in regard to the improvement of the educational system the wasteful destruction that inevitably accompanies violence could now be avoided if there were at least a modicum of foresight and action.

We say foresight *and* action because too much overbalance on intellect, or the cognitive, leads to discussion and the development of theories and usually stops there—with little action. Moreover, discussion and theories tend to be about an abstract rather than a real set of conditions. This is because those specialists engaged in the discussion, having chosen an occupation that centers on discussion and the intellect, have often at the same time rejected a mode of existence that involves less pleasant and less manageable work—the so-called "world of hard knocks." The contrast between the world of the authors of the following abstract of a study and the world of the author of the next excerpt is obvious.

Switching attention from one source of information to another requires time. . . . In this experiment, nonsense syllables were learned in a serial learning task in which syllables could be presented either visually or auditorially and under conditions that involved different frequencies of switching modality. . . . [The] procedure yields an estimate of switching time of 168 milliseconds—a value closely in accord with those previously derived from entirely different procedures (Reid and Travers, 1968).

The following account of how a Gestalt technique is used in a classroom is from *Anger and the Rocking Chair*, by Janet Lederman, a member of the Ford-Esalen project staff who taught a special class of children who could not be maintained or "contained" in regular classrooms in a school in an urban poverty area.

"I don't want to read that dumb book!"
Books are of little value to you as they do not relate to your present world.
"I hate my fucking sister. She beats me up."
You have just told an explicit story with words that have explicit meaning for you. I suggest that you write your story.
"I don't know how to spell the words."
I write the words on a separate piece of paper and you write them on your paper. I give you the words as you ask for them. This is also proof that I am listening to you. If you are ready, the same story can be expanded into fantasy. You may find other emotions available to you. As a result, your real works may expand.
"What would you like to do to your sister?"
"I can't do anything. She is bigger than I am."
"She is not here and this is just pretend. Tell her what you would like to do to her."
"I'd like to hit you."
"What else would you like to do?"

"I'd like to kick you."

"What else?"

"That's all, I'm finished."

Now you begin to write your story. You are full of energy. You are completing unfinished business.

Here is a professional teacher confronting a real problem where control of the situation is tenuous at best, but where a crossroads in a child's life is encountered. This contrasts clearly with the carefully controlled but manufactured problem described in the abstract.

Perhaps the earlier comment that intellect without emotion leads to abstract as opposed to real encounters should be modified. The former study does deal with real nonsense syllables. However, superficiality, no matter how rigorously pursued, cannot effect change where it is so substantively needed.

Furthermore, inaction—or superficial action, if you prefer—is dangerous. A practical dimension of democracy is that it allows for gradual change as the need for change becomes manifest. It *allows*, but it does not guarantee. For a democracy to function up to its potential, its separate institutions must likewise function, fully and in a way congruent with the nature of the democratic system. An educational establishment that insists on convergent thinking, that dehumanizes its student charges and its faculties, that postpones independent and responsible thinking until graduate school, that rewards status-quo values among its leadership, that selects administrative leaders for their public-relations skills (which means keeping relations between the public and the schools pleasant and harmonious rather than full of excitement and enthusiasm for the improvement of genuine learning); a school system that stubbornly resists change except for the meaningless rearrangement of content, which remains garbage no matter how packaged—this is an educational system more appropriate for a totalitarian state than for a democracy.

We are beginning to see an ominous reaction to this condition.

Negro parents revolt in New York City. College students plunge into violence on campuses throughout the nation. But more subtly ill-omened is the continuous cynical political manipulation of a thoughtless electorate by means of the creation of candidate images and other advertising techniques. These easily led voters are all products of our school systems. The health of our democracy continues to depend upon the decisions of its voters. Are they, then, to vote in a world of fantasy or in one of real issues and problems? And what are the consequences of this present tendency, when one compares what exists with the potential of (as the politicians like to say) our great nation? We may well be "great" by certain minimal standards. Yet, compared to the possible realization of our potential for greatness, we have only begun.

For learning to take place at all the learner must open himself to new experience. The nature of the experience may vary from the concrete to the abstract, but before he can learn anything a learner must be willing to expose himself to new experience. Teachers use a variety of methods, from enticement and reward to threat and reproof, to motivate students to take this step. There is unavoidably always some risk when one moves into the unknown, or not-yet-known, worlds of new experience. The most primal risk is that one will change. And the status quo is comfortable. Security, no matter how false or how well sustained by the denial of reality, seems preferable to "what might happen."

The ideal pedagogical condition is where a learner, fully possessed of feelings of personal adequacy as an explorer in the universe of experience, finds the adventure of new experience a prospect of challenge and excitement. Thus he learns. And he thirsts for yet more experience. He feels most alive when he is learning, whether what he learns be pleasant or unpleasant. This kind of vitalized learning involves both affective and cognitive dimensions. That is, the learner learns as a whole person, with both mind *and* feeling.

There is another kind of "learning," unfortunately that most commonly found in school classrooms, in which the student can discern nothing that is not superficial and usually irrelevant to him. Essentially rote verbalization, it consists, as Tillich says, of answers for which the learner has not yet asked the questions.

There is no magic wand, including the cudgel of violent revolution, that will make the person or institution committed to standing dead still suddenly convert to a passionate course of living, learning, and growth. The crusts of distorted, out-of-balance socialization and institutionalization have thickened with time. Once there was movement and life here. But even the echoes of the memories of those electric days have faded to the slightest of whispers. The immobilized, like babies, have to learn all over again—but without a baby's venturesome vitality. So each new risk must at first be a tiny one. Otherwise it would seem overwhelming. If the tiny new risk somehow fits into the familiar and the comfortable, there is a greater chance that the risk will be ventured.

This, then, was part of the strategy of the Ford-Esalen project. This is why we generally avoided isolating affective approaches to learning and presenting them as separate entities in the classroom. We endeavored instead to incorporate affective approaches with cognitive content and method. After examining conventional curricula, we explored ways to add the dimension of personal meaning and relevance by integrating appropriate personal and interpersonal feeling experiences into the teaching of the subject matter. When we did this well, the curriculum came alive. When we did it poorly, very little was lost, because often, in terms of the learner, there was little there to be lost in the first place.

When we view the appalling wastelands of the educational establishment, when we hear the monotonous drone of a teacher's voice, when we see classrooms with row on row of vacant eyes, when we experience the vast dullness dotted here and there by new gimmicks and techniques, we too, like Goodman, want to tear at the tedium and the waste. But the radical surgery he and others suggest cannot work, simply because there are not enough surgeons.

There are plenty of butchers about, however. And all the pent-up hostility toward the schools and toward those images of authority necessary to maintain the educational status quo lies seething close to the surface. All the frustrations of a compacted society—restricted living space, denied creativity, confusing dehumanization accompanied by a vague, aching awareness that there must be a better way to be and to live—all this tension and resentment is dammed up, waiting to burst out. And underneath this, steadily pushing and exerting more pressure, is the destructiveness of men who wish to eliminate the anxiety of powerlessness and isolation by eliminating by violence what they conceive to be its cause. McElroy, in *Existentialism and Modern Literature*, says:

> We strive to lose our identity by submerging our God-given individuality in the featureless mass of anonymous humanity; or we drown it in dope, lust, or senseless activity. And our destructiveness is as pervasive as our despair. . . .
>
> Our violence is everywhere: not just in our streets, in our homes, in our everyday lives; it is in our hearts, in our minds, and in our souls. We do not really fear the bomb, we lovers of violence, we worship it, and we secretly yearn for the day when we can destroy the world and ourselves in a great blissful flush of unholy consummation.

Suddenly to revolutionize education, as Goodman suggests, would take the cork off a volcano. Action would stimulate reaction, which would in turn increase action, and so on. The unreality of violence where humanity strikes out blindly just to strike out, where smashing is for the sake of smashing, when to the energy of a child in a tantrum are added the cunning and the power of the adult—all this adds up not to innovation but to sheer destruction.

If these destructive emotions could be confronted in the schools, using the approaches of confluent education as suggested in this book, they might not continue to fester.

In an attempt to bring about change without destruction—healthy and productive change—we have directed our course somewhere between the ends of a continuum having at one end the kind of curriculum innovation that focuses on content and uses a strategy of sweeping up teachers in a popular new wave (the "in" thing to do), usually stimulated by men of prestige in the disciplines and producing some necessary improvement in the curriculum though often neglecting the extrinsically manifested and consequently weak commitment on the part of the teachers; and, at the other end, "freedom for the children," a passionate plea that is sometimes a subtle substitute for the rejection of these same children but an attitude very real and functional to men like Neill of Summerhill. What is frequently ignored is the special context of these experiments. People usually see in them what they want to see, and often deny elements that do not fit in with what they would like. In our project we focused on both content and child, hoping to bring the two together. We have seen this work. However, there is much more that remains to be done. This is only a beginning.

AMERICANISM AND PATRIOTISM

What can be chauvinistic clichés, slogans deviously used to hide some scoundrelly act, or superficial verbalisms about what it means to live in a democracy make sense to us and were supported by the work in the project.

Discipline should be taught in the schools. To us this means a quality of discipline that emphasizes personal responsibility so that one respects law and order because one is committed to the democratic process that produces *and*, as needed, changes laws and the order that follows. The disciplined person that we hope will emerge as the result of confluent education will not need a policeman standing over him to see that he does not break the law. He will, however, be vitally concerned for the justice of our laws and will act and vote accordingly.

The individual comes before the state. We believe that the

uniqueness of the individual is a precious commodity and that for the state or any institution of the state to repress, inhibit, or distort the enormous potential of each individual for learning to do for himself and for his society is evil and wasteful. We believe that confluent education is an approach to the development of the individual's potential—not as a self-centered, greedy, manipulative malcontent, or as an unthinking member of a mob or movement, but as a whole person who thinks and feels for himself and who is also aware and capable of, in Buber's words, an "I-thou" relationship with others—a relationship all human beings need to help manifest their humanness.

Democracy is unreservedly preferable to a totalitarian state. The comments in the earlier part of this chapter make quite explicit our commitment to this position.

Concern for preserving the freedom of our country must permeate the very being of every citizen. Yes, *permeate*. Because a student can feel what it means to be free, as a citizen he will have a genuine understanding of the democratic process both as a theoretical construct and as an operational system with strengths and weaknesses. Furthermore, he will be committed to an open society for his fellow men not because he has *been told* to value the society but because he has *experienced* authentic contact with those who make up the society and knows the profound satisfaction of honest and open communication within that society.

9/

Proceed with Caution

One of the unfortunate aspects of the burgeoning interest in group techniques and the human-potential movement has been the creation of "instant" leaders. Persons who have attended only one or two workshops in such growth approaches as encounter groups, sensitivity groups, or sensory awakening want and feel competent to lead groups themselves. After all, it looks so easy. With all that wisdom and all that power, and with such devotion to the good of the members of the group, who can be condemned?

Aside from the more obvious reservations as to training and competency, there are equally salient considerations in regard to philosophical and ethical values. Where does one obtain the right to suggest, tell, or insist on how another person should behave? As a society we give this right to certain socializing institutions and their representatives—for example, to parents within the family or to teachers within a loosely defined educational structure. But now we introduce a new institution, the group.

Before examining the implications of this situation for classroom practices, let us take a look at the over-all movement in group work in general. The first question the would-be leader should ask of himself is, "What does it do for me to be a leader?" Notice that the question is not "Why do I want to be a leader?" There are a thousand wonderful reasons he can give himself—and probably already has—for why he should play the leadership role. Our skills at rationalizing our behavior are usually highly developed. So, instead, we ask that he get in touch with his feelings as he experiences himself, in actuality or in fantasy, as the leader. What are the personal "goodies" in this for him? What about his feelings of power? Does he enjoy the experience of control over others? Does he in some way feel "safe" from others as the leader? Can he experience the leaking out of negative feelings like aggression, hostility, or cruelty? Does he enjoy feeling superior, somehow "above" those he would lead? Or is he, rather, willing and eager to have the members of the group "use" him so that he can "give" to them through his personal sacrifice and depreciation, however these may manifest themselves? Or does he want to be "helpful"—that most subtly heinous act of all?

These questions illuminate one of the most urgent problems confronting the human-potential movement. The issue can be simply stated in the polarity of manipulation versus teaching. Does the teacher or leader teach or does he manipulate?

Manipulation may be defined as the influencing of others so that they will behave in ways that primarily satisfy the ego needs of the initiator. Although an act may have a residual positive effect on the others, the original intent, conscious or not, is toward satisfying the initiator's needs, in this case the needs of the leader. Teaching, in contrast, can be described as strategies, structures, or acts directed primarily toward the growth of others. It is true that a leader may get much satisfaction in the teaching role. His satisfaction can come from the practice of his art—group leadership contains many elements of an art—or from seeing another's growth. The difference, however, between this and an "ego trip" is the difference between "How great that Joe is finally getting in touch with some of his strengths" and "See how wonderful I am to be able to get Joe in touch." As an ego trip, the latter statement can in turn be contrasted with "I did well in selecting that particular exercise to help Joe get in touch and I appreciate my skill," which relates to satisfaction in the practice of one's art.

Sometimes these distinctions become fuzzy and confused. Although the extremes of manipulation and teaching can be readily defined, it is not so easy to know to what degree each is involved in the act of the moment. Much of the time a leader can be aware of whether he is manipulating or teaching, though in order to do this he must be able to get in touch with himself, and sometimes even well-known, experienced group leaders are skillful at avoiding that responsibility. This includes occasions when they allow or even encourage their groups to take over and literally or figuratively to push an individual around.

In relation to this, there is one rule that we strongly believe should be followed in this area, not only in the classroom but wherever work in affective experiences is done, and that is: *No one should be coerced to do anything he does not want to do*. With this rule as a criterion for examining himself, the teacher or leader can be more aware of which it is he is doing—pushing or allowing.

The justifications for such a rule are many. Ethically, if we have genuine respect for the individual, it would follow that we should allow him to decide for himself what he will or will not do. Politically, it is essential for the success of the democratic process that each citizen take responsibility for his decisions and actions. As we pointed out in Chapter 8, the issue of the relationship between freedom and responsibility is a crucial one. Each time we deprive an individual, whether adult or child, of the opportunity to make a decision that he could make himself, we negate the democratic process. Psychologically, we learn to assume responsibility by successfully assuming responsibility. As we learn to assume responsibility, we become aware that we can. This may seem simplistic, but in reality it is not. One of the great wastes in individuals and in society as a whole is that we are not in touch with our strengths, our resources—what is available to us for our use, both within ourselves and in our world. In the maturation process some of our strengths and abilities develop naturally if they are not interfered with; that is, babies learn to lift their heads, crawl, walk, and run, in that order. A baby "knows" when he is ready and apparently wants to move into each new developmental stage at that time. The analogy can be applied to other aspects of human behavior. Unfortunately, our socialization process, though undoubtedly intended to help the individual to become more mature, sometimes hinders or even prevents him from becoming so. Much has been written about this elsewhere. The point here is that when a person is ready, he will make his next move. Forcing him to move before he is ready is liable to make him overcautious or reluctant later, when he is faced with that next move. On the other side, and perhaps even worse, making the move for him, among other consequences, deprives him of the experience of knowing that he is capable of doing it himself.

This relates to our earlier comment about the subtly heinous act of being "helpful." We often become very skillful in manipulating others so that they will do things for us that we are perfectly capable of doing for ourselves. As we mentioned in Chapter 1, there are a number of ways to do this. We don't understand, we are helpless, flattering, seductive, so grateful, bullying, and so on. Of course, the more successful we are at getting others to do for us what we could do for ourselves, the more we cheat ourselves of realizing our own potential. It is easy to be sucked in by a manipulator and to give him the support he imagines he needs. Giving such support is not an act of love but rather an act of disrespect. If, instead, we refuse to be sucked in, he will experience the frustration of being denied the opportunity to manipulate and thus be faced with the necessity of standing on his own two feet. Then it is more likely that he will take the responsibility of doing things for himself. He faces a choice. He can give up, or if he wants whatever "it" is badly enough, he can exert himself. This is especially true if his attempts to manipulate continue to meet with frustrating "un-sucked-in" responses. Crucial here, however, is the decision of the "responder" as to whether the manipulator is capable of doing "it" himself. But we are usually capable of doing much more than we imagine we can do.

Pedagogically, we have known for a long time the importance of readiness in any learning activity. We even have the cliché, "The teacher takes the child from where he is and brings him as far as he can go." Although trite, this is nevertheless true. Each individual knows how much he can take or do at any given moment, and the wise teacher or leader is guided by that. There is an existential quality to this that fits in with the maturational approach to human development. The leader or teacher and the group or student can only consider what is at that moment. This is the only reality there is to work with. All else is fantasy, illusion, concept, or conjecture. At the same time it is a most hopeful and affirmative philosophical position, for there are an infinite number of fresh moments, one succeeding another, as long as there is life.

What, practically speaking, can a teacher or leader do when he encounters what he imagines to be manipulation, resistance, or avoidance? The trick here is to give feedback without at the same time seeming to judge the apparent resistance or avoidance. Judging connotes pressure or coercion to change, which to some degree deprives the individual of taking responsibility for his own behavior. The message, in its extreme, is, "Stop that avoiding!" The function of the teacher or leader is rather to help the individual become aware of what he is doing if in fact he really is avoiding. To do this effectively the teacher or leader must first be genuinely committed to the thesis that an individual is *the* expert on himself. Then feedback is given always within the context of "This is what it appears to me you are doing. Is this so?" Or, more simply, "How do you experience yourself?" or "What are you doing now?" And then, though the teacher may experience that individual differently, he is able to accept the individual's response. Remember, if you need reassurance, there are fresh moments coming. You can only do what is possible *now*. More important, even if the individual is not truthful, this is where he is at that moment.

There are motives other than the desire for control or power for wanting to lead others in affective experiences. Sometimes a participant finds his own involvement so exciting and rewarding that he cannot wait to share his experience with others. It is easy to become intoxicated with affective learning. It can be heady stuff. Most of us have suffered from affective deprivation. We have learned, for example, not to touch one another except perhaps in a sexual context. We deny or distort many of our feelings. And when all of a sudden we find ourselves in a situation where it is permissible to "let go" affectively, and at the same time apprehend the contrast between the substance of this kind of experience and that of our few socially acceptable times of release, such as New Year's Eve or football games, it is understandable that we could readily adopt a messianic role. Not only does it feel good, but there is sometimes a sense of relief that it can be legitimately incorporated with cognitive learning. Many of us have learned to be uneasy about enjoying a thing without any utilitarian value.

But even well-intentioned persons can ultimately do more harm than good, especially if they rush in as leaders or teachers while still in the euphoria of their own exciting experiences. They are then out of touch with those they would teach, who are now somewhere else. For the teacher this means not only the students in his class but also their parents, his colleagues, and the community as a whole.

The teacher who cannot provide on demand an intelligent, understandable rationale for his work in this area is not only heading for trouble himself; he will also create problems for those who do know what they are doing. They may be stereotyped and lumped into a single category, defined by his inadequacies.

This is one reason we recommend that affective learning not be isolated from the regular curriculum. If the teacher is forced to discipline himself by considering how affective experiences can be integrated with cognitive learning within the content of conventional curricula, then he will very likely be more in touch with the Now, at least the Now of the curriculum. And if he is student-oriented, he will also very likely get in touch with the individual Nows of his students with regard to how they experience the curriculum. He can then draw upon his affective experiences or invent new techniques that will add to his effectiveness as a teacher and improve the learning of his students.

That this learning has cognitive dimensions must not be denied. Just as there is no cognitive learning without an accompanying affective dimension—remember, it is the passion of the scholar that makes for great scholarship—there is no affective experience without its cognitive dimension. We have minds, and there is no way to turn these off even if we wanted to.

It might be well here to elaborate on a defense of the cognitive content of a curriculum. Granted, there is a great need for curriculum modification in order to eliminate much that is deadwood, to change some curriculum goals, and to improve methods of presenting content. Still, there is strong justification for having content for students to learn.

Unfortunately, in reaction to what seemed and may in fact have been irrelevant "stuff" to many of us who were forced to "learn" it, there are some who have swung to the other extreme and want to eliminate all prescribed curricula: "Let the child determine his own curriculum out of his own immediate needs. He will only learn that which is relevant to him anyway." Here relevance is too swiftly equated with what the child immediately perceives. It also implicitly defines the teacher's role as one of responding, while the child initiates the perception.

What is often overlooked by the "child-centered" or "emerging-approach" teacher is that the student does not exist in a vacuum. He must define himself in the context of his universe. A learner continually confronts his contextual universe, and the quality of these confrontations determines the quality of his learning and ultimately the quality of his life.

From the beginnings of the tribe, whoever assumed the teaching role—parent, older sibling, shaman, or tribal chief—was concerned first with transmitting knowledge as a means of survival and only secondarily for personal or tribal enhancement. For the preservation of the group as well as the individual, the tribe could not wait for that unique moment when the child would perceive, for example, the need for a hunting skill right there and then. The tribe knew from its experience of many skills which ones were essential for the survival of its members.

As civilization has developed and become more complex, enhancement has become more and more the focus of whoever represents society in the teaching role. This, of course, often leads to the narrowness of conventional wisdom. But much content can be relevant, for its source is in the reality of the universe. Somehow the teacher has to help the student to become aware of that reality, to get in touch with it.

Furthermore, learning content can be both exciting and personally satisfying. The child, as he matures, finds his universe fascinating. Because the content of curriculum has its source in the universe, this content can hold the same fascination. As we stated before, the problem is how to make the student aware of these potential fascinations through an effective teaching method, along with deciding what is to be taught, when, and to whom.

So there remains the question of selecting from the infinity of our universe that knowledge which will be of the greatest importance to the individual and to society. Philosophical, utilitarian, and social questions now arise that we cannot elaborate on more than we have in preceding chapters.

The point is that content can be readily justified. The teacher, the teaching staff, the board of education, or the appropriate agency will have to make the decisions as to what this will be. But there will be curriculum content.

We shall also not engage in debate here about how curriculum should be changed. At this stage of confluent education not enough is known. Much experimentation needs to be done, preferably by the empiricist and the clinician together. In the meantime, as a guideline for the teacher or teaching staff just beginning to work in the field of confluent education, we suggest starting with the present curriculum and working within that structure.

Related to this problem is the question of the difference between education and therapy. An easy way out of the dilemma of distinguishing between the two would be to claim, as many do, that therapy is nothing but teaching anyhow. But this may be begging the question. Is the teacher a therapist? And, if so, to what degree and depth should he become involved in the therapeutic relationship? A common criticism of teachers who use affective approaches in their teaching is that they are playing therapist. Sometimes this criticism is justified. Fundamental here are the points made earlier in this chapter. First, most teachers are not trained as therapists. What is perhaps more important, those who would play therapist can fall into the role of manipulator by using students for their own ego needs. Does this mean that the teacher avoids considering the student's emotions as he teaches? Obviously not. If such were the case, the whole *raison d'être* for confluent education would disintegrate. In actuality, whether a teacher is aware of it or not, he continually affects and is affected by his students' feelings. Miller and Dollard some time ago pointed out in their theory of social learning and imitation how children use older or more power-possessing people—"superordinated" people—as models for values and behavior.

The child who "fails" in the elementary school internalizes the stigma of failure as an integral part of his self-concept and responds to later schoolwork in terms of this concept of himself as a failure; the result, more failure. And each failure reinforces that part of his self-concept. Psychologically, he sinks to depths of self-deprecation and impotence. Furthermore, he is deeply scarred for life. Whatever he is or does after leaving school is nowhere near what he might have been or done in terms of his potential. What a waste of a human being, both for himself and for society. And this is but one of the more obvious psychological wounds for which schools and some teachers are responsible. Practically, because of the structure of schools and the organization of content and the inflexibility of these in the placement of students, once a student falls "behind" there is almost no chance for him to "catch up."

And we shall only comment in passing on what the system does to those who ostensibly do succeed: they are haunted by anxiety and the lurking fear of imminent failure, they become intellectually docile from playing it cool and playing the game, they exude the tacit arrogance that distinguishes the elite of the "successful," even though often only covertly so designated.

Whatever action a teacher takes in relation to his students has an affective dimension. Consequently, it would seem realistic for the teacher to be cognizant of the fact and to capitalize on it toward the end that his students may grow and learn.

Well, then, how does the teacher draw a distinction between being a therapist and being a teacher? The distinction Richard M. Jones makes between insight and "outsight" is helpful here. Insight is described as the consequence of an introspective act; in therapy the emphasis is often on discovering what is going on or has gone on in relation to the patient's pathological feelings about himself, and is primarily concerned with his history. Outsight is much more existential, and relates instead to how one responds emotionally to the portion of the universe one encounters at a given moment. Within the principles of Gestalt therapy—a contemporary approach in which the use of the term "therapy" is an exception—an individual defines himself in terms of the environment in which he finds himself, the environment including other human beings if they are present. The defining is not limited exclusively to how the environment responds to the individual but includes how the individual feels as he interacts with that particular environment at that particular moment.

If the teacher focuses on the outsight of his students, there is immediate justification for confluent education: (1) the cognitive content of the curriculum and the skills related to that content represent the environment, and (2) the affective dimension is the student's response to that environment.

We stated earlier how important it is for the person who assumes a leadership role in affective approaches to growth or learning to be in touch with himself, especially with what the role does for him. This getting in touch with oneself is invaluable in knowing how far one should go when teaching in the affective domain. In fact, it is often the only way to know, most teachers being without a colleague or supervisor in the classroom to give them feedback.

It is not difficult to sense when one is getting in over his head. This is the time to stop. And for the neophyte it is usually better to stop completely than to try at that moment to remedy the situation by modifying procedures or methodology.

Actually, affective techniques are not much different from what good teachers have done since teaching began. By promulgating confluent education and its affective dimension we are only making explicit what has long been implicit in excellent teaching.

The good teacher knows what is happening Now. He knows how his students are responding Now. And he knows what he is doing Now, how he is doing it, and how he feels as he does it. Experiencing the Now and taking responsibility for the Now are essential for successful teaching in confluent education.

10|

In Conclusion for Now

Perhaps, after the cautionary comments in the preceding chapter and because we have reached the last chapter in the book, this should instead be entitled, "Proceed with Caution but *Proceed*." As teachers, parents, administrators, students, or interested laymen, we are all faced with the condition "meanwhile back at the ranch." To each of us is given the choice to decide, for whatever reason, to accept the status quo and give up or to confront, engage, and creatively change what is going on back there.

If we choose creative change, we will work both with feeling and with intellect. To the degree that our feelings and our thoughts flow together, to that degree will our work also flow. The effectiveness of our work will, of course, also depend upon our authenticity as a feeling person, our cognitive intelligence, our experience and skills, and our commitment to the magnificent adventure of learning and teaching. But each of us, no matter what his position, status, or role, has something to contribute to the educational process.

We have attempted to provide an introduction to confluent

education—what it is and what it can do. And we have also to some extent presented a case for its existence.

Unfortunately, in presenting our arguments for the affective domain of learning, we are faced with the problem of translating experiences in the affective mode—feelings or emotion—into the cognitive mode—the symbols and abstractions of words and phrases. For the most part we do not write as poets or novelists or dramatists. And so we experience frustration with the inadequacy of our writing as well as with the imperfection of the medium we have chosen.

However, the significance of the affective dimension in human existence has become dramatically obvious. As we write this, the President's National Commission on Violence recommends that no prominent political figure appear in public but confine himself to television and radio communication. And the appeal to violence as a problem-solving approach meets with implicit violence in opposition to violence.

The reader may recall the technique "You've got it, I want it" for groups, described in Chapter 3. It can be a shaking experience to watch groups of middle-class, ostensibly civilized people work themselves into a primitive frenzy with group sounds and rhythm and relinquish their individual identities and responsibilities for the passion of the group. Fortunately, this was in a controlled situation and was used to help people get in touch with emotions that lie close beneath the surface. Nevertheless, to see this happening so rapidly and expressively is frightening. A similar phenomenon occurs in lynch mobs, certain militant groups, and pseudo-patriotic mass meetings. Our news media are full of examples.

One response to these primitive manifestations is, "Well, it's just human nature." A slightly more sophisticated theory is that through a series of minor explosions we as a society avoid a major explosion. Both explanations are explicitly fatalistic. They posit that human beings as individuals or in groups cannot become more civilized and more rational in their behavior. The tacit assumption here is that all that can be done is to struggle to maintain some kind of patchwork status quo.

This assumption negates the potential effectiveness of the educational process. The individual can change, can grow, can become a more mature human being. And societies—which are the sum of their individual components, the human beings who constitute them—can also become more mature in their functioning.

This is not wishful thinking or pie-in-the-sky ideology. It can be partially demonstrated. In this book we have described what can happen in the classroom. Other examples can be found in growth centers like Esalen, where it is not unusual for twenty-five strangers who begin a weekend workshop on Friday evening by Sunday noon to end up twenty-five friends who care for one another in the spirit of love as *agape*.

The paradox is that to achieve responsible rational behavior we must educate the irrational. And we must educate the irrational in conjunction with the rational. This is the major case for confluent education.

Another manifestation of the significance of the affective dimension in our society has been the growing reliance on drugs for "turning on." The use of alcohol, marijuana, barbiturates, and the so-called "hard" drugs is pervasive and permeates all classes and most subcultures. In a recent hearing before a Senate committee, Dr. Salvador Luria, a New York drug expert, testified to the need for a safe drug to satisfy the apparently unavoidable demands of our "hedonistic" society.

Drugs provide a substitute for "real" stimulation; that is, the stimulation of reality. To the extent that they are relied upon to avoid confronting reality, their use becomes a matter of serious concern. The situation is aggravated if a culture does not provide opportunities for learning how to encounter reality successfully and satisfactorily. And this cannot be done if the affective dimension is not a vital part of that encounter.

In writing this book, we have attempted to make a case for

confluent education with its affective dimension as vital and crucial for the schools, but we do not delude ourselves that we have more than begun. We speak honestly when we say that this book is not only an introduction to confluent education for the reader but also a prima-facie introduction to confluent education. It is only a beginning. We have come slightly beyond the alchemic stage. The baby has been born and has begun to crawl. Let us see where he goes.

This might be a good place to end. But we cannot resist the opportunity to make one last series of pleas and implorings.

Beginning teachers: Don't let the system smother you. Find at least one other person who can give you support and counsel. And then really "practice," the way a medical doctor practices. Intelligently try out appropriate innovations in your classroom.

Experienced teachers: Use what you know, but don't let it lock you in. You know teaching can be exciting, even if the excitement may not be as frequent as it once was. Do something about it. We've given you some ideas and suggestions. Now begin to create your own. And you too find someone with whom to share support and experiences. It is hard and lonely to be an innovator.

Administrators: Confluent education presents an opportunity for significant changes in your schools. Instead of simply rearranging or stirring up the cold, bland contents of the curriculum, you can help your teachers to heat up and flavor the dish so that students can satisfy their hunger for learning. And you can "teach" the parents and the community. Instead of conceiving public relations to be a series of "snow jobs," you can begin to confluently educate the public. Not easy, that's true! But what are your alternatives? There is much we still have to learn, and for now we can only learn by experience. This takes courage, but at the same time it promises excitement and satisfaction. Working with the public is no less a teaching act than what occurs in the classroom.

Researchers and theoreticians: There is much work that needs to be done. We need more sophisticated theory that is at the same time functional and that can be translated operationally. And we need a spate of empirical studies to test when, where, how, and with whom confluent education has effect. Our bias will not allow us to include "if." We are so prejudiced because of our clinical success that if empirical studies do not give evidence of effect, we will insist that something is wrong with the design or the evaluative instruments.

The rest of you good people: Share the book or at least tell people about it. Even if you do not agree with what has been presented, still, tell others what you think about it. Out of the controversy may come refinement and further explorations, adventures, and study. Become vocal in school matters, both in your local community and on the national scene.

We hope that for all readers this will be a provocative book. We hope it will be an incentive for others to go on. We conclude, as we did in the first chapter, with Fra Giovanni:

"There is a radiance and glory in the darkness could we but see, and to see we have only to look. I beseech you to look!"

APPENDIX
BIBLIOGRAPHY

Appendix

TRANSCRIPT OF FORD-ESALEN STAFF

WORKSHOP SESSION, MARCH 23, 1968,

ESALEN INSTITUTE, BIG SUR, CALIFORNIA

GEORGE (to visitors): Mid Squier teaches sixth grade in Goleta, the same district that Gloria teaches in. Aaron teaches high-school English. He works with next to dropout kinds of kids. These are kids that no one else can handle. Robin teaches junior-high social studies. Ann* teaches junior-high art in South San Francisco. Fundamentally, this project is directed toward exploring ways in the so-called affective domain—Esalen kinds of things—and seeing how they can be moved into the curriculum so that both the affective and cognitive can sort of swing together. And so the cognitive, the so-called academic kinds of things, can be even more real and more meaningful. What we do is meet here once a month and talk about things we've been doing, and try out some kinds of things, and brainstorm ideas. Our first session is usually a kind of reporting session, things that have been happening.

MID: I did something a couple of weeks ago using oranges. I think some of you may have even done the same one, but I hadn't

---

* Mrs. Ann Chestnut.

heard how you did it, so I did it pretty much on my own. I had the kids close their eyes and then I passed out oranges. Then I asked them to try to identify it without using their eyes, and they had no trouble at all because it had a real strong odor. And then I had them explore their oranges trying to get to really know them well. I had them first go over it with their hands and then over their face, and when they went over their face it really startled a lot of kids because it was so cold. They said, "Oh, this is neat!" and they had all these really wild expressions. They just rolled it over and I told them some things—like putting the navel part of the orange across their face and seeing if it felt different. Again it had a similar response. What else did we do with that? Oh. I asked them to try to become the orange itself and have somebody stare at them. What would it be like to be stared at? And I let them just think about this for a minute, and some kids were really shook up. They thought the person staring at them was kind of a creep. A few were *really* shook up, and some just couldn't do it. But a few were able to really get into it and had some comments. After we did that, we cut open the oranges, or they peeled the oranges, and they did much the same thing, only on their own. They were smelling it and tasting it and seeing how different it was.

GEORGE: You didn't give them any instructions? Just let them go?

MID: Well, I told them to peel it, and then I let them do what they wanted to do, and after that they ate it. But I think the kids really enjoyed it, because they came up to me and said, "I'd like to do that again with something else." They were really keyed up on it. This was kind of exciting for me, because they were really just great.

GEORGE: Have you thought about what you might go on with after this? Are you going to hitch this into your curriculum in any way?

MID: Well, I think basically what I was trying to do was just to tune in their senses, some of their physical senses that they don't use all the time. We use our eyes so much that we sometimes don't use our sense of taste or hearing or smell or touch on just typical everyday objects. I try to bring this in with other objects that we have. We were in the mountains on a field trip a few weeks ago, and instead of just looking at the trees and plants we had them touch them, and feel the difference of texture of the leaves, or the bark, or things like that. And if I had not mentioned this, I don't think many of them would have even thought of it. They would have just looked at them.

AARON: Did you tie that into a lesson in any way?

MID: No, I just planned it out to see what would happen. It was just an isolated thing.

BILL:* Do you think of, instead of using an orange, using each other?

MID: I didn't think of that. No.

BILL: If they would explore what other senses, what other people are like, what a class of kids are like . . .

MID: I think some people have done something like that.

ANN: I think you have to start out with something like this, though, and I think it would take a number of steps for them to feel relaxed exploring each other.

PEGGY: I did a little bit of sensory awakening with a sixth-grade class for ten minutes, and I had never been in the class before. I had them at the end close their eyes and sort of mill. This works up to touching, and they really enjoyed that. Just milling and feeling the room kind of thing and semi-touching each other when they were in proximity. But they would get really giggly at any kind of—like—feel where you're sitting on the chair. So you have to be pretty careful about your wording.

GLORIA: Mid, I really like your using the orange. I am being stared at. . . . You probably can use that again now that you've done that.

GEORGE: It's a good opening, I imagine, to the whole business

* William Schultz, of Esalen Institute (a visitor).

of avoiding contact or making contact. You could move that into—
What are you doing in social studies now?

MID: Mexico.

GEORGE: This would be great. How do Mexicans respond in this kind of way? What context, and how do we respond in our own culture, and are there alternatives in how you feel about it? You know, this whole "mishegass"?

GLORIA: We have a lot of that in Mexican American. You know. . . . How do your Mexican children feel? I think you could use that, too. You've put the first stone in, and you can go a long way with that now. It's really hard to tie it in. I've tried it. So what? What's next? I'm having problems with that, too.

ANN: Do you work with art with this? Or do you have an art teacher?

MID: No, I do their art with them.

ANN: Something in art could be tied in with experiencing the form, making some kind of a drawing or some kind of a painting, and then tasting it, and making it another hue or color, and see if they experience it differently.

GEORGE: Get some rocks. Is there a place with some big rocks nearby?

MID: There's a creek. There are probably some rocks in there.

GEORGE: You have the jungle gyms out there. You could have them go out and sort of paint those, but also have them experience them with their bodies, not the usual way, but sort of rubbing up and feeling—you know, this whole thing.

ANN: Like with this science thing, too. Experiencing the leaves and the bark. There are some of the most beautiful patterns and things in the bark of the trees or in the branches. The negative pattern between the branches, and things like this. They could experience them for the science and express them in art, too. Tie things together like that.

GLORIA: I just want to share that I had my parents in. It was March 8. I had all but two parents come. I asked them to write comments of the doubts. (That was on Friday, and I was out Monday and Tuesday with the flu.) And so when I did them later on, it was Wednesday.

GEORGE: Excuse me, I don't think some people know what you did. Do you all know what she did?

GLORIA: To get them to come, I had a lot of parents come in on how you teach reading and how you teach math. So from nine-thirty to nine forty-five we had a reading session, and from nine forty-five to ten we had a math session. Parent working with the child, sitting side by side. Then the children went out to recess, and when they came back the parent sat across from the child, and Peggy and I had taped down paper between them. The parent had a crayon in each hand, and the child had a crayon in each hand, and the child drew for ten seconds, and then the parent was to draw for ten seconds on the same paper. Then the child and mother joined hands and drew together for ten seconds. Then the child used his other hand, Mother used her other hand, and then together. It started out with ten seconds, and I tried to feel what was happening with them. I had about fifty-five people I was working with. It started out with ten seconds, and I could tell ten seconds was interminable for some of them, and it worked out so that at the end they were working together for a minute. They were having all kinds of fun with it. One mother and daughter got going in great big circles, and they were going off their paper, laughing, round the desk. You know, they were just great! Their papers were just covered. They got away from it had to be a picture thing easily because you couldn't make it be a picture. It just turned into this swirly and straight-up-and-down kind of thing.

From there we moved over to the cafeteria. The children were blindfolded and the parents closed their eyes, and I brought a big bag of objects in. They all closed their eyes, and I gave each one of them an object, and then I clicked sticks and they passed their objects to the right. I asked them if they could go beyond the labeling of what they had—to actually experience the object itself.

And just taking a spoon, for example—be aware of the part that you put in your mouth and the part that you hold in your hand. The roundness, the straightness, the hardness of it. I was very pleased. I was standing by this one mother who had a block of wood and a nail that had come out, and she moved herself out from the circle and got up with her knees over this block, with her eyes closed, and fitted the nail back into the hole, and thought that was so much fun she took all four nails out and then did it again, and then moved back into the group, passed her object on, and kept playing the game. From there I had the children move out with their mothers and this feeling of each other. Blindfold your mother —I started with mothers blindfolded. And having the child take his mother's hand and feel her, feel you. We've done this in the room, too, finding lots of textures. And from there they got up and started bringing objects. Well, they moved out in circles. There were objects strewn all over the cafeteria, and they would bring things to their mother. Then they got up and started leading their mothers around. It had just poured the day before, so I didn't know if we could do a blind walk outside. I had told them that they might not be able to go out, but some of them went on out anyway, rain or no rain. Then after about twenty minutes I had the mother take the child. And in one of the letters that came back, the mother said that she realized that she trusted her child but that the child didn't trust her. She had lost a lot of contact with this boy since having the new baby in the home. She had been very disturbed about his behavior and had asked on several occasions about it. And I had noticed a change in this boy but hadn't tied it to any-thing. I didn't know what was happening. And then just this last Thursday I got this letter from her. Then they came in, and we had been doing some work with sheets, which I reported on to the group—having them get under the sheets and grow, getting under the sheets and feeling being alone, and what it feels like when people intrude in their space, and how you feel when you bump into somebody else. The beginning of the sheet work was this random play, getting on the sheets and sliding, and having somebody pull you on the sheets. I had this lesson all worked out about what I was going to do with the parents with the children on the sheets, but it threw them into a complete play session, just like the kids had. The mothers pulled the kids back and forth across the cafeteria. There was one that said "You gotta be kidding!" when she walked in and saw these kids pulling their mothers all over the place. The next thing I knew, this woman was running across the cafeteria. She got to the end and went to the left, her son fell off the sheet and went to the right, and she got down in the corner and just doubled over in laughter. She was just broken up! And Peggy said this was the one that said she just couldn't believe it when she saw what was going on. Then I had this one father who came because the mother is a teacher and couldn't get off. He had on a suit and a white shirt and tie, and he was pulling his son on a sheet, and another boy was on a separate sheet, hanging on. He had his knees up like this and his elbow on his knee, hanging on to the other sheet, and they were going all around the cafeteria. They were just wild! They had such a good time. Then the children pulled their parents. This was funny, too. They became aware of "My goodness, how much Mommy weighs," you know, and how hard it was to pull Mommy. This one mother, the one that had taken the nails out of the block of wood, her son couldn't pull her. She had worn a parka because it was quite cold in the rain. She took her parka off. She was about from the wall to the table that was over here, and she threw it from where she was over toward the table just to get it out of the way. She got up on her knees, and she began pumping just like the kids had done. I couldn't get over the similarities between what the mothers did and what the children did on the first day on the sheets. So they became pretty exhausted with all this running and winding the kids around and being pulled and pulling. One mother had recently had a heart attack. She had had a change-of-life baby, now six years old, and she said that she felt pretty bad because she couldn't involve herself in this kind of activity, and her little girl felt kind of left out of things. I looked up at the clock, and we had about twenty minutes left of our two hours, and I said, "Why don't you two go over to the room and bring out the cookies and punch?" The children had made cookies, and Peggy had done a lot with them on that, making cookies two days before to have refreshments for them, and later she told me that this was marvelous because she and Marilyn were able to resolve the conflict. Marilyn was resentful and angry with her mother because she couldn't do what the other mothers were doing. And yet to be able to have her mother all to herself and to do something for the other children was very pleasant. She was very thankful for the opportunity of being able to work with Marilyn in another way. I hadn't even thought of other ways of having mothers work with their children who might not have been able to move into this. Then they had cookies and punch together. The mothers were amazed that the children had made the cookies themselves. One said, "Did you mix everything, and just have the kids make the cookies?" They were amazed that the children had measured the flour, and Peggy and I kidded each other. I said all I did was break the eggs, and Peggy said, "Not my group. They broke the eggs themselves."

AARON: Gloria, you mentioned there were two students whose parents didn't show up. What did you do with them?

GLORIA: Well, Peggy took one, and I sent the other one, because he's such a disturbance in the classroom many times, into a second-grade classroom—first-second combination, next door. And I talked to him about it. He was rather glad to go.

AARON: Any connection between the fact that the parent didn't show up and the disturbances he caused?

GLORIA: The children didn't say anything. This boy is used to his mother. He has a stepmother, and she hasn't been there long, and she's not really interested in him, and he had this for a long time, so he and I talked about it. I asked George if he would come on Tuesday to be Jimmy's father, because he wasn't able to participate last time, and I would like him to be in on some of it. One mother didn't come at the last moment, and Peggy took Tom. Another mother said she would share Tom with her daughter—take her daughter and Tom, too—but she soon found she had all she could do. She was very much involved with her own daughter, and it was not possible. You just couldn't take two children in that kind of a situation. I wasn't free enough to take a child, either. We did have one boy whose parents knew they were coming, and they didn't come until we were working with the sheets, which was around ten. Then both parents came. He fitted in, though. He's pretty self-sufficient. Didn't need any attention, and he could just join in with whatever they were doing and sat alongside another child. Then Peggy took both the boys when the mothers and the children went that way—the situation was to have one in each hand. But fitting it into the art work would have been difficult. And I got these letters back. We'd like you, if you have time, to go over them. It's very rewarding. They enjoyed what they did. There were some questions about how it ties in, and I would like to work on that this weekend. I asked you to write down a statement that you made yesterday, Robin. This kind of material I think should be written down.

BILL: Gloria, did you try what might be the rainy-day blind walk of falling backwards?

GLORIA: Well, we thought about that, but I didn't know how to do the child-parent. You know, the catching of the adult by the children.

GEORGE: You have to have about six kids.

GLORIA: Yeah. You know, just pulling, it took three or four kids just to pull a mother on a sheet. . . . Well, this was funny because we had written this down. A step for getting the children to lead the blind walk themselves, which occurred about a month ago. We had written this as being a part of trust, and this was something we thought we really should look at before they could do this. Doing this touching of each other and this catching bit was to be the next day's lesson—you know, experiencing of this. And when they were doing the touching of each other and this kind of thing, it just went into a blind walk, and all of a sudden I looked around and there were kids leading each other all over the place. So we have never gone back to the catching exercise. Someday we probably will throw it in.

BILL: I think it's a little bit different.

GLORIA: I thought of all kinds of things when it was raining. You know, what in the world was I going to do to get the same kind of a thing. I know when I've gone with the children what a tremendous feeling it is, and I told the parents before they came this was one reason why I wanted them to come, because I've done things with their children that I wish they would do with their own children. And I've felt such a lot of warmth for their children that I want to share it with them. I want them to experience this, too. I think it happened, from the letters they wrote.

BILL: They had more physical contact with the head of the family.

GLORIA: Yes, and even their art work, in touching. I could try not to be predetermined in what they're doing. Just let it happen. I could see them moving into it from being stiff and self-conscious. There were quite a few of the mothers who wrote about their watching other mothers with children, and what a reassuring thing it was. This is one reason why I started having my parents come in early and helping out on P.T.A. night. Just to talk about what is a six-year-old or what is a seven-year-old right now. What kind of problems are you having with your children? And when they find out that five or six others are having the same kind of thing happening, it's not nearly so frightening when your child is being negative. Your child's behavior is rapidly changing, and you don't understand it. When they know that other mothers are having this same kind of thing, it helps. Peggy, you did some real good things with the cookies you might want to share.

PEGGY: After they had baked the cookies, I had them go back

to the room and do sort of a two-step thing. One was "What would the batter say to the spoon?" You know, get a conversation going between the spoon and the batter. I was going to do that as a class kind of story that they could all write together, and then have them go out on their own with what one cookie would say to another cookie as they're on the sheet in the oven. We never got to that because the spoon and the batter thing was so good that the kids just wanted to stay with that. But it ended up sort of as a class story. The batter says to the spoon, "Stop beating me," and the spoon replies, "I can't, the arm is turning me," and then the spoon says to the arm to stop turning me, and the arm says, "I can't"— I've forgotten exactly how it goes—"the teacher is making me." You know. I guess it was the teacher's arm. It just progressed to that point, and the kids really enjoyed the idea.

BILL: It's for your own good. (Laughter.)

PEGGY: So that's about all that really happened from that.

GLORIA: We had just done a lot of this smelling and feeling, and it was really great, because after the children made the batter for the cookies, Peg took a group and I took a group, and we baked them, and she worked with them while they were baking them, and we took them out hot and dropped them into their hands hot. How does the cookie feel, and how does it smell, and how does it taste? They were just marvelous! They loved that, and I think we'll do some more of this before the year is out. You get so many parts of them involved.

PEGGY: The other thing that happened kind of spontaneously was going around saying what kind of foods they liked and what they didn't like. It just sort of happened. Somebody said, "Oh, I don't like this," and I said, "Well, what foods do you like?" It turned out that they would say, "I like popcorn," and everyone would say, "Popcorn, wow!" "I don't like spinach." "Spinach, boo!" It was a kind of chant thing, all around the group.

GLORIA: Some of the things mentioned, like "I don't like macaroni and cheese," and then when we came around to the likes,

macaroni and cheese was mentioned again. And this was great—
to get into some of these. How do we judge what's good, how do
we judge what's bad, what's beautiful, and what's ugly? Some of
these things that we arbitrarily apply names to. That what you like
he doesn't like. Is it good or is it bad? Can you say? It really went
into some nice things.

ANN: I did some work with this kind of thing in that family-
life class, where they express some of their likes or dislikes, but
there's no right or wrong about it. It's not . . . you know . . . can
you give a right answer or something. It seemed to be helping
them to see how different they were from each other. Some of them
were so surprised when someone would say their favorite food was
pizza, or something like that, and then some of the others would
say, "Oh-h-h," but they seemed to be able to accept that someone
else liked something that they didn't like, and we did that with a
number of things. I'm trying to think of what else we did that with,
and they seemed to enjoy that, too. They weren't expected to give
any one answer, as they are so often.

BILL: Did anyone like both? Like and dislike the same thing?

GLORIA: We got to this when we were talking about trust. Who
do I trust the most, and who do I trust the least? When we were
working on building of trust, they would say, "I trust my mother
the most," "I trust my mother the least." We got into some of that
then.

BILL: Then they could accept that?

GLORIA: I guess so. We didn't really go into it. Another thing
Peggy did was use the opaque projector on a blur and then ask
the kids, "What do you see?" Then she sharpened the focus somewhat. "Now what do you see?" And then sharpened the focus some
more. "Now what do you see?" And then with a clear focus. That
was good. It was interesting that the children named a buggy a
wagon. They said, "I see a boy and a girl and a dog in a wagon"
while it was still pretty fuzzy. Even when it came to sharp focus,
they were still calling the buggy a wagon. Peggy didn't pick it up,

but we've gotten into this deal on labeling and have brought it up in a lot of different ways. They called it a wagon, and now what we're finding out is if they saw it as a wagon. You know . . . they said it was a wagon. Did they block out the visual of seeing the buggy, or were they seeing the buggy and calling it a wagon? Although I know they know the difference between a buggy and a wagon. This is the same thing we got into with a television commercial. I really have no idea what's going on. Were they blocked? We asked them what they saw on a "To Catch a Thief" commercial. It had hitting, guns, and kissing.

GEORGE: This is where you were trying to get into the listening skills. Hearing voices.

GLORIA: Yes, hearing voices, and what do you see—both. They said they heard the gun. They didn't mention they saw the gun. They saw the man bouncing on the trampoline, but they didn't mention the fact that he had been socked onto the trampoline. I just don't know what's happening on things like that. We haven't done enough of it to come to any conclusion about it.

GEORGE: That's very good. One of the things we're trying to get at in this thing is to get kids to move from preconception to perception. That is, from seeing things they think ought to be there to seeing things that are really there. This is the real essence of what we're trying to do. Experiencing what's real as opposed to experiencing what you think ought to be or should be or must be— something like that.

GLORIA: Well, this is what happened with the wagon and buggy. The same thing with the TV commercial. All the violence that was in it. Did they block it? What I wonder is did they see it and block it, or did they not even see it?

GEORGE: I would suggest you do this whole thing again, and take some time. Individually sit down with them and find out. Maybe I can work with you sometime, because I'm very curious about this.

GLORIA: I am, too.

GEORGE: Because have our first-graders really been that much distorted and pressed into selected perception that they are now beginning to . . .

ANN: Maybe with the wagon it's just an object that will pertain more to them and their age and it was the first thing that came to their minds, and a buggy goes back to babies or little children and it's not something that really still pertains to them.

GEORGE: You said they know the difference.

GLORIA: I'm sure this group knows the difference.

ANN: Not knowing the difference, but the idea that a buggy hasn't something to do with them any longer, but maybe a wagon is a special toy that they have.

GLORIA: They tend to be more identified by their wagons at this age. A buggy and wagon are both kind of behind them now.

PEGGY: That's right.

BILL: What's the motivation for being accurate?

GLORIA: Well, there wasn't any particular motivation. You know, it was just interesting that this happened again. I can see the end product, but I don't know what's happening to the child, what's gone on, why he is labeling . . .

BILL: What I'm thinking of is if I were the child and I saw this blurry thing and said it was a wagon . . .

GLORIA: No, this was in sharp focus. They called it a wagon while it was still blurry, then pretty clear.

BILL: No, but it's the sequence. I first identified it as a wagon and it's all blurred; then it gets closer and closer. It's not quite a wagon. It's something like it, but I don't know. Why not just call it a wagon? I don't feel in identifying with the child that there is need to be accurate any closer than I already have been.

GLORIA: It depends on what you're working on. If you're working on visual, you know, you're getting kids to become aware of what they're looking at, which is what we were doing, and you want them to see that it is not a wagon, that it is a buggy. There is a girl and there is a dog and there is a buggy in the picture. This is a language-development lesson and— Well, other things, too.

But there are times when it doesn't matter what they call it, and even then I didn't see any need to say, "Look at that thing. What is it?" And even to call particular attention to their error. I just noticed it happening again. This isn't the first instance of it. Being in a classroom, I wonder what's happening.

ROBIN: There's a friend of mine who uses that blur technique for getting into short stories and poems and things. He takes nature slides and projects them in a very definite blur, and then he never brings them into clear focus. He leaves them in enough of a blur so that it's a kind of a mystical thing. It looks kind of mystical to the kids, anyway. Then they write about it or make up a song, or they do something like this. It seems to be pretty effective.

GLORIA: What do you find is more effective than using the opaque projector with the picture? Because with the first-graders, anyway, the need to know what it was was so great they couldn't get into it. The kids were sitting by the opaque projector and insisted on getting up and looking underneath to see what it was rather than to . . . We do a tremendous amount of work trying to get them to be . . . not knowing, you don't have to have a right answer. It's amazing the conditioning that first-graders have had, because we're continually working, like with the blindfolds, getting their eyes closed. Just to get them to close their eyes was about a six-week procedure. Now the one who kept yelling, "I can't! I can't!"—my Timmy—now can. You know the idea we were doing, the game from *Put Your Mother on the Ceiling*, and here he was the whole time, just way out somewhere. I thought, "Well you can, Timmy. I wish you knew you could."

GEORGE: What's happening with that book?

GLORIA: Oh, we're still having a good time with it. I asked one of my children in a science lesson, "Can a puppy have a cat for a parent?" And David said, "Yes." The others were all saying no, and I said, "Dave, why did you say yes?" He said, "In your imagination you can." So I said, "Well, let's play that game later. Now we're reading science."

PEGGY: I had the imagination of this little guy that was giving us so much trouble. Just couldn't work. He was all over the room. He's small, should be really in kindergarten, but he's in first grade. I went up to him and said, "Tommy, what's your problem? Is there anything I can do to help you?" "No." "Is there anything you can do to help yourself?" "I don't know." "Well, what's really bothering you?" "It's my imagination." And I said, "What's the problem with your imagination?" "Gets into fights with my mind, then I can't work."

GEORGE: Is that what he said? It's incredible!

PEGGY: I had your reaction. I just sat there, so I didn't really hear what he went on to say. Then he talked for a while, and I said, "You feel any better?" and he said that he did.

GEORGE: Boy, is that beautiful! Because there's the whole scene right there. Between the mind and all the other things that go on. Even though they're in the first grade, they've had their parents just pushing and pushing and pushing at this cognitive thing. You've got to know. You've got to test it out, use your mind, make sense.

AARON: You know what is a good illustration of that bit? When Rosemary* was teaching kindergarten in San Francisco, they had to have grade cards for kindergarten, and they had to put on them M for most of the time and P for part of the time and N for none of the time, and they were passing out grade cards to kindergarten kids. She said one day in class one of the kids came up and said, "Mrs. Hillman, when are we going to get some more of those good M's?" She felt like burning down the school that day.

GEORGE: There's a developmental thing, too. This phenomenon called synesthesia, where there's confusion between the sense modalities. That is, you talk about seeing music and hearing a color, or you touch something and it somehow brings an odor to you.

ANN: I hear music when I see colors.

GEORGE: Well, great poetry is based on this, you see. The whole

* Mrs. Hillman.

business of the so-called confusion between the sense modalities. Kids have this, and it's great. And what we do instead of teaching them when it's appropriate and that it is all right sometimes is just stomp on the whole thing. You've got to use your head, use your mind. Obviously you can't smell a color. You know, that kind of thing.

ROBIN: Obviously your little imaginary playmate doesn't exist.

GEORGE: Yes.

GLORIA: We've really gotten into a lot of . . . you know, the imagination that's been expressed. The thing that DeMille was after was to do that between reality and imagination, and I think with the first-grader he knows the difference quite well. In DeMille's book, he writes as though there is a confusion, that people have problems in working strictly with imagination. They want to tie it back to reality. Like in the game, it says, "Go to the store." "Put on a hat." "What color is it?" "Now change the color." Then he has you ask, "How did you change the color?" If the child says the lady came up and took the red one off and put the green one on, he makes them go back. "No, do it in your imagination. Just change the color. It's changed."

BILL: How do you deal with something like Santa Claus?

GLORIA: I don't. I ignore it.

BILL: What if they ask you about it?

GLORIA: If they ask me if I believe in Santa Claus, then I say that I believe in the spirit of Christmas and that Santa Claus is more than just one thing. And that just kind of adds to their confusion and they mull that over.

BILL: But I mean, is Santa Claus real or imagined?

GLORIA: If they ask me that point-blank, I tell them it's imagination. Same way with the Easter bunny. And this with the teeth and all, the missing teeth in first grade.

AARON: The only difference is my kids know what a fairy is!

GEORGE: It's somebody that touches. It's a man that touches another man.

BILL: Well, that would seem consistent. It's part of the cultural things acting against it. If Santa Claus is real, or maybe even God . . .

GLORIA: Well, my little girl has asked me about this. Is God real or is God in your imagination? Because I play these games with her. How do you answer that? How do you know God is real? Or where do you see God?

GEORGE: One thing I think can help in this is if you talk about the whole business of knowing—I think you can talk even with first-graders. How do you know anything? You can know with your mind, you can know with your touch, you can know with your feelings, and you can know with your imagination, and they're all perfectly legitimate ways to know.

GLORIA: But we're really getting into this mixed-signal business, which I think is so important, and it's taken a long time.

GEORGE: What do you mean by mixed signals?

GLORIA: A double-message thing. One little girl was saying, "I don't want you to sit next to me." And Mary looked at her and looked at me, and then this big smile came on Mary's face. And I said, "What's happening?" And she said, "Judy is saying with her voice that she doesn't want me to sit next to her, but her face doesn't say that." Mary was just beaming, because even if she was hearing these awful things, she was getting another message from Judy's face. So I said to Judy, "Do you know what's happening?" And Judy said, "Yeah, I'm smiling." And I said, "Do you know what you are feeling?" And she said, "I'm feeling funny." What she meant was "I'm playing with her and I know it," and so they sat down together, and this was really great—that Mary knew how to get the double signal and read it accurately.

BILL: I would think that this is a way you could tie in the orange thing. You could talk about how that could be related, the whole issue of knowing. How do you learn, how do you know something? And it's certainly demonstrated by that. So that would be a way of tying in this problem.

GLORIA: Well, we always get these double things. Very rarely is it a straight kind of thing, no matter what you're doing. Any one thing you're doing, other people do it another way. And for the children to see the difference is very important.

GEORGE: We found, Bill, in the project, that we can go from both ends. Sometimes we can't move, but we can start with a conventional bit of curriculum, look at it, and say, "Now what could we do here to bring more of the feeling . . ." Or we can start with a technique and say, "now where could we plug it in." You know, it works both ways. Actually, what I had hoped we'd be able to do—maybe we won't be able to do too much of it this year—but I hope if we do get re-funded that we can look at the thing in a much broader perspective. You know, in terms of units, where we can go into some big chunks of things, things leading from one thing to another.

AARON: I mentioned this to George last night. The assistant superintendent is working so Bob Goodwin and I can have five days off to write units out of the classroom.

GEORGE: You sent me one that was very good.

AARON: Take a week off from the classroom and simply write units.

GEORGE: While we're on this, you want to share some of the things you've been doing?

AARON: Yeah, I did one thing with them. But there isn't anything we haven't done this last month. Well, these are tenth-graders. We had the opportunity to tape a thirty-minute television show this last month. So I set it up artificially and got nine of the kids, mixed races, and we went through the listening series that Sev and Al Drucker sent up. I worked it out of *Death of a Salesman* and the lack of communication between father and sons and the family itself. Everybody was talking but no one was listening. In the first sequence, a Negro and a Mexican American girl came on camera. The Negro girl was the mirror and Felicia Lopez was looking into the mirror. They were on camera with this mirror in silence for some time. Then the second group—a white girl and a white boy—were on camera. I asked them to close their eyes. I was off camera, but the kids were there. I asked them to reach out and touch hands with their eyes closed, and then to get acquainted with their hands. They got to know each other. If you like each other, now do a dance together. They were dancing with the hands, simply with the hands. I said, "You don't like each other for some reason. You probably stepped on his toe. Have a fight. . . . You're sorry now. Make up. . . . You've got to part. You're feeling very sorry about it." And they started pulling away. I said, "Say so long. You regret to go." And they withdrew very slowly, and they were very good at that. I went through this revolving-discussion sequence, in this case between a Mexican American girl and a white boy. I had him state his opinion of fathers who live through sons. He stated his opinion, and then Juanita answered only to the point of how much she agreed with him and asked him questions about where she didn't understand. When that was through, then she stated her disagreement. They reversed the role. Then we went from there into improvisational theater from *Death of a Salesman*. This one boy just tickled the hell out of me. It was Johnny Herman and he is black. He can't read or write, and he's a tenth-grade kid. But he's pretty good. He's got an excellent brain. I really enjoyed him being on the show. He had been kicked out of school that day for coming to school early and he had a crap game going on over at the cafeteria.

BILL: During school hours?

AARON: Yeah, some of them come the first period, the second period, or the third period. He came two periods early so he could make his lunch money for the day. He and a white boy. I had them play brothers from the play *Death of a Salesman*. The white boy was Biff. Now, this is the bum, the no-good guy. Johnny was Happy, who stayed at home with his parents in the same town, was trying to be a success the same way as Willie Loman. I said, "Now you're upstairs in your bedroom, and you haven't seen each other for a long time. You hear your father downstairs in the kitchen. You know he's going to commit suicide. You take it from there." And so the white boy says, "Why don't you go down and take care of Dad?" And Johnny says, "Let him take care of himself." And they played this thing, and they were just beautiful. We moved on from that to another book, *Lord of the Flies*. In the book a group of English schoolboys are on a deserted island, no adults, nothing, and you're on your own. You've got to do something, but you're on your own. I said, "It's your problem." I was off camera, and the kids were there. So they winged it, and they did great. The black boy did exactly what would happen. The kids wanted to get somebody to lead the group. Johnny said he wanted to go off and do something else, and he wasn't going to cooperate with the group. He worked that, and they worked themselves up to exactly what would happen. One boy was very cynical. "We'd kill each other off." Exactly what probably would happen in a group like that is what they went through. When the thing was shown—and from the principal of the school we got beautiful reactions. From the kids we got reactions, from the community we got some reactions, and every one of them was positive. There wasn't one negative reaction from the whole community.

GEORGE: The principal didn't object to the fact that you used a kid that he had kicked out of school that day?

AARON: He never mentioned it. I'm not so sure that the dean of boys even told him. We have a swinger for the dean of boys, I might add. He was some sort of executive with Revlon, couldn't stand it any more, and got out and went to school. But I just enjoyed that so much. Rosemary and I took the nine kids out afterward, and we went to a restaurant. We all had filet mignon. We sat around a table for three hours.

GEORGE: Had they ever had filet mignon at any time?

AARON: No. They asked, "How do you pronounce it?" "What is it?"

GEORGE: Did they save that tape by any chance?

AARON: I'm going to find out.

GEORGE: If they did, I'd like to hear it. Tell them we'll pay them for it if they've got it. Call them when you get back, will you? They're probably stupid enough to destroy a beautiful thing like that.

AARON: It was beautiful. We talked about what we were going to do—we had gone through both books, of course—but we didn't stage it in any way.

GEORGE: I'm really curious about this. Now, these are kids that have a really rough time reading. How do you get through the books with them? Do you read to them? Do they read? I've never seen you do that when I've been in your classroom.

AARON: We are going through *Moby Dick* right now, and the boys really enjoy *Moby Dick*. Just to give you an example, we started out yesterday in class with a chapter, and I said, "O.K., here we are in Chapter 28 of *Moby Dick*." They don't read it. They don't have the book. I'm the only one with a book, and this is a good idea. We got to Chapter 28, and we hadn't met this Captain Ahab. It's the first time he appears on the scene. The first thing we ought to start with is Captain Ahab's name. Who was he? Where did the name come from? Ahab was the old Israelite king back in the Old Testament. He was a good king except that he brought in pagan gods. They started worshiping other gods. It was predicted that he would die a violent death. It said he'd die a warrior's death on the battlefield, and according to the Old Testament the dogs drank his blood.

GEORGE: Oh, the kids must have loved that!

AARON: So I said, your homework assignment for the weekend is to write at least a one-page paper on the subject of warriors. Ahab, when we first see him, has two things that strike you about him. One thing, he's only got one leg. His leg was torn off by a whale, and they cut off a whale's jaw and fashioned him another leg. That's kind of a good idea. His leg was torn off by a whale, so they replaced it by a whale's jaw. Well, that's our discussion exercise for the day when we get to that.

BILL: What did you discuss with that?

AARON: Whatever came up.

GEORGE: Just their reactions to the whole thing.

BILL: Balance of payments.

GLORIA: I've got it, you want it. You took it.

AARON: So that was the discussion exercise for the class. Then the other thing about Ahab is a very livid scar that ran from his cap down to his collar, so I explained what the word "livid" means. That was their writing exercise. Anything they wanted to make out of that. I haven't read what they've done yet. The third item was that Ahab in the Old Testament was predicted to die a violent death. I said, "It occurs to me"—or thought, when I was speaking about this—"Can any death be called peaceful?" We take that up for a daily diary that we keep. Can any death be peaceful? Let's work on that. Those were things we were doing in class. Then I had the television on, a television tape. The school had it set up in the classroom, and we worked through some experiences with that. Improvisational theater. You only have one leg. Be a one-legged man. You've got it. He wants it. Let the kids go. All right, then they play with it for a while. I said, "Arch, you're the whale, Moby Dick." "You're Captain Ahab. Moby Dick's got it, you want it."

GEORGE: What struck me when you were talking was that it could be very exciting. I don't know if they could do it or not, but you might have them do some kind of fantasy work with dying. In one case dying violently, in another case dying peacefully. Seeing if they could get into this would be a fascinating thing for us to do.

AARON: What's that quote about death? You were saying, for many people it's man's first real adventure.

GEORGE: Oh, yeah. H. G. Wells's *Tono-Bungay*. There's a thing in there—a scene . . . Do you know the book? It's really his best novel. This is about Tono-Bungay, the very first patent medicine, and the guy who invents it and uses a kind of advertising. He's kind of a go-getter, one of the first. He does all kinds of things. One of the things he does is to fly one of the first airplanes across the English Channel. He's doing this in this rickety old airplane, and the Channel is rough. He's feeling all the excitement of this, how exhilarating this is, and it's kind of stream-of-consciousness. He's thinking that many people have only one adventure in their whole life, and that's on their deathbed. It's the one time that they can't help risking moving into the unknown. Maybe tonight would be a good time to die. That's really exciting.

BILL: Tell me, what is your conceptual basis for this? I mean, I can see different things happening, acting it out, hopping around on one leg, and so forth, but how do you—why do you do this? It seems like it's good entertainment and the kids are enjoying it, but do you connect it with curriculum, or what's the rationale for it?

AARON: The rationale? There are a thousand and one things, but for reading purposes and for writing, we get into it, find it's something else besides a lot of words you don't understand. And to live it, to get in and live what is there. It does have meaning.

BILL: So they understand the stories better.

GEORGE: Not only that. They understand the process is something that's real, not something that's imposed on them.

AARON: The simple thing of being able to express themselves in front of the group. Trying to get them up in front of a group is a real chore.

BILL: Well, let me ask you more specifically, then. Supposing they act out the *Death of a Salesman* scene. Do you talk about the connection between that and their own lives, or do you talk about that as a way of understanding the play?

AARON: Absolutely everything is tied in with their lives.

BILL: Then you do specifically connect all of these things with their other lives, with their everyday lives. I see.

ANN: This "other lives" thing is really bothering me. I'm wondering which is the best thing they've gained from this going out to dinner. Is it the fact that they're doing something that maybe they haven't done before, or the fact that it's a kind of carryover of their relationship with you in the classroom but outside the classroom? It seems to me like this is so important. Yet, because they come to school and they're in these classes for a short period each day—and maybe they become very much involved—and though some of this may be very meaningful to them, soon they are gone. I don't know how often the carryover of whatever they do in school isn't their life at all, you know, outside of school. Or if school then becomes almost some kind of fantasy, and so much of the rest of the time spent outside of school . . .

GEORGE: The thing that's happened is that curriculum, everything we do in school, originally came from some kind of reality, but in the process it became so ritualized that it is being done for its own sake. It once was a means toward an end, and then the means became the end itself. It's what a poor English professor does to a book. Now they take this and put it in its own context as if it were no part of our universe. Aaron is taking all this stuff and putting it back where it was in the first place. And it's something that shouldn't be just for disadvantaged kids. All kids should be having this. Fortunately, the disadvantaged kids are so dramatically out of it that it's an excuse. If you were to do it with so-called college-bound kids, then people would say you're not doing the right thing. These guys have sort of given up, so you can go ahead and do anything.

ROBIN: We do it with college-bound kids.

GEORGE: I know you're doing it, but I mean generally.

BILL: What I'm concerned about is that as far as I know from the research in my experience, if you want to get generalization, you really have to specifically teach for it. It's not often that kids will see the connection between what you do and what they live. Feeling like having one leg would probably be connected with being disadvantaged some way—having some connection with being black, being Mexican, and that kind of thing. I wonder if, in the discussion that follows, that sort of connection is made. Or just how is it handled? Or does it stay as just *Moby Dick?*

GEORGE: You see, the trouble with that, in my concern, is that the research is generalization. They started out with wanting to make this connection to this, and then they go ahead and teach. What's happening, I suspect, at Aaron's—I've watched him—is that all kinds of generalizations are being allowed to emerge as he just hitches these things together in a very gross way.

AARON: I have taken an eclectic approach. Everything and anything ties in some way or another. I don't know whether this fits in or not, but we went out, spent two hundred and twenty-five dollars for a stereo, and put it in the classroom, and that really boomed up the place. We were talking about sailing on the sea, so I got hold of *La Mer* and we played the record and listened to the sea. Talking about the relationships between Ishmael and Queequeg, Ishmael being the man, Queequeg the animal, we talked a little about Negroes, talked about lynching. Then we got hold of Josh White's record of "Strange Fruit." Strange fruit means Negroes hanging from trees in that folk song. We played it and talked about that. It tied right in with the book—the relationship between Ishmael and Queequeg—and we talked and wrote about Ishmael saying he would rather sleep with a sober cannibal than a drunken Christian.

GEORGE: That's the best line in the whole book.

AARON: I think so. They said to crowd as much as we can into the time. That damnable fifty minutes. That's why I like this federal-government grant. It allows us so much more time by scheduling things on Saturdays. We're all going out on a picnic next Saturday. We thought on the way we'd drop into a couple of the missions. This month we have done so much, it's been wild. There isn't anything we haven't done.

ROBIN: This has probably been the most productive month in my life, too. I hardly know where to begin. Everything is so much a piece of one thing, and yet there are some significant events that happened during the month. We finished up with our government stuff, and the English teachers were starting on *Julius Caesar*. They knew ahead of time that this thing was going to be boring as hell for the kids unless they did something good. This English teacher and I took three groups of kids, about fifty-five or sixty, to the cafeteria to begin this whole thing. We started out by calling up to the front all the kids that were in Theater Arts—about eight or nine of them—as a beginning group. Then we started out by saying, "Imagine now that you people are going to be reading or acting out a scene from *Julius Caesar*. How do you feel about that?" Some of them were really excited, so we let them do a couple of these scenes.

I have to back up, because the very beginning of the unit was with everybody in the auditorium. We could see a lot of comparisons and similarities between Julius Caesar and President Kennedy, so we showed scenes of Kennedy's assassination and read lines from the play. We brought it into a little closer context with what they were doing, where they were. There were a couple of days' discussion of that. We then moved into what I was talking about before. One girl got up in front, and I gave her an improvisation to do. The improvisation was: "Your best friend has just been killed. You walk out of your house and see that everybody is celebrating his death. They're having a ball. They're having a party. You're going to naturally react. O.K., react. Go!" So she really got into it and really bawled out the class. After they had reacted to that, we went back and read Scene 1 of the play, which was exactly that—the guy comes out after Pompey's death and bawls out the citizens of Rome for celebrating Pompey's death and the rise of Caesar. We went from that into a bunch of other things like that. One thing that we finally got into was getting the rest of the class involved in doing some of these improvisations or some of the acting out of the actual scenes. Of course, we ran into the stage-fright problem. So I did some of the stage-fright things that Fritz does.

GEORGE: Like what?

ROBIN: The first thing I did was to put a chair on top of the table. I said, "All right, put yourself in the chair. You're up there in the chair and you're reading from this play, but you're on top of the table in this chair in front of seventy-five kids. Put yourself in the chair. Just really get yourself up in there." They all were concentrating on the chair, and I could see faces that exhibited terror and some that were smiling, and various other expressions. I had them experience that for a while, and then I said, "How many of you could actually get up there and do that?" Very few raised their hands. So I gave them the top dog–underdog thing and had them carry on a conversation between the top dog and the underdog about getting up there. "Yes, I should get up there because it would be a good thing to do. No, I don't want to because I'm scared." That kind of thing. After that had gone on for a while, I asked all the ones who still had stage fright to raise their hands, and I just pulled them all up in front, lined them up, and had them stand up and tell everybody their name. Finally, we had only two or three kids that still had serious stage fright, so we were able to get on with all kinds of play and interaction and things like that. As we got a little farther, we came to the scene of the death of Caesar. We had a ritual murder—ritual assassination—and a dummy that Pat made up out of paper and cloth. We put it in the middle of the floor, and all the kids grouped around. We got some shamans, and they were the conspirators in the play. We got those people out there, and the kids wrote their gripes on pieces of paper, and we chanted the gripes and put them in the dummy. Then everybody tore the dummy all apart. Everybody was really with it, and they were yelling the line from the play, "Speak, hands, for me! Speak, hands, for me!" and tearing this thing up. There was paper and cloth all over the cafeteria. We could get with the feeling of this murder, this mass slaughter, that they were in. They really got with it. After they had experienced that for a while, I read them the funeral oration from the play: "Oh, pardon me, thou bleeding piece of earth, that I am meek and gentle with these butchers," and all that kind of thing. And they went from this hilarity—"Boy, this is great!"—to "My God, what have we done?" Then I brought them back to the love-hate thing: What you really love you also have the capacity of hating, and what you really hate you can love; the opposite of love is indifference and not hate. Then I brought them back to the play itself again. Lots of kids still talk about that. They thought that was really something!

Later on the girls were working with the idea of the chaos in the middle of the play, and as I was doing something else, I didn't really know what they were doing. It could have gotten out of hand, because they didn't bring it back for evaluation at the end, and I always try to do that. They had two leaders. One of them was the good-guy leader type, the teacher-pleaser type, where you have all the good shoulds and should-nots over on this side. They gave the other guy a record player and some ice cream and all this stuff, and he was promising the group, "If you elect me leader, you can do anything you want to do. You can have free ice cream; you can have records and dancing all the rest of the period. You can do anything you want to do." So they had this huge thing, the kids just milling all around all over the campus, running around pulling people this way and that way. I didn't know any of this stuff was going on. I was someplace else working with a small group that I'll talk about in a minute. But what eventually happened was that the kids did not choose the leader that promised them all this stuff. They chose the one they thought was the most responsible. So they, in a sense, had their own evaluation. But I thought they should have brought them back and talked about what they had experienced. But instead they had them write about it, which took two or three days, and by that time the immediacy was gone, and I felt that was a mistake. But that was dealing with some of the cognitive material. We've been doing a lot of other things. At the same time there have been several groups of kids who came up to me and said, "Mr. Montz, where did you get all of these things that we're doing?" So I told them about our project and what we do, and how I come here once a month and we talk about this stuff. And they said, "You know, we would like to get together just as a group of people and do some more of this." So I said, "O.K." There was another group of kids who were really problems—troublemakers—totally negative about almost everything. So I pulled that group together, and when I called them in the first time they said, "Are we in trouble? Are we going to get kicked out?" I said, "No, of course not." So we sat down. We started playing the blaming game: my resentments—the whole thing. We got into some good stuff with that particular group.

GEORGE: Did you do the sequence? The resentment, the should, the appreciation?

ROBIN: Yes.

GEORGE: This is something that Fritz Perls worked on with us last time. You start with resentments. Then, after you state them all, you tell people, whomever you resent, how they should be— get that out—and then move into how you appreciate what they are.

ANN: What did Fritz say about this? That this is the basic something-or-other of unfinished business. What did he call resentment?

GEORGE: It's fundamentally the unfinished thing. You can't make contact, he feels, and I agree with him. A teacher cannot make contact with kids until the resentments are out. The kid that stays behind the resentment is a kind of barrier to contact.

ROBIN: At any rate, what happened the first day was all negative. The resentments just poured out. We tried to get to appreciations, but they just couldn't get to them at all. I felt extremely unfinished about the whole thing, and I know they did too. So the next day I called them in again, and we sat down and started getting around to the appreciations. But their main resentment in school was— They had a lot of resentment against teachers and authority figures, but their major resentment was against a group of kids called the Socias, that ran everything. They felt like they were totally out of it. They had a lot of ideas that were good, and they had no way of getting them out and letting them work. So they started coming around to "We don't have to do this. We don't have to sit around and not do anything. Let's do something about it, let's get some ideas." I said, "Sure, what are they? Put them down on paper, and I'll take them to the principal and we'll work them out." So now they have come up with a whole list of things that they would like to do—to raise money for the class, to get the class spirit going—a whole bunch of good things. They've gone to see the principal, sat down and talked to him for an hour and went over these things, and we're now in the process of working them out so they can actually carry them through. Their attitude is just a hundred-and-eighty-degree reversal in ninety per cent of them. There are one or two kids who still are pretty bad, and I'm burdened by all that.

GEORGE: Well, sometimes there are pathological things going on that you can't touch. It's just out of your context.

ROBIN: That's true.

BILL: Do you have them confront the Socias at any point?

ROBIN: Yeah, I have a little bit, but not as much as I will. Right now it's partly "Gee, we're going to be able to do something for a change." It's partly that, and it's also partly "We'll show those Socias." The other group was a group of girls that are very much interested. Some of them were turned on to drugs . . .

GEORGE: These are ninth-graders?

ROBIN: Some, yes. Some of them are on drugs, and some of them are just having some hangups. But they all want to get together and do some things, so I pulled them together last week and talked a little bit about the potential we have if we can get everything together into a Gestalt, the idea of fragmentation and the idea of how we need to put things together in a meaningful whole.

BILL: What drugs do you mean? Pot?

ROBIN: Pot, LSD, speed, and lots of things. I'm not sure what, but I do know they've tried them, and some of them are on them pretty steadily.

GEORGE: This is not a lower-class-neighborhood school. It's at least middle class.

ROBIN: Middle to very high. There are some low-class areas in the district. We started working through some basic techniques. The listening thing, back to back, then the eyes, the touching, and all that. We went on and on through this, and I pulled one girl in. I didn't really plan to, but about two days before this, during one of my free periods, I was walking around outside. She was sitting on the lawn with a friend of hers, and I could see that she was just about ready to cry. I usually play it pretty much by intuition. I felt that this was the time that I needed to say, "Is there anything wrong?" So I sat down on the grass with these two girls and started talking. She had gone through some kind of thing with the vice-principal where she happened to be right and the vice-principal wrong. This girl has a tremendous block against releasing any kind of aggression at all, or giving any kind of argument. She's always very sweet and very, very nice. It's a genuine sweetness, but it's a tremendous frustration to her that she can't release some of these feelings of hers. So I played the part of the girl's vice-principal and I tried to get her to attack me, but she just wouldn't do it. She couldn't do it. In the meantime— This is where I got called a Pied Piper, because I was sitting there with these two girls and soon two or three others drifted over, and then five or six others, and by the time the period was over there were forty-five kids sitting around me on the grass. They came out of drama class. It happened that they were all working on individual projects, and it ended up by the end of the period that we were all sitting around having a really great conversation. The drama teacher is a very good friend of mine, and he came out and I said, "Look, are these people supposed to be doing anything?" And he said, "No, it's fine." Then in half-jest he called me a Pied Piper, which I thought was kind of interesting. Just lots of situations like this. Oh, on this other group that I pulled the girl into, we made a circle and left a chair empty, and we did the thing about telling your most terrible fault—confessing it to the group. How would you feel if you were doing this? Put yourself in the empty chair and imagine yourself doing this. The conversation was between top dog and underdog. They really got into it.

GEORGE: They did? They didn't have any trouble?

ROBIN: No. At first they did, but by the time it was almost the end of the period they were really versed in these things. I had other warm-up things before this. This one girl, Jean, who had had this block about aggression . . . We went around after we went through it, and I asked them how they felt. Some of them said they felt a lot better, others said they felt kind of silly or something. Jean said, "I'm really afraid." So I said, "What is it that you're afraid of?" And she said, "I'm afraid that if I told anybody that, no one would like me, absolutely no one would like me." And so I said, "Well, group, why don't we tell Jean what we think about her?"

BILL: And they told the secrets, or just talked?

ROBIN: No, nobody told about it. So I said, "Why don't you tell Jean what you think of her?" I crossed my fingers. This positive bombardment started spontaneously, and the tears started, and it was just a beautiful thing.

GEORGE: You know, I think that kids are much more open to the positive bombardment. They are so willing to give.

ROBIN: They really are. They said, "Jean, you're really a beautiful person! You're just a wonderful person! I've never heard anyone say anything bad about you! You're just warm, open, friendly . . ." The tears started, not only with Jean but with several of the girls in the group, and it was a happy kind of tears. So I tied the whole thing together and closed it off a little bit, as it was time for them to go. As she went out, Jean looked at me through those teary eyes and said, "Thank you, Mr. Montz," and then went on. Lots of things like this have been happening this month. One girl came to me while I was with a large group of kids. There were two or three of us in there, and she said, "Mr.

Montz, I've just got to talk to you." So I said I'd be with her in a minute, let the other guys know I was splitting out, and went with her. She was having some kind of hangup in the home situation, and she really wanted to talk about it, but she also wanted to find out about herself, too. She was afraid to find out about herself— explore her own personality, and find out what she was like. I suggested that she go home that night and make a list of all the good things she felt about herself and all the bad things she felt about herself and bring it back and we'd talk about it the next day. So she did, and we got together at noon and talked about those things. Then the next day it got to a kind of obvious conflict with the mother, so I had her put her mother in the chair and have a conversation with her, and then be her mother and talk back to her—the whole thing like this. It was really good. She got out a lot of the resentment, frustration, and anger. I want to continue some more with her, but I want to do it in a group context. At that time I didn't know that was going to happen, or I would have had it in a group context to begin with. With one group of girls I pulled together I had this in mind, but she happened to be absent that day.

GEORGE: What are you going to do if a parent comes to you and says, "What are you doing here, Montz, running group therapy?"

ROBIN: Well, I'll explain what the situation is, that's all.

GEORGE: You don't feel uneasy about this?

ROBIN: No. I'm not really getting too deep with it. I feel comfortable with what I'm doing.

BILL: Can I make a comment on this? That sounds very good, and I want to say a few things to even deepen it. If you have a group this far, it sounds like you could go farther than you have already. For example, telling secrets. I think if they've already talked that much about them it isn't hard, and I'm also sure that one person's secret is not nearly as bad as he thinks it is. It's just like so many others.

GEORGE: Robin, do you know the technique where people write

secrets on a piece of paper and put them together and everyone draws? Then you take the secret and read it? It's not your secret you're reading but someone else's secret, and you put yourself into this thing. That's kind of the next step before moving into the actual. Then if they want to volunteer that it's their secret, it's O.K. Or you could even play with this whole idea of how to use secrets. The whole thing is just kind of off the top of my head. Take two or three people and work with two or three secrets. Let them respond individually to the same secret. It's something you could improvise with.

BILL: Another thing is the strength bombardment. You can do it nonverbally as well.

ROBIN: I felt that that group wasn't quite ready. I tried some nonverbal things in the warmup, and they weren't quite as ready as they were with the verbal. I tried to get away from using words, and they did fairly well, but I think that will come later.

GEORGE: You've done a lot of nonverbal things, though. You've done a lot of gibberish games, too.

ROBIN: I had them work with gibberish for a while the other day, and that's very effective.

MIKE:* It sounds like you're able to respond spontaneously with what is appropriate at the time.

ROBIN: Well, I feel that I am. That's what I've tried to do, and I feel I'm quite successful.

The group went to lunch.

* Michael Murphy, president of Esalen Institute (a visitor).

Bibliography

Assagioli, Roberto. *Psychosynthesis.* New York: Hobbs, Dorman, 1965.

Association for Supervision and Curriculum Development. *Perceiving, Behaving, Becoming: A New Focus in Education.* Yearbook. Washington, D.C.: National Education Association, 1962.

Bessell, Harold. "The Content Is the Medium: The Confidence Is the Message," *Psychology Today*, January 1968, pp. 32–35.

Borton, Terry. "What Turns Kids On?" *Saturday Review*, April 15, 1967, pp. 72–74.

Bronfenbrenner, Urie. "The Split-Level American Family," *Saturday Review*, October 7, 1967, pp. 60–66.

Brown, George I. "A Plague on Both Your Houses," *Improving University and College Teaching. International Quarterly Journal*, Oregon State University, Corvallis, Oregon, Spring 1970.

————. Awareness Training and Creativity Based on Gestalt Therapy," *Journal of Contemporary Psychotherapy*, Vol 2, Summer 1969, pp. 25–32.

————. "Operational Creativity: A Strategy for Teacher Change," *Journal of Creative Behavior*, Vol. 2, Fall 1968, pp. 263–70.

Carmichael, Joel. "An Opinion by Joel Carmichael on Religion," *Mademoiselle*, September 1965.

DeMille, Richard. *Put Your Mother on the Ceiling: Children's Imagination Games.* Chicago: Walker, 1967.

Dewey, John. *Art as Experience.* New York: Minton, 1934.

Enright, John B. "An Introduction to Gestalt Therapy." San Francisco: Langley Porter Neuropsychiatric Institute. Unpublished.

Fantini, Mario, and Gerald Weinstein. "Reducing the Behavior Gap," *NEA Journal*, January 1968, pp. 23–25.

———. *Toward a Contact Curriculum.* New York: Anti-Defamation League of B'nai B'rith, 1968.

———. *A Strategy for Developing Relevant Content for Disadvantaged Children.* New York: Fund for the Advancement of Education, Ford Foundation, 1968.

Gendlin, Eugene T. "A Theory of Personality Change." In *Personality Change*, edited by Philip Worchel and Donn Byrne. New York: John Wiley, 1964.

Gordon, William J. J. *Synectics: The Development of Creative Capacity.* New York: Harper & Row, 1961.

Gunther, Bernard. *Sense Awakening and Relaxation.* Esalen paper. Big Sur, Calif.: Esalen Institute.

———. *Sense Relaxation.* New York: Collier, 1968.

Hall, June. "Three Bags Full," *Arts and Activities*, September 1967, pp. 36–39.

Hentoff, Nat. *Our Children Are Dying.* New York: Viking, 1966.

Huxley, Laura Archera. *You Are Not the Target.* New York: Farrar, Straus, 1963.

Ivey, Allen E. *Micro-Teaching and the Student Development Center: Programming Human Relations in the School.* University of Massachusetts. Unpublished paper.

James, William. *The Varieties of Religious Experience.* 1902. Reprint, New York: New American Library.

Jones, Richard M. *Fantasy and Feeling in Education.* New York: New York University Press, 1968.

Krathwohl, David R., Benjamin S. Bloom, and Bertram B. Masia. *Taxonomy of Educational Objectives; Handbook II, Affective Domain.* New York: David McKay, 1956.

Lederman, Janet. *Anger and the Rocking Chair.* New York: McGraw-Hill, 1969.

Leonard, George. *Education and Ecstasy.* New York: Delacorte, 1968.

———. *Education for the Year 2000.* Esalen monograph. Big Sur, Calif.: Esalen Institute.

Lowen, Alexander. Synopsis of three lectures given at Hotel Biltmore, New York, October 21, October 28, November 4, 1965. New York: Institute for Bio-Energetic Analysis. Unpublished program announcement.

McElroy, Davis Dunbar. *Existentialism and Modern Literature.* New York: Philosophical Library, 1963.

Maslow, Abraham. *The Goals of Humanistic Education.* Esalen monograph. Big Sur, Calif.: Esalen Institute.

Miller, N. E., and J. Dollard. *Social Learning and Imitation.* New Haven: Yale University Press, 1941.

Myers, R. E., and E. Paul Torrance. *Can You Imagine?* Minneapolis: Perceptive Publishing, 1963.

Naranjo, Claudio. *I and Thou, Here and Now.* Esalen paper No. 2. Big Sur, Calif.: Esalen Institute.

Neill, A. S. *Summerhill: A Radical Approach to Child Rearing.* New York: Hart, 1960.

Otto, Herbert. *Group Methods Designed to Actualize Human Potential.* Chicago: Stone-Brandel, 1967.

——— and John Mann. *Ways of Growth.* New York: Grossman, 1968.

Perls, Frederick S. *Ego, Hunger, and Aggression.* New York: Random House, 1969.

———. *Gestalt Therapy and Human Potentialities.* Esalen paper No. 1. Big Sur, Calif.: Esalen Institute.

———. *Gestalt Therapy Verbatim.* Lafayette, Calif.: Real People Press, 1969.

———. "Group vs. Individual Therapy," *Review of General Semantics,* Vol. 24, 1967, pp. 306–312.

———, Ralph F. Hefferline, and Paul Goodman. *Gestalt Therapy: Excitement and Growth in the Human Personality.* New York: Julian Press, 1951.

Polanyi, Michael. *The Tacit Dimension.* Garden City, N.Y.: Doubleday, 1966.

Reid, I. E., and R. M. W. Travers. "Time Required to Switch Attention," *American Educational Research Journal*, Vol. 5, March 1968, pp. 203–212.

Reps, Paul. *Zen Flesh, Zen Bones.* Garden City, N.Y.: Anchor Books.

Rogers, Carl R. *Client-Centered Therapy.* Boston: Houghton Mifflin, 1951.

——. *On Becoming a Person.* Boston: Houghton Mifflin, 1961.

Rolf, Ida P. *Structural Integration.* New York: Ida P. Rolf, 11 Riverside Drive, 1962.

Schultz, William. *Joy.* New York: Grove Press, 1968.

Simkin, James S. *Introduction to Gestalt Therapy.* Big Sur, Calif: Esalen Institute. Unpublished paper.

Spolin, Viola. *Improvisation for the Theater.* Evanston, Ill.: Northwestern University Press, 1963.

Tumin, Melvin. "Teaching in America," *Saturday Review*, October 21, 1967.

Von Franz, M. L. "Time and Synchronicity in Analytic Psychology." In *The Voices of Time*, edited by J. T. Fraser. New York: George Braziller, 1966.

Whitehouse, Mary. "The Tao of the Body," 1958; "Physical Movement and Personality," 1966; "Creative Expression in Physical Movement Is Language without Words," 1966. Los Angeles lectures.